OSINT People Finder: Advanced Techniques for Online Investigations

Algoryth Ryker

The internet remembers everything. Whether it's a decades-old forum post, a forgotten MySpace account, or a leaked database entry, our digital footprints linger—sometimes in places we least expect. Open-Source Intelligence (OSINT) has become a powerful tool for uncovering personal details, tracking movements, verifying identities, and even solving real-world cases.

From journalists uncovering corruption to private investigators searching for missing persons, OSINT techniques offer a non-intrusive yet highly effective way of piecing together digital trails. However, finding people online is both an art and a science. It requires knowing where to look, how to pivot between data points, and how to cross-reference information while respecting privacy and ethical boundaries.

This book is a deep dive into people-focused OSINT—helping you master the skills needed to find, verify, and analyze personal information using publicly available data. Whether you're an investigator, researcher, or simply curious about digital footprints, you'll discover the most effective techniques for tracking down people online, from social media reconnaissance to deep web searches.

Chapter Summaries & Key Takeaways

1. Finding People Online: The Basics

Before diving into complex investigations, understanding digital footprints is essential. This chapter introduces the foundations of OSINT people searches: how online identities are built, how individuals leave data traces across the web, and the best practices for structuring an efficient search workflow. Key concepts include:

- Recognizing different types of digital footprints
- How usernames, emails, and metadata create a personal web history
- The difference between surface web, deep web, and dark web searches
- Ethical considerations: What is legal and what crosses the line?

2. Public Records & Government Databases

Governments and institutions store vast amounts of personal information, much of it accessible through public records. This chapter covers:

- How to search court records, business filings, property ownership, and voting registrations
- The best tools for accessing birth, marriage, and death records

- How to cross-reference criminal, arrest, and civil litigation databases
- Real-world case study: Finding someone using business registrations and corporate filings

3. Social Media Profiles & Cross-Platform Analysis

People reveal more about themselves on social media than they realize. This chapter focuses on:

- How to find hidden social media accounts
- Using Facebook Graph Search (even after its removal)
- Tracking Twitter (X) hashtags, mentions, and geolocation data
- Investigating LinkedIn profiles for employment verification
- **Case Study**: Exposing a fraudulent social media account

4. Email & Username Investigations

An email address or username can reveal a complete digital identity. Learn how to:

- Reverse search email addresses to uncover linked accounts
- Track username patterns across different platforms
- Use leaked data breaches to find hidden connections
- **Case Study**: Tracing an online scammer

5. Phone Number OSINT & Reverse Lookups

With the right tools, phone numbers can provide geolocation, messaging apps, and social media connections. This chapter covers:

- How to conduct reverse phone lookups
- Identifying VoIP and burner numbers
- Investigating phone numbers in leaked data breaches
- Using APIs to automate phone number OSINT

6. Geolocation Tracking & Travel History

A single photo or social media check-in can reveal a person's location. This chapter explains how to:

- Extract GPS metadata from images

- Use Google Maps & satellite imagery to verify locations
- Identify travel history using online data points
- **Case Study**: Finding a person's real location through OSINT

7. Employment & Educational Background Verification

Many people fabricate their resumes. This chapter teaches:

- How to verify employment history & job credentials
- Identifying fake degrees & diploma mills
- Using corporate filings & LinkedIn cross-checks
- **Case Study**: Exposing a fake job candidate

8. Facial Recognition & Biometric OSINT

AI-powered facial recognition is a game-changer in OSINT. Learn how to:

- Use reverse image search to find online profiles
- Identify AI-generated fake profile pictures
- Extract photo metadata for geolocation
- **Case Study**: Tracking a missing person using facial recognition tools

9. Dark Web & Identity Theft Investigations

The dark web is a hotbed for identity theft, fraud, and data leaks. This chapter covers:

- Searching for stolen credentials on underground marketplaces
- Investigating hacked accounts, passport fraud, and cybercrime
- Monitoring data breaches to prevent identity theft
- **Case Study**: Recovering stolen identity information

10. Social Engineering & Behavioral Analysis

Understanding human behavior can help OSINT analysts extract key information. This chapter explores:

- Identifying psychological patterns in online behavior
- How people unknowingly expose personal data
- Manipulating online conversations to gather intelligence
- **Case Study**: Using social engineering to verify a fake identity

11. OSINT & Missing Persons Investigations

OSINT is widely used in missing person and skip tracing investigations. Learn how to:

- Track missing individuals using digital footprints
- Identify alias names, changed identities, and online behavior shifts
- Work with law enforcement and families to locate missing people
- Case Study: Finding a missing person using social media clues

12. Case Study: High-Profile People OSINT

This final chapter examines real-world OSINT investigations, focusing on high-profile figures:

- How journalists track politicians, criminals, and celebrities
- Techniques for exposing fraudulent social media influencers
- Investigating public figures for accountability and transparency
- **Final OSINT Challenge**: Apply all techniques to a real-world case

Final Thoughts: The Ethics of People-Focused OSINT

OSINT is powerful, but with great power comes great responsibility. While this book equips you with the skills to find and analyze personal data, it also stresses the ethical and legal boundaries of investigations. Whether you're using these techniques to protect, investigate, or verify, always ensure your actions remain lawful, responsible, and ethical.

Now, let's begin the hunt.

1. Finding People Online: The Basics

In the digital age, almost everyone leaves a trace online, whether through social media, public records, or hidden data points scattered across the web. This chapter introduces the core principles of online people-finding, covering essential OSINT (Open-Source Intelligence) techniques, key resources, and ethical considerations. You'll learn how to leverage search engines, social networks, and public databases to locate individuals while maintaining operational security and respecting privacy laws. Mastering these foundational skills will set the stage for more advanced investigative techniques in later chapters.

1.1 Understanding Digital Footprints & Online Identities

In the modern digital era, almost every individual leaves behind a unique trail of information known as a digital footprint. This footprint consists of online activities, social media interactions, public records, and various other forms of data that can be traced, analyzed, and interpreted. Understanding digital footprints and online identities is fundamental for OSINT professionals, as it provides the foundation for people-finding investigations. By recognizing how individuals interact with the internet, investigators can efficiently track their targets, uncover hidden details, and map out their online presence.

This subchapter explores the concept of digital footprints, differentiates between active and passive footprints, and discusses how online identities are formed and maintained. It also delves into the risks, ethical considerations, and practical methods for analyzing digital trails to gather intelligence.

What is a Digital Footprint?

A digital footprint refers to the traces of an individual's activities left behind as they navigate the internet. These traces can be either active (intentionally shared information) or passive (unintended data collected by websites and services).

Active Digital Footprint: This includes any data that a person willingly shares online, such as social media posts, comments, blog entries, forum discussions, and website registrations. Every time someone updates their LinkedIn profile, tweets an opinion, or uploads a picture to Instagram, they are actively contributing to their digital footprint.

Passive Digital Footprint: This refers to information collected without the user's direct input. Websites, search engines, and apps track browsing habits, location data, and metadata, often without explicit consent. Cookies, IP addresses, and analytics tools log online behavior, creating a trail that can be analyzed by investigators.

Both types of footprints are critical for OSINT analysts, as they provide insights into a person's habits, affiliations, and identity, often revealing more than the subject realizes.

Online Identities: The Digital Representation of a Person

An online identity is how an individual presents themselves across various digital platforms. Most people maintain multiple online identities, either intentionally or inadvertently, through social media, professional networks, and other digital interactions.

Types of Online Identities:

- **Real Identity**: Some users operate under their real name and personal details, making it easier to verify their authenticity. LinkedIn profiles, government databases, and professional websites often feature real identities.
- **Pseudonymous Identity**: Many individuals use aliases, screen names, or usernames to separate their online activities from their real-world identity. This is common in gaming communities, forums, and social media platforms.
- **Anonymous Identity**: Some users attempt to remain entirely anonymous by using encryption tools, VPNs, and burner accounts. While true anonymity is challenging to maintain, advanced OSINT techniques can often link anonymous profiles to real identities.

By analyzing username patterns, profile photos, writing styles, and online behaviors, investigators can often connect different online identities to a single individual.

How Digital Footprints are Created and Expanded

A person's digital footprint grows every time they engage with online platforms. Some of the most common contributors to a person's digital footprint include:

- **Social Media Activity**: Facebook, Twitter, Instagram, LinkedIn, and TikTok collect extensive user data, including posts, likes, comments, and connections.
- Search Engine Queries: Google and other search engines log searches, creating a record of interests, inquiries, and potential intent.

- **E-commerce Transactions**: Online purchases, product reviews, and shopping habits provide insights into an individual's preferences and financial behavior.
- **Public Records and Databases**: Government databases, property records, court documents, and business registries contribute to a person's discoverable information.
- **Metadata from Images and Files**: Digital images often contain EXIF metadata, which can reveal location, time, and device information.

Each of these elements provides valuable clues when conducting OSINT investigations, allowing analysts to reconstruct a person's online history and habits.

Tracking and Analyzing Digital Footprints

To effectively analyze a person's digital footprint, OSINT professionals rely on a combination of manual research and specialized tools.

Step 1: Identifying Key Data Points

Start by gathering basic information such as:

- Full name or known aliases
- Email addresses
- Usernames
- Phone numbers
- Social media handles

These details serve as anchor points for deeper investigations.

Step 2: Cross-Referencing Information Across Platforms

By searching for the same username or email across different platforms, investigators can uncover linked accounts. Websites like Have I Been Pwned, WhatsMyName, and Sherlock help identify accounts associated with specific usernames or emails.

Step 3: Examining Metadata and Hidden Clues

- Reverse Image Searches (using Google Images, Yandex, or PimEyes) help find other accounts using the same profile picture.
- EXIF Data Analysis can reveal location and device details in images.

- IP and Geolocation Tracking using OSINT tools can approximate where an individual is accessing the internet from.

Step 4: Behavioral Analysis and Pattern Recognition

A person's posting frequency, writing style, online interactions, and digital habits can reveal significant insights. Behavioral patterns help confirm identities and detect deception attempts, such as sock puppet accounts (fake identities created to manipulate online discussions).

Ethical Considerations & Privacy Issues

While OSINT techniques provide powerful tools for tracking individuals, it is essential to adhere to legal and ethical guidelines. Investigators must:

- Ensure that data is obtained from publicly available sources.
- Respect privacy laws and terms of service for different platforms.
- Avoid engaging in doxxing (publishing private or personal information without consent).

Understanding and mitigating the risks of digital footprints is also crucial for individuals who want to maintain privacy. Educating the public about how their data is collected and used can help prevent identity theft and unauthorized surveillance.

Digital Footprint Management & Privacy Protection

For those looking to minimize their online exposure, several steps can help control their digital footprint:

- Regularly audit social media privacy settings to limit public access.
- Use alias emails and usernames for different services to compartmentalize online identities.
- Opt-out of data collection services and request removal from public databases.
- Use VPNs and privacy-focused browsers to minimize tracking.
- Be mindful of what is shared online, as even deleted content can persist in archives or backups.

By understanding how digital footprints are formed and used, individuals can take proactive measures to protect their online presence while OSINT investigators can refine their tracking techniques.

Conclusion

Digital footprints and online identities play a crucial role in modern investigations. Every piece of data a person leaves behind contributes to a vast web of information that can be analyzed and connected. By mastering the ability to track, analyze, and interpret digital footprints, OSINT professionals gain a significant advantage in people-finding investigations. However, with great power comes great responsibility—ethical and legal considerations must always guide the investigative process.

1.2 How People Leave Traces on the Internet

Every online action leaves a mark, whether intentional or unintentional. From social media posts to browsing habits, people continuously generate data that can be traced, analyzed, and linked to their real-world identity. Understanding how individuals leave digital traces is crucial for OSINT professionals conducting online investigations.

This chapter explores the various ways people unknowingly expose information on the internet, including social media activity, website interactions, metadata leaks, and data breaches. We'll also discuss techniques for identifying and analyzing these traces while considering the ethical implications of OSINT investigations.

1.2.1 Social Media & Public Posts

Social media platforms are among the richest sources of digital traces. People frequently share personal details, locations, and opinions without realizing the extent of their exposure.

Types of Exposed Data on Social Media:

- **Personal Information**: Names, birthdays, locations, relationships, and workplace details.
- **Activity Logs**: Check-ins, likes, comments, and posts that reveal behavior patterns.
- **Images & Videos**: Often contain metadata (e.g., GPS coordinates, timestamps).
- **Friend Networks**: Connections and interactions help establish personal and professional relationships.

OSINT Techniques for Social Media Analysis:

- **Username Investigations**: Searching for usernames across different platforms (using tools like Sherlock or WhatsMyName) to find linked accounts.
- **Reverse Image Search**: Identifying other accounts using the same profile picture (Google Reverse Image Search, Yandex, or PimEyes).
- **Metadata Extraction**: Using tools like ExifTool to analyze hidden data in images.

1.2.2 Website Interactions & Online Behavior

Even passive browsing leaves a footprint. Websites track users through various means, often storing information that can be accessed or analyzed later.

Common Ways Websites Track Users:

- **Cookies & Tracking Pixels**: These track browsing behavior and can be used to build a digital profile of a user.
- **IP Addresses**: Websites log visitor IP addresses, which can reveal approximate locations and ISPs.
- **Browser Fingerprinting**: Sites collect details like operating system, browser version, and screen resolution to uniquely identify visitors.
- **Login Credentials & Account Activity**: Many sites log user login attempts and interactions, creating a timeline of digital activity.

OSINT Techniques for Tracking Website Interactions:

- **Checking Cookie Policies**: Investigating what data a website collects.
- **Analyzing IP Addresses**: Using tools like Shodan to find associated network activity.
- **Tracking Online Mentions**: Using Google Alerts or Mention to monitor when a name, email, or phone number appears online.

1.2.3 Metadata & Hidden Digital Traces

Metadata is hidden data embedded in files, images, and documents that can reveal significant details about an individual.

Types of Metadata:

- **Image Metadata (EXIF Data):** Contains GPS coordinates, camera model, timestamps, and more.

- **Document Metadata**: PDFs, Word files, and Excel sheets may include author names, timestamps, and revision history.
- **Email Headers**: Provide details about the sender's IP address, email service provider, and routing path.

OSINT Techniques for Extracting Metadata:

- **ExifTool & Jeffrey's Image Metadata Viewer**: Extract EXIF data from images.
- **FOCA & Metagoofil**: Analyze document metadata for hidden information.
- **Email Header Analysis Tools**: Investigate email origins and trace senders.

1.2.4 Data Breaches & Leaked Information

Many individuals unknowingly leave traces on the internet due to data breaches and leaks. Hackers frequently expose sensitive data, which can then be accessed through various OSINT resources.

Common Types of Leaked Data:

- **Emails & Passwords**: Often found in breached databases.
- **Personal Identifiable Information (PII):** Addresses, phone numbers, and financial details.
- **Private Messages & Conversations**: Leaked from hacked accounts or insecure databases.

OSINT Techniques for Finding Breached Data:

- **Have I Been Pwned**: Checks if an email or password has been leaked.
- **DeHashed & LeakCheck**: Advanced search tools for finding breached credentials.
- **Pastebin & Dark Web Monitoring**: Searching for exposed data in hacker forums.

1.2.5 Search Engines & Cached Data

Search engines index vast amounts of information, including content that users may believe has been deleted.

How Search Engines Preserve Data:

- **Cached Pages**: Older versions of web pages stored for quick access.

- **Web Archives (Wayback Machine):** A historical record of websites, even after deletion.
- **Publicly Indexed Documents**: PDFs, spreadsheets, and reports stored in search engine databases.

OSINT Techniques for Leveraging Search Engines:

- **Google Dorking**: Using advanced search operators to find hidden data.
- site:example.com (Search within a specific website)
- filetype:pdf (Find specific file types)
- intitle:"index of" (Find open directories)
- **Wayback Machine**: Retrieve deleted pages for investigative purposes.

1.2.6 Online Reviews, Forums & Dark Web Activity

Beyond mainstream platforms, people leave traces on discussion boards, product reviews, and even the dark web.

Common Platforms Where Traces are Found:

- **Online Marketplaces**: eBay, Craigslist, and Facebook Marketplace.
- **Forums & Message Boards**: Reddit, 4chan, and niche communities.
- **Dark Web Markets**: Contain leaked personal information and fraudulent activity.

OSINT Techniques for Analyzing Forum & Marketplace Activity:

- **Searching by Username**: Identifying the same user across multiple platforms.
- **Tracking Digital Transactions**: Looking at cryptocurrency transactions linked to a target.
- **Monitoring Discussion Trends**: Analyzing behavioral patterns in posts.

1.2.7 Ethical Considerations in Tracing Online Activity

While OSINT is a powerful tool, it must be used responsibly. Analysts should always:

- Adhere to legal and ethical guidelines.
- Respect privacy laws and platform terms of service.
- Avoid doxxing or exposing sensitive information unnecessarily.

Conclusion

People constantly leave traces on the internet, often without realizing it. By understanding how these digital breadcrumbs are created, OSINT professionals can efficiently track and analyze online activity. However, ethical considerations must guide every investigation to ensure responsible and lawful intelligence gathering.

1.3 The OSINT Workflow for Finding People

The process of finding individuals online using Open-Source Intelligence (OSINT) requires a structured and methodical approach. Without a clear workflow, an investigation can become overwhelming, leading to missed details or inefficient research. A well-defined OSINT workflow ensures accuracy, efficiency, and ethical compliance while navigating vast amounts of public data.

This chapter outlines a step-by-step process for conducting OSINT investigations on individuals. From defining objectives to analyzing data and verifying findings, this workflow provides a systematic approach to tracking digital footprints and uncovering useful intelligence.

1.3.1 Defining the Investigation Scope & Objectives

Before starting an OSINT investigation, it is essential to clearly define its purpose and limitations. This prevents scope creep and ensures ethical and legal compliance.

Key Questions to Define Scope:

- Who is the subject of the investigation? (Full name, alias, username, email, phone number, etc.)
- What specific information is being sought? (Current location, contact details, employment history, etc.)
- Are there any legal or ethical restrictions on collecting this information?
- What sources will be used? (Public records, social media, data leaks, etc.)

Ethical Considerations:

- Always adhere to legal and ethical standards.
- Respect privacy laws and platform terms of service.
- Avoid unauthorized data access or doxxing.

1.3.2 Initial Data Collection: Establishing a Starting Point

Gathering initial data is crucial for building a foundation for deeper investigations. Start with whatever known details are available.

Common Starting Points for OSINT Investigations:

- **Full Name & Aliases**: Search for legal names, nicknames, and pseudonyms.
- **Usernames & Social Media Handles**: Many users recycle usernames across platforms.
- **Email Addresses**: Often tied to social media accounts and data breaches.
- **Phone Numbers**: Can be used for reverse lookups and carrier identification.
- **IP Addresses (if available)**: Help approximate geographic location.

OSINT Tools for Initial Data Collection:

- **Google Dorking**: site:facebook.com "John Doe" to find public Facebook profiles.
- **WhatsMyName**: Identifies username matches across multiple platforms.
- **Have I Been Pwned**: Checks for compromised email addresses in data breaches.
- **OSINT Framework**: A collection of tools categorized by investigation type.

1.3.3 Expanding the Investigation: Cross-Referencing Data

Once an initial profile is built, the next step is cross-referencing the collected data across multiple sources.

1.3.3.1 Social Media & Online Presence Analysis

- **Profile Identification**: Matching usernames, profile pictures, and bio descriptions across different platforms.
- **Friend & Follower Analysis**: Identifying connections, interactions, and networks.
- **Activity Monitoring**: Analyzing posts, likes, comments, and location check-ins.

OSINT Tools for Social Media Analysis:

- **Social Searcher**: Finds social media mentions of a name or keyword.
- **PimEyes**: Reverse image search for profile photos.
- **TweetDeck**: Monitors Twitter activity in real time.

1.3.3.2 Public Records & Government Databases

Official records provide valuable data points such as addresses, legal documents, and business registrations.

Sources of Public Records:

- **Property Records**: Land ownership databases.
- **Business Registries**: Company affiliations and director roles.
- **Court & Criminal Records**: Legal disputes and criminal background checks.

OSINT Tools for Public Record Searches:

- **OpenCorporates**: Searches global company records.
- **PACER (USA):** Provides access to federal court records.
- **UK Companies House**: Lists business information for UK entities.

1.3.3.3 Email & Username Investigations

Email addresses and usernames often provide crucial links to other accounts and data leaks.

Investigation Methods:

- **Email to Username Matching**: Finding other accounts linked to an email.
- **Data Breach Analysis**: Checking for leaked passwords and associated platforms.

OSINT Tools for Email & Username Investigations:

- **Hunter.io**: Identifies professional email addresses.
- **Dehashed**: Searches breached databases for emails, usernames, and passwords.

1.3.4 Analyzing & Verifying Collected Data

Not all information found online is accurate. Verification is a crucial step in ensuring reliability before drawing conclusions.

Verification Techniques:

- **Cross-Check Across Multiple Sources**: Ensure consistency between different data points.
- **Reverse Image Search**: Confirm profile pictures aren't stolen or fake.
- **Metadata Analysis**: Extract hidden data from images and documents for validation.
- **Time & Date Verification**: Ensure timestamps align with real-world events.

OSINT Tools for Verification:

- **InVID**: Verifies and analyzes images and videos.
- **FotoForensics**: Examines image metadata and potential manipulation.

1.3.5 Mapping & Visualizing Connections

To better understand an individual's network and digital footprint, it's helpful to visualize the relationships between various data points.

Benefits of Data Mapping:

- Identifies hidden connections between individuals, locations, and organizations.
- Helps track behavioral patterns over time.
- Highlights inconsistencies or anomalies in a person's online presence.

OSINT Tools for Data Visualization:

- **Maltego**: Graph-based link analysis tool for mapping connections.
- **Hunchly**: Organizes and tracks OSINT investigations systematically.

1.3.6 Ethical Reporting & Documentation

Once an investigation is complete, properly documenting findings is essential for transparency, legal compliance, and credibility.

Best Practices for OSINT Documentation:

- **Maintain Detailed Notes**: Record sources, timestamps, and investigation steps.
- **Use Screenshots & Archived Links**: Preserve evidence before it's deleted or altered.
- **Cite Sources Accurately**: Ensure findings can be independently verified.

- **Follow Legal & Ethical Guidelines**: Avoid sharing or storing sensitive information irresponsibly.

OSINT Tools for Documentation & Reporting:

- **Wayback Machine**: Captures and archives web pages.
- **Hunchly**: Logs browsing activity for evidentiary purposes.
- **Obsidian or Notion**: Organizes notes and case files efficiently.

The OSINT workflow for finding people is a structured process that involves defining objectives, collecting initial data, cross-referencing sources, verifying findings, mapping connections, and ethically documenting results. By following this systematic approach, OSINT professionals can conduct effective and responsible investigations while minimizing errors and ethical risks.

1.4 Free vs. Paid Data Sources for People Investigations

OSINT professionals rely on a variety of data sources to track individuals online. These sources range from publicly accessible databases to premium services that provide in-depth background checks. Understanding the advantages and limitations of both free and paid sources is crucial for conducting efficient and cost-effective investigations.

This chapter explores the key differences between free and paid data sources, their reliability, ethical considerations, and when to use each type.

1.4.1 Understanding Free Data Sources

Free OSINT tools and databases are the foundation of most investigations. These sources provide publicly available data, often collected from government databases, social media platforms, and open records.

Advantages of Free Data Sources:

- **Cost-Effective**: No financial investment required.
- **Accessible to Everyone**: Open to the public without restrictions.
- **Diverse Information Sources**: Covers a wide range of data, from social media to public records.

Limitations of Free Data Sources:

- **Time-Consuming**: Requires manual searching and verification.
- **Limited Data Depth**: May not include historical or sensitive records.
- **Incomplete or Outdated Information**: Some sources are not frequently updated.

Examples of Free OSINT Data Sources:

1. Social Media & Online Platforms

- **Facebook, Twitter, Instagram, LinkedIn**: Profile information, connections, and activities.
- **Pipl (Limited Free Search):** Finds publicly available information linked to names, emails, and usernames.

2. Public Records & Government Databases

- **US Public Records (data.gov, PACER):** Access to legal documents and business filings.
- **UK Companies House**: Company ownership and director details.

3. Search Engines & Archives

- **Google Dorking**: Advanced search operators for hidden online data.
- **Wayback Machine**: Retrieves archived web pages.

4. Email & Username Lookups

- **Have I Been Pwned**: Checks if an email has appeared in data breaches.
- **WhatsMyName**: Finds username matches across multiple platforms.

5. Phone Number & Address Lookups

- **TrueCaller (Limited Free Search):** Identifies caller information.
- **WhitePages (Basic Free Lookup):** Provides limited address and phone number details.

1.4.2 Exploring Paid Data Sources

Paid OSINT tools offer enhanced capabilities, such as deep web searches, historical records, and automated data aggregation. These services are commonly used by law enforcement, private investigators, and corporate security teams.

Advantages of Paid Data Sources:

- **Access to Deep & Private Records**: Includes financial history, criminal records, and court filings.
- **Time-Saving Automation**: Aggregates data from multiple sources into a single report.
- **Historical & Deleted Data**: Retrieves information that may no longer be publicly available.

Limitations of Paid Data Sources:

- **Subscription Costs**: Can be expensive, often requiring monthly or yearly payments.
- **Restricted Access**: Some services require professional credentials or legal justification.
- **Potential Ethical Concerns**: Paid databases may collect data from questionable sources.

Examples of Paid OSINT Data Sources:

1. People Search & Background Check Services

- **Intelius, Spokeo, TruthFinder**: Aggregates data from multiple sources for personal background checks.
- **Pipl Pro**: Advanced search capabilities for professionals.

2. Data Breach & Cybersecurity Intelligence

- **DeHashed, LeakCheck**: Searches leaked databases for compromised emails, passwords, and personal data.

3. Reverse Phone & Email Lookup Services

- **CocoFinder, BeenVerified**: Provides detailed reports on phone numbers and email addresses.

4. Financial & Property Records

- **LexisNexis Accurint (Professional Access Only):** Extensive reports on assets, financial records, and legal filings.
- **TLOxp**: A high-level investigative tool for verifying personal and business records.

1.4.3 When to Use Free vs. Paid Data Sources

The choice between free and paid data sources depends on the depth of information needed and the nature of the investigation.

Use Free Data Sources When:

- Conducting preliminary searches to gather basic information.
- Investigating social media activity and public online presence.
- Searching for open government records and company registrations.
- Checking usernames, emails, or phone numbers in data breach databases.

Use Paid Data Sources When:

A deeper level of verification is required (e.g., criminal history, financial records).
The subject has a low online presence, requiring access to private or premium databases.
Time-sensitive investigations demand quick and automated data aggregation.
Cross-referencing public data with hidden or deleted records is necessary.

1.4.4 Ethical & Legal Considerations in Data Collection

Using OSINT tools—whether free or paid—must be done within ethical and legal boundaries.

Key Ethical Concerns:

- **Privacy Violations**: Avoid collecting or publishing sensitive data without proper authorization.
- **Legality of Data Access**: Some paid services aggregate data that may not be legally obtained.
- **Terms of Service Compliance**: Respect platform rules when gathering information.

Best Practices for Ethical OSINT Investigations:

- **Verify Data Sources**: Ensure that information comes from legally accessible records.
- **Avoid Unauthorized Data Access**: Never attempt to bypass paywalls or access restricted databases unlawfully.
- **Use Data Responsibly**: Do not share or misuse personal information obtained through OSINT research.
- **Respect Privacy Laws**: Understand jurisdictional differences in data protection laws, such as GDPR (Europe) or CCPA (California).

Conclusion

Free and paid data sources both play an essential role in OSINT investigations. While free sources provide a valuable starting point, paid services offer enhanced capabilities for deeper research. However, it is critical to use all OSINT tools ethically and legally to ensure responsible intelligence gathering.

1.5 Common Challenges & Mistakes in People OSINT

Finding people online using OSINT can be a powerful but complex process. While modern tools and techniques provide unprecedented access to public data, many challenges can hinder an investigation. From dealing with false information to ethical pitfalls, OSINT practitioners must be aware of common mistakes to ensure accuracy and effectiveness.

This chapter explores the most frequent challenges in people investigations, the mistakes analysts often make, and strategies to overcome them.

1.5.1 Common Challenges in People OSINT

1.5.1.1 False or Misleading Information

Not all data found online is accurate. People often use fake names, old addresses, or outdated profile information. Additionally, disinformation campaigns, deepfake images, and manipulated data can mislead an investigation.

How to Overcome It:

- Cross-reference sources to confirm accuracy.
- Use metadata analysis to verify images and documents.

- Check timestamps and activity history for outdated information.

1.5.1.2 Multiple Individuals with the Same Name

Common names lead to confusion when trying to locate the correct individual. Searching for "John Smith" without additional identifiers can generate hundreds of results.

How to Overcome It:

- Use additional data points such as location, job history, or known associates.
- Apply Google search operators (e.g., "John Smith" AND "New York" site:linkedin.com).
- Use facial recognition or profile picture comparisons where available.

1.5.1.3 Limited or No Online Presence

Some individuals have minimal online activity, making them difficult to track. Privacy-conscious users may delete social media accounts, use aliases, or limit publicly available information.

How to Overcome It:

- Search for old web archives (Wayback Machine) to find deleted profiles.
- Investigate known associates to uncover indirect traces of the subject.
- Look into business records and property ownership databases for additional clues.

1.5.1.4 Data Fragmentation Across Multiple Platforms

People often use different usernames, emails, and aliases on various platforms, making it challenging to connect their accounts.

How to Overcome It:

- Use username enumeration tools (e.g., WhatsMyName) to track cross-platform identities.
- Conduct reverse image searches to match profile pictures across sites.
- Utilize data aggregation tools like Maltego for mapping connections.

1.5.2 Common Mistakes in OSINT Investigations

1.5.2.1 Failing to Define the Investigation Scope

A lack of clear objectives can lead to inefficient research and wasted time. Analysts may gather unnecessary data instead of focusing on key details.

How to Avoid This Mistake:

- Define specific goals before starting an investigation.
- Use a structured OSINT workflow to stay focused.
- Avoid collecting excessive data that is irrelevant to the case.

1.5.2.2 Relying on a Single Source

Some investigators depend too much on one platform, such as Facebook or LinkedIn, without cross-checking other sources.

How to Avoid This Mistake:

- Use multiple data sources (e.g., social media, public records, breach databases).
- Validate findings with different tools to avoid misleading results.
- Be cautious of confirmation bias, where information aligns with assumptions rather than facts.

1.5.2.3 Ignoring Privacy & Legal Boundaries

Some OSINT techniques may violate privacy laws, terms of service, or ethical guidelines. Accessing restricted databases or engaging in social engineering without permission can lead to legal consequences.

How to Avoid This Mistake:

- Always follow legal and ethical standards when conducting investigations.
- Understand data protection laws such as GDPR (Europe) and CCPA (California).
- Use only publicly available data and avoid unauthorized access to private accounts.

1.5.2.4 Poor Data Organization & Documentation

Failing to record sources, timestamps, and investigative steps can make it difficult to retrace findings or verify data later.

How to Avoid This Mistake:

- Keep structured notes using tools like Obsidian, Notion, or Hunchly.
- Store screenshots and archived links as evidence.
- Organize findings using graphs or link analysis tools such as Maltego.

1.5.2.5 Not Verifying Findings Before Reporting

Incorrect or incomplete data can lead to false conclusions, misidentifying individuals, or spreading misinformation.

How to Avoid This Mistake:

- Always verify data across multiple independent sources.
- Double-check spelling variations and alternative names.
- Confirm geolocation details using IP lookup tools or public travel history.

1.5.3 Overcoming OSINT Challenges with Best Practices

✅ **Use a Structured OSINT Process**

- Start with basic information and expand as necessary.
- Follow a step-by-step workflow for consistency.

✅ **Cross-Verify All Data**

- Never trust a single source; always compare findings.
- Use reverse image search and metadata tools for verification.

✅ **Respect Privacy & Legal Boundaries**

- Follow ethical guidelines for intelligence gathering.
- Be aware of regional laws that regulate data access.

✅ **Stay Updated on OSINT Tools & Techniques**

- OSINT is constantly evolving; continuously learn new tools.

- Participate in OSINT communities and training programs.

Conclusion

While OSINT is a powerful method for finding people online, it comes with significant challenges. Avoiding common mistakes—such as relying on a single source, failing to verify findings, or overlooking privacy laws—ensures ethical, efficient, and accurate investigations.

1.6 Ethical & Legal Considerations in People Investigations

Conducting OSINT investigations to find people online comes with significant ethical and legal responsibilities. Investigators must balance the need for information with the privacy rights of individuals and the legal frameworks governing data access. Misuse of OSINT techniques can lead to privacy violations, legal consequences, and ethical dilemmas.

This chapter explores key ethical considerations, relevant laws and regulations, and best practices for conducting responsible and lawful OSINT investigations.

1.6.1 Ethical Considerations in OSINT Investigations

1.6.1.1 Respecting Privacy & Consent

Even if information is publicly available, it does not always mean it is ethical to collect, use, or share it. Investigators must consider whether gathering certain data infringes on a person's right to privacy.

Ethical Best Practices:

- Avoid unnecessary collection of sensitive data (e.g., health records, private messages).
- Respect personal boundaries when investigating non-criminal subjects.
- Obtain consent when appropriate, especially in corporate or journalistic investigations.

1.6.1.2 Avoiding Doxxing & Harassment

Doxxing—the act of publicly exposing private information about an individual without their consent—is an unethical and potentially illegal practice. OSINT should never be used to harm, intimidate, or harass individuals.

Ethical Best Practices:

- Do not publicly share personal details unless legally justified (e.g., exposing fraud).
- Avoid targeting individuals for personal, political, or financial gain.
- Ensure data is used for legitimate investigative purposes, such as missing persons cases.

1.6.1.3 Transparency & Accountability

OSINT professionals should operate with transparency and be accountable for their investigative methods. Using deception or misinformation can damage credibility and lead to ethical violations.

Ethical Best Practices:

- Clearly define the purpose of an investigation before starting.
- Be transparent about sources and methodologies in reports.
- Take responsibility for mistakes and correct misinformation when discovered.

1.6.2 Legal Considerations in OSINT Investigations

Laws governing OSINT vary by country and region. Understanding relevant regulations is essential to ensure compliance and avoid legal risks.

1.6.2.1 Data Protection Laws (GDPR, CCPA, etc.)

Many countries have strict data protection laws that limit how personal information can be collected, stored, and used.

Key Regulations:

General Data Protection Regulation (GDPR) – Europe

- Restricts collection and processing of personal data without consent.
- Requires data minimization and purpose limitation.

California Consumer Privacy Act (CCPA) – USA

- Gives consumers the right to know what personal data is collected and request its deletion.

Personal Data Protection Act (PDPA) – Singapore & Other Regions

- Regulates the collection, use, and disclosure of personal information.

How to Stay Compliant:

- Collect only necessary data and avoid storing sensitive information.
- If using third-party data providers, ensure they comply with privacy laws.
- Follow data retention policies and delete information when no longer needed.

1.6.2.2 Computer Fraud & Unauthorized Access Laws

Accessing protected data without authorization is illegal in most jurisdictions. This includes hacking, bypassing login restrictions, or using stolen credentials.

Relevant Laws:

Computer Fraud and Abuse Act (CFAA) – USA

- Prohibits unauthorized access to protected computer systems.

UK Computer Misuse Act

- Criminalizes unauthorized access and data theft.

Cybercrime Laws in Various Countries

- Many nations have similar laws prohibiting unauthorized data access.

How to Stay Compliant:

- Only access publicly available data—never attempt to bypass security measures.
- Do not engage in credential stuffing, phishing, or brute-force attacks.
- Follow website terms of service when conducting OSINT research.

1.6.2.3 Social Engineering & Deception Laws

Social engineering—manipulating individuals into revealing information—can cross legal and ethical boundaries. In some cases, it may violate fraud or wiretapping laws.

Legal Risks:

- **Impersonation laws**: Using a fake identity to obtain information can be illegal.
- **Wiretapping & eavesdropping laws**: Recording conversations without consent is restricted in many places.
- **Fraud statutes**: Misrepresentation for personal gain can lead to legal penalties.

How to Stay Compliant:

- Avoid impersonating others or using deceptive pretexts.
- Follow laws regarding recording and intercepting communications.
- Obtain explicit permission when engaging in social engineering for security testing.

1.6.3 Responsible OSINT Practices

To ensure ethical and legal compliance, OSINT investigators should follow best practices that promote responsible intelligence gathering.

✓ Use Only Legal & Publicly Accessible Data Sources

- Stick to open-source intelligence—do not access protected systems.
- Be mindful of terms of service for platforms and tools.

✓ Follow a Clear Ethical Framework

- Operate under ethical guidelines, such as The OSINT Framework's best practices.
- Ensure proportionality—only collect information necessary for the investigation.

✓ Respect the Rights of Individuals

- Do not publish or share sensitive personal information unless legally justified.
- Protect the privacy and security of individuals involved in investigations.

✓ Stay Informed on Legal Changes

- Laws and regulations change frequently—stay updated on data protection and cybercrime laws.
- Join OSINT communities and legal forums to stay informed.

Conclusion

Ethical and legal considerations are at the core of responsible OSINT investigations. Analysts must respect privacy rights, follow data protection laws, and avoid unauthorized access or deceptive practices. By adhering to ethical guidelines and legal frameworks, OSINT professionals can ensure their work remains credible, lawful, and effective.

2. Public Records & Government Databases

Public records and government databases are invaluable resources for OSINT professionals conducting people-finding investigations. These repositories contain vast amounts of information, including birth and death records, property ownership, business registrations, court filings, and more. In this chapter, you'll learn how to navigate official databases, access publicly available records, and interpret the data effectively. We'll also discuss jurisdictional differences, potential legal restrictions, and ethical considerations to ensure responsible and lawful investigations.

2.1 What Public Records Are Available Online?

Public records are a valuable resource for OSINT practitioners conducting people investigations. These records, often maintained by government agencies, organizations, and third-party aggregators, contain a wealth of information about individuals, including their legal history, property ownership, business affiliations, and more.

This chapter explores the different types of public records available online, where to find them, and how to use them effectively in investigations while remaining compliant with legal and ethical guidelines.

2.1.1 Types of Public Records Available Online

Public records vary by country and jurisdiction, but generally, the following categories of information can be accessed online:

2.1.1.1 Government-Issued Identification Records

While personally identifiable information (PII) such as full Social Security numbers (SSNs) or passport details is typically restricted, some identification-related records are available.

Examples:

- Voter registration databases (availability depends on jurisdiction)
- Professional licenses and certifications (e.g., medical licenses, legal bar records)
- Publicly registered businesses and corporate filings

Where to Find Them:

- State or local election offices
- Licensing board websites (e.g., medical, legal, real estate regulators)
- Business registration databases (e.g., SEC EDGAR, Companies House UK)

2.1.1.2 Property & Land Records

Property ownership records can provide valuable insights into an individual's assets, financial status, and residential history.

Examples:

- Deeds and mortgage records
- Property tax assessments
- Land ownership and real estate transactions

Where to Find Them:

- County assessor's websites (USA)
- Land registry databases (UK, Canada, Australia)
- Third-party property search tools like Zillow or Redfin

2.1.1.3 Court & Legal Records

Court records can reveal a person's involvement in lawsuits, criminal cases, divorces, and bankruptcies.

Examples:

- Criminal records (availability varies by jurisdiction)
- Civil litigation cases (e.g., lawsuits, restraining orders)
- Bankruptcy filings
- Divorce and family court records

Where to Find Them:

- Federal and state court websites (PACER for U.S. federal cases)
- Local county court databases
- Third-party legal research tools (Justia, CourtListener)

2.1.1.4 Business & Corporate Filings

Public business records can provide details about an individual's professional activities, ownership of companies, and financial standing.

Examples:

- Business incorporation records
- SEC filings for publicly traded companies
- Executive and director information
- Licenses for regulated industries

Where to Find Them:

- SEC EDGAR (U.S. securities filings)
- Companies House (UK)
- State business registries (varies by country)

2.1.1.5 Birth, Marriage & Death Records

Vital records can help confirm relationships, identify next of kin, and track changes in personal status.

Examples:

- Birth and death certificates
- Marriage and divorce records
- Obituaries and genealogical records

Where to Find Them:

- State or national archives
- Genealogy websites (Ancestry, FamilySearch)
- Local government offices

2.1.1.6 Professional & Academic Records

Many professional and academic achievements are documented in public records, which can help verify credentials and work history.

Examples:

- University graduation records
- Professional licenses (e.g., medical, legal, engineering certifications)
- Patent filings and research publications

Where to Find Them:

- University alumni directories
- Google Scholar & ResearchGate (for academic work)
- U.S. Patent and Trademark Office (USPTO)

2.1.1.7 Political Contributions & Campaign Donations

Political donations and affiliations are often recorded in public databases, offering insight into an individual's political activity.

Examples:

- Federal and state political donations
- Lobbying and advocacy group affiliations

Where to Find Them:

- Federal Election Commission (FEC.gov, USA)
- OpenSecrets.org (tracks campaign finance data)
- Local government political contribution records

2.1.1.8 Social & Government Benefits Records

Some records related to government benefits, grants, and contracts are publicly accessible.

Examples:
- Government contracts and procurement records
- Public welfare and grants (limited availability)

Where to Find Them:

- USA Spending.gov (federal contracts)

- Local government procurement portals

2.1.2 How to Effectively Use Public Records in OSINT Investigations

2.1.2.1 Cross-Referencing Data for Accuracy

- Compare multiple sources to verify the authenticity of the information.
- Look for inconsistencies in names, dates, and addresses.
- Use timeline analysis to track movements and life events.

2.1.2.2 Searching with Variations of Names & Addresses

- Use maiden names, nicknames, or aliases.
- Try different formats of an address (e.g., "123 Main St." vs. "123 Main Street").

2.1.2.3 Leveraging Archived & Historical Records

- Use the Wayback Machine (archive.org) to retrieve old versions of websites.
- Check property records for previous owners and tenants.

2.1.2.4 Staying Within Legal & Ethical Boundaries

- Avoid restricted or confidential data (e.g., sealed court records).
- Respect data protection laws like GDPR and CCPA.
- Do not engage in unauthorized access or social engineering.

Conclusion

Public records are an essential resource in OSINT investigations, offering insights into an individual's background, assets, legal history, and professional activities. By understanding what information is available, where to find it, and how to use it ethically and legally, investigators can enhance their ability to locate and verify individuals efficiently.

2.2 Searching Birth, Marriage & Death Records

Vital records—birth, marriage, and death records—are essential resources in OSINT investigations. These records help confirm identities, establish relationships, and track life events. Many government agencies and genealogy platforms provide access to such records, although availability varies by jurisdiction and privacy laws.

In this chapter, we will explore where to find birth, marriage, and death records, how to search them effectively, and ethical considerations when using this data.

2.2.1 Understanding the Importance of Vital Records in OSINT

Vital records serve several investigative purposes, including:

- **Identity Verification** – Confirming an individual's legal name, date of birth, and familial ties.
- **Genealogical & Family Research** – Tracing lineage and establishing historical connections.
- **Missing Persons & Fraud Investigations** – Detecting cases of identity fraud or verifying whether someone is deceased.
- **Legal & Financial Matters** – Establishing next-of-kin relationships in cases of inheritance or legal disputes.

2.2.2 Where to Find Birth, Marriage & Death Records Online

2.2.2.1 Government Databases & Official Records

Most countries maintain centralized repositories for vital records, although access restrictions vary. Some allow public access, while others require proof of relationship or legal interest.

Key Sources by Region:

United States

- **National Center for Health Statistics (CDC)** – Guides where to request official records.
- **State Vital Records Offices** – Each state maintains its own database.
- **Social Security Death Index (SSDI)** – Lists deceased individuals with U.S. Social Security numbers.

United Kingdom

- **General Register Office (GRO)** – Holds records for England and Wales.

- **Scotland's People** – Scottish government's official genealogy records.
- **Public Record Office of Northern Ireland (PRONI)** – Manages birth, marriage, and death records.

Canada

- **Provincial Vital Statistics Offices** – Records are maintained at the provincial level.
- **Library and Archives Canada** – Some historical birth, marriage, and death records are available.

Australia

- **State and Territory Registries** – Each Australian state maintains its own records.
- **National Archives of Australia** – Some older records may be available for research.

European Union & Other Countries

- **National or Local Civil Registry Offices** – Birth and marriage records are often stored at municipal offices.
- **Church Records** – Some European countries have extensive church-based documentation.

How to Access These Records:

- Some jurisdictions allow online searches for index records but require official requests for full certificates.
- Older records (typically over 100 years old) are often publicly available in historical archives.
- Death records are generally easier to access than birth or marriage records due to lower privacy restrictions.

2.2.2.2 Genealogy & Historical Archives

Genealogy websites compile vast databases of birth, marriage, and death records, often digitizing historical documents.

Top Genealogy Resources:

- **Ancestry.com** – Extensive global record collections (paid access).
- **FamilySearch.org** – Free genealogy database maintained by The Church of Jesus Christ of Latter-day Saints.
- **FindMyPast.com** – Specializes in UK and Irish records.
- **MyHeritage.com** – International records with DNA testing integration.
- **The National Archives (UK, USA, etc.)** – Historical records accessible online.
- **Cyndi's List (cyndislist.com)** – A directory of online genealogical resources.

Pros & Cons of Genealogy Databases:

✅ Advantages:

- Easy access to indexed and digitized historical records.
- Many records available for free or low-cost subscriptions.
- Often include scanned copies of original documents.

✖ Limitations:

- Some databases require paid access.
- Accuracy depends on transcription quality and source material.
- Modern records (less than 50-100 years old) may be restricted.

2.2.2.3 Newspapers, Obituaries & Cemetery Records

Obituaries, cemetery records, and newspaper archives provide additional sources for birth, marriage, and death information.

Key Sources:

Obituary Search Websites

- **Legacy.com** – Global obituary database.
- **Tributes.com** – U.S.-based obituary records.
- **NewspaperArchive.com** – Digital newspaper archives.

Cemetery & Burial Databases

- **FindAGrave.com** – Crowdsourced burial records and tombstone photos.
- **BillionGraves.com** – GPS-based cemetery records.

- **Interment.net** – Compilation of global cemetery records.

How to Use These Sources:

- Obituaries often include birth and death dates, family relationships, and residence history.
- Cemetery records can confirm dates of death and burial locations.
- Digital newspaper archives may contain wedding announcements or death notices.

2.2.3 Searching Strategies for Birth, Marriage & Death Records

To maximize success when searching for vital records, follow these key strategies:

2.2.3.1 Name Variations & Spelling Differences

- Try different spellings (e.g., "Smith" vs. "Smyth").
- Search using maiden names or married names.
- Consider initials or abbreviations used in historical records.

2.2.3.2 Date Range Adjustments

- Birth records may be delayed in registration (search a few years before/after).
- Marriage records may be under the bride's or groom's surname.
- Death records might list only the year, not the full date.

2.2.3.3 Location-Specific Searches

- Start with known cities, counties, or states and expand outward.
- Use local historical societies for regional data.
- Cross-check census records if available.

2.2.3.4 Cross-Referencing Data

- Use multiple databases to verify the same information.
- Compare birth certificates with census records for consistency.
- Check obituaries for family names that appear in marriage records.

2.2.4 Legal & Ethical Considerations in Accessing Vital Records

While many vital records are public, some are restricted due to privacy laws.

Key Privacy Laws Affecting Access:

- **GDPR (Europe)** – Limits access to recent personal data.
- **CCPA (California, USA)** – Protects personal information of living individuals.
- **HIPAA (USA)** – Restricts medical and death-related records.
- **State/Provincial Privacy Laws** – Vary widely in record access policies.

Best Practices for Ethical Research:

✓ Use public records responsibly—do not misuse personal data.

✓ Do not impersonate family members to gain access to restricted records.

✓ Ensure compliance with legal regulations when obtaining documents.

✓ Avoid sharing sensitive information without consent.

Conclusion

Searching for birth, marriage, and death records is a fundamental part of OSINT investigations, offering valuable insights into identities, relationships, and historical data. By leveraging government databases, genealogy platforms, and newspaper archives, investigators can efficiently locate and verify key personal details.

2.3 Court, Criminal & Arrest Record Lookups

Court, criminal, and arrest records provide valuable insights into a person's legal history, including past lawsuits, criminal charges, and incarcerations. These records can help investigators verify identities, uncover hidden connections, and assess potential risks. While some records are publicly accessible, others are restricted due to privacy laws.

This chapter explores where to find these records, how to search them effectively, and the ethical and legal considerations when using them in OSINT investigations.

2.3.1 Understanding the Types of Legal Records

Legal records fall into three primary categories:

- **Court Records** – Includes civil lawsuits, divorces, probate cases, and business disputes.
- **Criminal Records** – Covers charges, convictions, and sentencing information.
- **Arrest Records** – Documents police interactions, including detentions and charges filed.

2.3.2 Where to Find Court, Criminal & Arrest Records Online

2.3.2.1 Court Records

Court records provide information about legal disputes and judicial decisions. These records can be accessed through federal, state, and local court databases.

Examples of Court Records:

- **Civil Cases** – Lawsuits, restraining orders, probate cases.
- **Divorce & Family Court Records** – Custody battles, alimony settlements.
- **Bankruptcy Filings** – Financial status and insolvency cases.

Where to Find Court Records:

- **PACER (Public Access to Court Electronic Records)** – U.S. federal case database
- **State court websites** (e.g., California Courts, New York Unified Court System)

Local county court databases

- Justia.com, CourtListener, and RECAP for free case law research

Challenges in Accessing Court Records:

- Some jurisdictions require in-person requests.
- Divorce and family court records may be restricted.
- Sealed and expunged records are not publicly available.

2.3.2.2 Criminal Records

Criminal records document offenses, including misdemeanors and felonies. Availability varies by jurisdiction, with some databases providing free access while others require requests through law enforcement agencies.

Examples of Criminal Records:

- **Convictions** – Documented offenses and sentences.
- **Parole & Probation Records** – Status and terms of supervised release.
- **Sex Offender Registries** – Publicly available information on registered offenders.

Where to Find Criminal Records:

- **Federal Bureau of Prisons (BOP.gov)** – Inmate locator for federal prisoners

State Department of Corrections websites

- National Sex Offender Public Website (NSOPW.gov, U.S.)
- Interpol & Europol databases for international offenders

Challenges in Accessing Criminal Records:

- Many records are only available to law enforcement or authorized agencies.
- Juvenile and sealed records are generally inaccessible.
- Some states restrict access to conviction details.

2.3.2.3 Arrest Records & Police Reports

Arrest records document instances where an individual has been taken into custody but do not necessarily indicate a conviction.

Examples of Arrest Records:

- **Police incident reports** – Details of the arrest and charges.
- **Mugshots & Booking Records** – Photos and case details from law enforcement agencies.
- **Warrant Searches** – Active warrants for an individual.

Where to Find Arrest Records:

- Local police department websites (some publish daily arrest logs).
- Sheriff's department databases (county-level arrests).
- FBI's Most Wanted List (FBI.gov) for fugitives.
- Third-party aggregator sites like Arrests.org & BustedMugshots.com.

Challenges in Accessing Arrest Records:

- Many jurisdictions do not publish arrest details online.
- Arrests that did not result in charges may be removed.
- Some states prohibit third-party sharing of mugshots.

2.3.3 Searching Strategies for Legal Records

To maximize efficiency when searching for legal records, consider the following strategies:

2.3.3.1 Use Name Variations & Aliases

- Search using different spellings, middle names, and maiden names.
- Use known aliases or nicknames.
- Try searching with and without middle initials.

2.3.3.2 Narrow Down by Jurisdiction

- Criminal cases are typically handled at the state or local level.
- Federal crimes appear in the PACER system.
- Arrest records may be stored at city, county, or state law enforcement agencies.

2.3.3.3 Check for Record Expungement or Sealing

- Some individuals may have their records expunged, making them inaccessible to the public.
- Juvenile records are usually sealed and not publicly available.

2.3.3.4 Cross-Reference with News Reports

- Arrests and high-profile court cases are often reported in local news.
- Use Google News archives and LexisNexis for historical case details.

2.3.4 Legal & Ethical Considerations in Accessing Legal Records

While many legal records are public, accessing and using them must comply with privacy laws and ethical guidelines.

Key Legal Restrictions:

- **Fair Credit Reporting Act (FCRA, U.S.)** – Restricts the use of criminal records in employment background checks.
- **General Data Protection Regulation (GDPR, EU)** – Limits public access to personal legal records.
- **State-specific privacy laws (e.g., California Consumer Privacy Act, CCPA)** – May restrict access to arrest and conviction records.

Ethical Best Practices:

✓ Use only publicly available records – Do not attempt unauthorized access.

✓ Respect individual privacy – Avoid unnecessary exposure of sensitive data.

✓ Verify information before acting – Legal records may contain errors or outdated data.

Conclusion

Court, criminal, and arrest records play a critical role in OSINT investigations, helping analysts verify identities, track legal disputes, and assess risks. While many records are accessible online, ethical and legal considerations must be respected.

2.4 Business & Corporate Registration Investigations

Investigating business and corporate registrations is a crucial component of OSINT when tracking individuals, verifying financial ties, uncovering fraud, or assessing risks. Business records can reveal ownership structures, financial status, licensing details, and even hidden connections between individuals and entities.

This chapter will explore where to find corporate registration records, how to analyze them effectively, and the legal and ethical considerations involved in using business OSINT for investigations.

2.4.1 Understanding Business & Corporate Records

Corporate records document essential details about companies, including:

- **Business Registration Information** – Name, address, type of business entity, and formation date.
- **Ownership & Directorship Data** – Names of founders, directors, shareholders, and executives.
- **Financial & Tax Filings** – Annual reports, financial statements, tax registrations, and bankruptcy filings.
- **Licenses & Regulatory Compliance** – Industry-specific permits, regulatory filings, and government contracts.
- **Legal History & Lawsuits** – Litigation records, fraud investigations, and compliance violations.

These records can provide critical insights into an individual's financial interests, business dealings, and potential conflicts of interest.

2.4.2 Where to Find Business & Corporate Registration Records

2.4.2.1 Government Business Registries

Many governments maintain public databases where businesses must register their corporate details. These databases vary in accessibility—some provide open access, while others require registration or payment.

Key Government Sources by Region:

United States:

- **SEC EDGAR (Securities and Exchange Commission)** – Public company filings and reports.
- **State Business Registries** – Each state has a corporate registration portal (e.g., California Secretary of State, Florida Division of Corporations).
- **IRS Exempt Organizations (IRS.gov)** – Nonprofit business filings.
- **Federal Procurement Data System (FPDS.gov)** – Government contract awards.

United Kingdom:

- **Companies House (companieshouse.gov.uk)** – Business ownership, financials, and registration details.
- **Financial Conduct Authority (FCA)** – Regulated financial firms and compliance records.

European Union:

- **European Business Register (EBR)** – Corporate records from multiple EU member states.
- **Transparency Register (EU)** – Lists lobbyists and their financial affiliations.

Canada:

- **Corporations Canada (canada.ca)** – Federal and provincial business registrations.
- **Provincial Registries (e.g., BC Registry, Ontario Business Registry)** – Regional business data.

Australia & New Zealand:

- **Australian Business Register (ABR.gov.au)** – Business names, Australian Business Numbers (ABNs), and tax records.
- **ASIC (Australian Securities & Investments Commission)** – Corporate financial reports and directors.
- **New Zealand Companies Office (companies.govt.nz)** – Business registrations and directorships.

How to Access Government Business Records:

- Many registries allow free searches for basic company details.
- Detailed reports or ownership information may require a paid subscription.
- Some records are restricted due to privacy laws, requiring authorized access.

2.4.2.2 Third-Party Business Databases & OSINT Tools

In addition to official government registries, several third-party platforms aggregate corporate data and provide investigative tools.

Popular Business Intelligence & OSINT Tools:

- **OpenCorporates (opencorporates.com)** – World's largest open database of company records.
- **Orbis (Bureau van Dijk)** – Corporate ownership structures and financials (paid).
- **Dun & Bradstreet (DNB.com)** – Business credit reports and risk analysis.

- **Bloomberg & Reuters Business Databases** – High-level corporate financial data.
- **Trade Registries & Import/Export Data** – International trade filings, shipping records, and customs reports.

Advantages of Third-Party Business Intelligence Tools:

✓ Global coverage, including offshore businesses and shell companies.

✓ Historical data, including company name changes and dissolved entities.

✓ Cross-referencing capabilities with other business and financial data.

Limitations & Challenges:

✗ Some services require expensive subscriptions.

✗ Data accuracy depends on the source and jurisdiction.

✗ Offshore businesses often use secrecy jurisdictions to obscure ownership.

2.4.2.3 News, Leaks & Dark Web Sources

Investigative journalists and leaked data sources often provide valuable insights into businesses involved in corruption, fraud, or illicit activities.

Where to Look:

- **The Panama Papers, Paradise Papers & Other Offshore Leaks** – Exposes hidden offshore companies and tax evasion schemes.
- **ICIJ (International Consortium of Investigative Journalists)** – Investigations into corporate fraud and financial crime.
- **Transparency International** – Reports on corruption and money laundering networks.
- **Dark Web Marketplaces** – Illicit business dealings and identity fraud services.

How to Use This Data Responsibly:

- Verify information from multiple sources before drawing conclusions.
- Be aware of legal risks when using leaked or hacked corporate data.

- Follow ethical guidelines to avoid unauthorized access or misuse of sensitive records.

2.4.3 Investigative Techniques for Business & Corporate OSINT

To effectively analyze business records, use the following OSINT techniques:

2.4.3.1 Cross-Referencing Corporate Ownership

- Identify patterns in company directorships and shareholders.
- Use tools like OpenCorporates to find connections between businesses.
- Investigate shell companies or offshore entities that may be used for fraud.

2.4.3.2 Tracking Business Relationships & Financial Transactions

- Look for contracts, procurement records, and vendor agreements.
- Analyze tax filings and financial statements for irregularities.
- Check SEC filings for insider trading, mergers, or fraud allegations.

2.4.3.3 Social Media & Business Networking Analysis

- LinkedIn, Twitter, and corporate websites can reveal executive connections.
- Identify hidden relationships between business associates and investors.
- Monitor business reviews and complaints for reputational risks.

2.4.3.4 Identifying Fraud & Money Laundering Risks

- Investigate frequent name changes or dissolved/reincorporated entities.
- Search for businesses registered at residential addresses or PO boxes.
- Compare declared revenue with known business activities for inconsistencies.

2.4.4 Legal & Ethical Considerations in Business Investigations

Investigating businesses must be done within legal and ethical boundaries.

Key Legal Issues to Consider:

- **Data Privacy Laws (GDPR, CCPA, etc.)** – Regulate access to personal and financial data.
- **Financial Disclosure Laws** – Some corporate financial records are restricted.

- **Anti-Money Laundering (AML) & Know Your Customer (KYC) Regulations –** Govern financial investigations and due diligence.

Best Practices for Ethical Business OSINT:

✅ Verify sources before using business intelligence in reports.

✅ Avoid accessing protected financial data without authorization.

✅ Respect corporate confidentiality and trade secrets.

✅ Use only publicly available and legally accessible records.

Conclusion

Business and corporate registration investigations are essential in OSINT for uncovering financial networks, verifying identities, and exposing fraud. By utilizing government registries, business intelligence tools, and investigative techniques, analysts can reveal hidden connections and assess corporate risks.

2.5 Property, License & Voter Registration Records

Property records, professional licenses, and voter registration records are valuable OSINT sources for identifying individuals, verifying identities, and uncovering financial or residency details. These records can reveal where a person lives, their real estate holdings, their professional qualifications, and even their political affiliations.

This chapter will explore how to access and analyze these records, where to find them, and the ethical and legal considerations involved in their use for investigations.

2.5.1 Property Records & Real Estate Ownership

2.5.1.1 What Information Property Records Contain

Property records document ownership, transactions, valuations, and tax assessments of real estate. These records can help OSINT investigators:

- Verify an individual's residence or business location.
- Identify undisclosed assets or property holdings.
- Track financial transactions linked to real estate.

- Uncover hidden connections through joint property ownership.

2.5.1.2 Where to Find Property Records

Most property records are maintained by county tax assessors, local land registries, or real estate offices. Some jurisdictions provide free access, while others require fees or in-person requests.

U.S. Property Record Sources

- **County Assessor Websites** – Search for property tax records, ownership history, and valuations.
- **Bureau of Land Management (BLM.gov)** – Federal land records.
- **Zillow & Realtor.com** – Public real estate listings and estimated property values.
- **PropertyShark & LexisNexis Real Estate Solutions** – Paid databases with ownership details.

International Property Record Sources

- **UK Land Registry** (gov.uk/search-property-information-land-registry)
- **Canadian Land Titles Offices** (Provincial Registries)
- **Australian Property Registry** (state-based land titles offices)
- **European Land Registries** (varies by country, some restricted access)

2.5.1.3 Investigative Techniques for Property OSINT

- Cross-reference names with real estate holdings to identify assets.
- Analyze property transfer records to track financial movements.
- Check for mortgage liens or unpaid taxes that indicate financial stress.
- Look for ownership structures using shell companies or trusts.

2.5.2 Professional Licenses & Business Permits

2.5.2.1 What Professional Licenses Reveal

Professional licenses verify an individual's qualifications, employment, and regulatory compliance. Investigators use these records to:

- Confirm if someone holds a valid professional certification (e.g., doctors, lawyers, real estate agents).

- Uncover past disciplinary actions or revoked licenses.
- Validate employment claims and business activities.

2.5.2.2 Where to Find Licensing Records

Most professional licenses are managed by state, national, or industry-specific regulatory bodies.

Common Licensing Databases

U.S. License Registries

- **National Plan & Provider Enumeration System (NPPES)** – Medical provider registry.
- **State Bar Associations** – Lawyer licensing and disciplinary records.
- **FINRA BrokerCheck (brokercheck.finra.org)** – Financial advisor and stockbroker credentials.
- **FAA Airmen Inquiry (registry.faa.gov)** – Licensed pilots.
- **Real Estate Commissions** – State-level real estate license lookups.

International License Registries

- **UK General Medical Council (GMC-uk.org)** – Physician licensing.
- **Law Society of Canada (lawsociety.ca)** – Lawyer credentials.
- **Australian Health Practitioner Regulation Agency (AHPRA.gov.au)** – Medical professionals.

2.5.2.3 Investigative Techniques for Licensing OSINT

- Verify claims of professional experience by cross-referencing licenses.
- Check for disciplinary actions, license suspensions, or fraud allegations.
- Use license numbers to track professional history and associations.

2.5.3 Voter Registration & Political Affiliations

2.5.3.1 What Voter Records Reveal

Voter registration records can provide information about:

- A person's residency and electoral district.

- Political party affiliation (in some countries).
- Voting history (e.g., participation in elections but not actual votes cast).

Voter records are useful for:

- Confirming a person's location and residency.
- Identifying political leanings and affiliations.
- Investigating political influence or activism.

2.5.3.2 Where to Find Voter Registration Records

Access to voter records varies by country and jurisdiction. Some governments provide public access, while others restrict records to government officials or political campaigns.

U.S. Voter Registration Sources

- **State Election Offices** – Some states allow public access to basic voter registration details.
- **Political Party Databases** – Party-affiliated organizations sometimes maintain voter records.
- **Campaign Finance Databases (FEC.gov)** – Tracks donations and political affiliations.

International Voter Registration Sources

- **UK Electoral Roll (edited version)** – Limited public access.
- **Canadian Elections Canada Registry** – Restricted access for political and research purposes.
- **Australian Electoral Commission (AEC.gov.au)** – Voter roll access under strict conditions.

2.5.3.3 Investigative Techniques for Voter OSINT

- Cross-check voter records with property and business data to confirm residency.
- Analyze political donations to assess ideological leanings.
- Use voter registration history to track migration patterns.

2.5.4 Legal & Ethical Considerations in Accessing These Records

2.5.4.1 Data Privacy Laws & Restrictions

- **GDPR (Europe)** – Limits the use of personal data from public records.
- **CCPA (California)** – Restricts access to personal information without consent.
- **FCRA (U.S.)** – Governs the use of public records in background checks.

2.5.4.2 Ethical Best Practices

✓ Use only legally accessible databases.

✓ Verify data from multiple sources before acting on it.

✓ Avoid doxxing or exposing private information irresponsibly.

✓ Be aware of potential biases in voter registration and property records.

Conclusion

Property records, professional licenses, and voter registrations provide key insights into individuals' locations, professions, and political ties. These sources, when used responsibly, can significantly enhance OSINT investigations.

2.6 Case Study: Finding a Person Through Public Databases

Public databases are powerful tools for locating individuals, uncovering hidden connections, and verifying identities. This case study walks through a real-world scenario where an OSINT investigator uses publicly available records—including property records, business registrations, professional licenses, and voter registration—to track down an individual.

By following a structured OSINT workflow, this investigation demonstrates how different data sources intersect, creating a comprehensive digital footprint.

2.6.1 Case Scenario: The Missing Business Partner

Background

A private investigator is hired by a client to locate his former business partner, John Reynolds, who disappeared after dissolving their joint company. The client wants to determine John's current location and business activities to resolve financial disputes.

Known Information

- **Full Name**: John Reynolds
- **Former Business Name**: Reynolds Tech Solutions
- **Last Known Location**: Dallas, Texas
- **Possible Industry**: IT Consulting

2.6.2 Step 1: Searching Business Registration Records

Database Used:

- Texas Secretary of State Business Registry (SOS Direct)
- OpenCorporates (opencorporates.com)

Findings:

A search for Reynolds Tech Solutions reveals that the company was dissolved six months ago. However, an associated business, Reynolds Digital Consulting LLC, was registered in Austin, Texas, a month after the dissolution.

New Business Details:

- **Owner**: John M. Reynolds
- **Registered Address**: 1523 Oakwood Lane, Austin, TX
- **Business Type**: IT & Software Consulting
- **Filing Date**: One month after the original business dissolved

Analysis:

John may have moved to Austin and started a new company under a different name.

2.6.3 Step 2: Investigating Property & Real Estate Records

Database Used:

- Travis County Assessor's Office (Austin, TX Property Search)
- Zillow & Realtor.com (for market trends and historical transactions)

Findings:

A property search for 1523 Oakwood Lane confirms that it is a residential property owned by John M. Reynolds, purchased three months ago. The mortgage lender is Lone Star Bank, suggesting recent financial stability.

Analysis:

This supports the theory that John relocated to Austin and is actively establishing himself there.

2.6.4 Step 3: Checking Professional Licensing & Employment Records

Database Used:

- Texas Department of Licensing and Regulation (TDLR)
- LinkedIn & Industry Directories

Findings:

John Reynolds holds an active Certified IT Security Specialist license, renewed recently. A LinkedIn search for "John Reynolds IT Consultant Austin" reveals a profile with minimal public details but confirms his employment at Reynolds Digital Consulting LLC.

Analysis:

John is actively working in the IT sector and maintains a digital presence, though limited.

2.6.5 Step 4: Voter Registration & Political Contributions

Database Used:

- Texas Voter Registration Database
- Federal Election Commission (FEC) Contribution Records

Findings:

- John is registered to vote in Travis County, confirming his residence in Austin.
- He made a recent $250 donation to a local political campaign, listing 1523 Oakwood Lane as his address.

Analysis:

This verifies his presence in Austin and suggests civic engagement, which may indicate social media activity or public event participation.

2.6.6 Step 5: Social Media & Additional Public Mentions

Database Used:

- Google Dorking (Advanced Search Queries)
- Facebook, Twitter, Instagram, LinkedIn
- Local News & Community Websites

Findings:

- A Facebook search reveals that John recently attended an IT networking event in Austin.
- A Twitter handle (@JohnReynoldsTX) matches his profession and location, but the account is mostly inactive.
- A local business journal interviewed him regarding IT startups in Austin.

Analysis:

Although John keeps a low digital profile, his professional activities still generate public mentions.

2.6.7 Conclusion: Assembling the Profile

By piecing together multiple data sources, we now have a solid profile of John Reynolds:

- **Current Location**: Austin, Texas (confirmed via business registration, property records, and voter registration).
- **Business Activities**: Operating Reynolds Digital Consulting LLC (business registry, LinkedIn).
- **Home Address**: 1523 Oakwood Lane (property records, political donations).
- **Financial Standing**: Recently purchased a home with a mortgage (real estate data).
- **Public Engagement**: Attended IT events and was featured in a business journal (news and social media).

2.6.8 Ethical & Legal Considerations

While all information gathered is from public records, OSINT investigators must adhere to ethical guidelines:

✓ **Legality**: Ensure that all data is legally accessible and not obtained through unauthorized means.
✓ **Privacy Concerns**: Avoid doxxing or exposing personal information unnecessarily.
✓ **Verification**: Cross-check multiple sources before drawing conclusions.
✓ **Responsible Use**: Use findings strictly for legal and ethical purposes.

Final Takeaway

This case study demonstrates the power of OSINT in tracking individuals through public databases. By following a structured approach—starting with business records, then verifying property, licensing, voter registration, and social media—an investigator can construct a detailed profile while remaining within ethical and legal boundaries.

3. Social Media Profiles & Cross-Platform Analysis

Social media platforms serve as digital footprints, often revealing crucial insights about a person's identity, location, and connections. This chapter explores methods for discovering, analyzing, and cross-referencing social media profiles across multiple platforms. You'll learn how to track username patterns, uncover hidden profiles, and extract valuable metadata from posts, images, and interactions. Additionally, we'll discuss techniques for mapping relationships and identifying linked accounts, enabling a more comprehensive view of an individual's online presence.

3.1 How to Search for Hidden Social Media Accounts

Social media is one of the most valuable sources for OSINT investigations, but many individuals attempt to hide their accounts by using aliases, limited personal details, or privacy settings. However, through various techniques, investigators can uncover hidden social media profiles by analyzing usernames, email addresses, phone numbers, and other digital breadcrumbs.

This chapter covers step-by-step methods to locate hidden social media accounts using advanced OSINT techniques, including username enumeration, metadata analysis, and cross-platform correlation.

3.1.1 Understanding Why People Hide Social Media Accounts

Before searching for hidden profiles, it's important to understand why individuals may conceal their accounts:

- **Privacy Concerns** – They want to keep personal details hidden from the public.
- **Fraud & Deception** – Some create hidden accounts to engage in scams or impersonation.
- **Multiple Identities** – They maintain different profiles for personal, professional, or anonymous use.
- **Avoiding Detection** – Criminals, whistleblowers, or dissidents may hide accounts for security reasons.

Knowing these motivations helps investigators determine where and how a person may attempt to conceal their online presence.

3.1.2 Searching by Username & Variations

Method 1: Username Reuse Across Platforms

Most people reuse usernames across multiple websites. If you find a username linked to one social media profile, you can check if the same username exists on other platforms.

Tools & Techniques:

OSINT Username Search Engines:

- **WhatsMyName (whatsmyname.app)** – Checks username availability across multiple websites.
- **Namechk (namechk.com)** – Searches for usernames across social media, gaming, and online services.
- **KnowEm (knowem.com)** – Identifies username usage across 500+ platforms.

Manual Google Searches:

- "username" site:facebook.com
- "username" site:instagram.com
- "username" site:tiktok.com

Variations to Check:

- JohnDoe → John.Doe, John_Doe, JohnDoe123, J_Doe
- Modify numbers (birth year, area code)

Method 2: Reverse Searching Usernames

Once you find a username, you can:

- Check profile pictures for matches on Google Reverse Image Search.
- Search the username in data breach databases (e.g., HaveIBeenPwned).
- Look for forum posts, blogs, or gaming accounts linked to that username.

3.1.3 Searching by Email Address

Method 1: Social Media Login Lookup

Many platforms allow users to check if an email is associated with an account:

- Try the "Forgot Password" option on major platforms (Twitter, Instagram, Facebook).
- If the email exists, the platform may display a masked username or profile hint.

Method 2: Email Lookup Tools

Several OSINT tools can check whether an email is linked to social media accounts:

- **IntelX (intelx.io)** – Searches for leaked data related to an email.
- **Hunter.io** – Finds professional accounts linked to an email.
- **EmailRep (emailrep.io)** – Assesses reputation and associated accounts.

3.1.4 Searching by Phone Number

Method 1: Social Media Contact Syncing

- Create a new contact with the target's phone number and enable contact syncing on WhatsApp, Facebook, Instagram, or Telegram.
- If the number is linked to an account, the platform may suggest it as a friend/contact.

Method 2: Reverse Phone Lookup

- **TrueCaller** (truecaller.com) – Finds linked names and profiles.
- **Sync.me** – Identifies social media accounts tied to phone numbers.
- **OSINT tools like Scylla.sh** – Searches phone numbers in breach databases.

3.1.5 Reverse Image Search for Social Media Profiles

If you have a photo of the person, you can conduct a reverse image search to find social media profiles.

Tools to Use:

- Google Reverse Image Search

- Yandex Reverse Image Search – More effective for facial recognition.
- TinEye (tineye.com) – Finds image matches across the internet.

Steps to Conduct a Search:

Upload the image to Google Images (images.google.com).
Check LinkedIn, Facebook, Twitter, and other social sites for matching profile pictures.
Use Yandex for better facial recognition, as it often identifies accounts Google misses.

3.1.6 Investigating Social Media Metadata & URL Structures

Finding Hidden Facebook Profiles

Use Google Dorks:

- "John Doe" site:facebook.com
- intitle:"John Doe" site:facebook.com

Check Facebook Graph Search URLs (if available).

If you find a Facebook profile ID (numeric), plug it into:

- https://www.facebook.com/profile.php?id=[ID]

Finding Hidden Twitter Accounts

- Check Twitter advanced search for tweets mentioning the person's name.
- If a LinkedIn profile exists, check for a linked Twitter handle.
- Try Twitter ID converters to find old handles.

Instagram & TikTok Hidden Accounts

- If the person follows an influencer, their profile may show up in comment sections.
- Instagram & TikTok accounts often use the same bio, emojis, or hashtags—search these across platforms.

3.1.7 Case Study: Uncovering a Hidden Social Media Account

Scenario:

An OSINT investigator is hired to verify the online presence of a suspect named Michael Carter. The client suspects that Michael has a hidden Instagram and Twitter account that he uses under a different name.

Investigation Steps:

✓ Step 1: Check Known Usernames

- The investigator finds an old email from a data breach that contains "MikeC89" as part of the username.
- Searching "MikeC89" site:instagram.com and Twitter username checkers reveals inactive accounts.

✓ Step 2: Reverse Image Search

- A LinkedIn photo of Michael is uploaded to Yandex, which returns an Instagram profile: "mike_c_photography".

✓ Step 3: Cross-Platform Checks

- Searching "mike_c_photography" on Google shows a Twitter profile linked to an art community.
- A Pinterest account under the same username is found, containing Michael's personal artwork, confirming ownership.

✓ Step 4: Verifying Phone Number Linkage

- A Telegram contact search using Michael's phone number reveals an account with the same profile photo.

Conclusion:

The hidden social media accounts were identified using username reuse, image searches, and metadata analysis.

3.1.8 Ethical & Legal Considerations

☐ **DO NOT:**

✗ Hack, breach, or illegally access private data.

✗ Impersonate someone to gain unauthorized access.

✗ Publicly expose private information irresponsibly.

✅ DO:

✓☐ Use only legal and public OSINT techniques.
✓☐ Verify findings with multiple sources before drawing conclusions.
✓☐ Respect privacy laws (GDPR, CCPA, etc.).

Conclusion

Finding hidden social media accounts requires creativity, patience, and multiple OSINT techniques. By leveraging username searches, email lookups, reverse image tools, and metadata analysis, investigators can uncover concealed profiles while remaining within legal and ethical boundaries.

3.2 Facebook OSINT: Analyzing Profiles, Groups & Posts

Facebook remains one of the richest OSINT (Open-Source Intelligence) sources, offering valuable insights into a person's digital footprint. While privacy settings have evolved, investigators can still extract useful information from profiles, posts, groups, and interactions. This chapter covers step-by-step methods to analyze Facebook data, including profile enumeration, group monitoring, post tracking, and metadata extraction.

3.2.1 Understanding Facebook's OSINT Value

Facebook provides several types of publicly accessible data:

- **Profile Information** – Name, bio, profile picture, cover photo, workplace, education.
- **Friends & Connections** – Friend lists (if public), mutual friends, tagged associations.
- **Groups & Pages** – Public group memberships, liked pages, comments on public posts.

- **Posts & Media** – Status updates, images, videos, and shared links.
- **Check-ins & Locations** – Places visited, geotagged posts, and location-based content.

By analyzing these elements, OSINT investigators can build a comprehensive profile of a target individual.

3.2.2 Extracting Facebook Profile Information

Step 1: Locating a Target's Facebook Profile

Google Dorking Techniques:

- "John Doe" site:facebook.com
- "John Doe" AND "City Name" site:facebook.com
- inurl:"facebook.com/public" "John Doe"

Facebook's Built-in Search:

- Use keywords like name, workplace, education, or phone number.
- If known, search by their email or username in the search bar.

Step 2: Analyzing a Profile Page

Even if a profile is private, the following elements may still be visible:

- **Profile Picture & Cover Photo** – Can be cross-referenced using reverse image searches.
- **Intro/Bio Section** – May contain workplace, location, relationship status.
- **Education & Work History** – Often visible under the "About" section.
- **Friends List** – If public, check for connections and potential aliases.
- **Liked Pages** – Reveals interests, affiliations, and possible workplaces.

Step 3: Checking Profile Metadata

Right-click on a profile picture and copy the image URL.

The URL contains a Facebook User ID (UID) in this format:

https://www.facebook.com/photo.php?fbid=1234567890&id=987654321

Extract the UID and use it in the following query:

https://www.facebook.com/UID

This may reveal alternative profiles, business pages, or old accounts.

3.2.3 Investigating Facebook Groups

Finding Groups Associated with a Person

Check the "Groups" tab on a target's profile (if public).

Use Google Dorks to find group membership:

- "John Doe" site:facebook.com/groups
- "Joined this group" site:facebook.com

Analyze posts within public groups for comments, reactions, or discussions involving the target.

Monitoring Group Activity

- Some private groups allow public post previews—check for discussions and member lists.
- Use Wayback Machine (archive.org) to see past group discussions.
- Look for patterns—group membership often reveals political, religious, or professional affiliations.

Extracting Group Member Lists

- Open a public group and scroll through the Members section.
- Cross-reference names in other social media searches.
- Identify frequent posters or admins who may have closer ties to the target.

3.2.4 Tracking Facebook Posts & Interactions

Searching for a Target's Past Posts

Use Facebook's built-in search with filters for year, location, or content type.

Google Dorks for posts:

- site:facebook.com "John Doe" "Just posted"
- "John Doe" site:facebook.com/posts

Finding Posts They've Liked or Commented On

Even if a profile is private, their interactions on public posts remain visible.

- Go to news pages, public figures, or community groups where they may have commented.

Use Facebook search with keywords:

"John Doe commented" site:facebook.com

Track patterns—do they frequently interact with a specific individual or page?

Extracting Post Metadata

Every Facebook post has a unique post ID.

Right-click on a post's timestamp, copy the link, and extract the Post ID:

https://www.facebook.com/username/posts/1234567890

The ID can be used to track edits, shares, and discussion threads.

3.2.5 Reverse Image & Video Analysis on Facebook

Reverse Image Search on Facebook

If you suspect a photo belongs to a certain profile:

- Download the image from Facebook.
- Use Google Reverse Image Search, Yandex, or TinEye.
- Check for matching photos on LinkedIn, Instagram, or dating sites.

Extracting EXIF Metadata (If Applicable)

- Facebook removes metadata from uploaded images, but screenshots from mobile uploads may retain geotags.
- Cross-check profile photos with social media image databases (e.g., PimEyes, Betaface).
- Tracking Facebook Videos
- If a video is uploaded natively to Facebook, extract the video URL and check for reposts using InVID verification tools.
- Look for hidden metadata in captions (e.g., location tags, event mentions).

3.2.6 Case Study: Uncovering a Hidden Facebook Profile

Scenario:

An OSINT investigator is hired to track Lisa Matthews, a missing person. The client believes Lisa may have an alternate Facebook account.

Investigation Steps:

✅ **Step 1: Google Dorking & Username Search**

- "Lisa Matthews" site:facebook.com returns multiple profiles.
- Searching "LisaM89" site:facebook.com" leads to an abandoned account with a similar profile picture.

✅ **Step 2: Checking Friends & Tagged Photos**

- The old account is connected to Emily R., a known close friend.
- Checking Emily's profile reveals Lisa was tagged in a recent post, but under a different name.

✅ **Step 3: Extracting Metadata & Analyzing Groups**

- Lisa's new profile (under alias Lisa Marie) is a member of local fitness and travel groups.
- A public group discussion confirms she recently traveled to Los Angeles.

Conclusion:

By using Dorking, friend connections, and group analysis, Lisa's hidden profile was discovered, providing critical location details.

3.2.7 Ethical & Legal Considerations

☐ **DO NOT:**

✖ Hack, breach, or use phishing to access private accounts.

✖ Engage in unauthorized scraping of Facebook data (violates ToS).

✖ Publish or misuse personally identifiable information (PII).

✅ **DO:**

✓☐ Use publicly accessible information and legal OSINT methods.
✓☐ Verify information across multiple sources before making conclusions.
✓☐ Adhere to data privacy laws (GDPR, CCPA).

Conclusion

Facebook remains a goldmine for OSINT investigations, offering deep insights into a person's digital behavior. By leveraging advanced search techniques, metadata extraction, and group analysis, investigators can uncover hidden profiles, connections, and activities while staying within ethical boundaries.

3.3 Twitter & X OSINT: Tracking Mentions, Hashtags & Followers

Twitter (now rebranded as X) remains one of the most powerful platforms for OSINT investigations. With its real-time updates, open API, and public-by-default posts, investigators can extract valuable data on individuals, organizations, and events. By tracking mentions, hashtags, and follower relationships, OSINT analysts can uncover hidden connections, identify trends, and monitor social behaviors.

This chapter covers advanced techniques for extracting intelligence from Twitter/X, including keyword searches, metadata analysis, and follower tracking strategies.

3.3.1 Why Twitter/X Is Valuable for OSINT

Twitter/X is a goldmine for intelligence gathering due to its:

- **Public Nature** – Most tweets, replies, and interactions are publicly accessible.
- **Real-Time Data** – Fast updates make it useful for tracking breaking news and live events.
- **User Engagement Patterns** – Replies, likes, retweets, and follows reveal relationships.
- **Geotagged Posts** – Some tweets contain location data, useful for tracking movements.
- **Hashtag & Trend Analysis** – Helps identify viral topics and sentiment shifts.

3.3.2 Finding & Analyzing Twitter/X Profiles

Step 1: Locating a Target's Twitter/X Account

Google Dorking Techniques:

Use the following queries to locate Twitter/X profiles:

- "John Doe" site:twitter.com
- "John Doe" AND "City Name" site:twitter.com
- "JohnDoe89" site:twitter.com (if you suspect a username)

Twitter/X Search Operators:

Twitter's search bar supports advanced filters:

- from: – Find tweets from a specific user.
- from:JohnDoe
- to: – See tweets directed at a user.
- to:JohnDoe
- since: and until: – Filter tweets by date.
- from:JohnDoe since:2023-01-01 until:2023-12-31
- filter:links – Show only tweets with URLs.
- from:JohnDoe filter:links

Step 2: Extracting Profile Metadata

A Twitter/X profile may reveal:

- **Username & Handle** – Check for variations across platforms.
- **Profile & Cover Photos** – Reverse image search them for matches.
- **Bio & Location** – May contain job titles, interests, or city names.
- **Join Date** – Helps verify authenticity.
- **Pinned Tweets** – Often showcase important personal or professional details.

3.3.3 Tracking Mentions & Conversations

Method 1: Searching for Mentions of a Target

To find who is talking about a person or brand, use:

- **@JohnDoe** – See direct mentions.
- **"John Doe"** – Find tweets containing their name.
- **"John Doe"** -from:JohnDoe – Exclude their own tweets to see what others say.

Method 2: Monitoring Replies & Conversations

- Open a tweet and check the "View Replies" section.
- Look for hidden replies (Twitter/X often hides flagged content).
- Use thread readers (like Thread Reader App) to extract long conversations.

Method 3: Real-Time Mentions Monitoring

- Use TweetDeck (free) or tools like Hootsuite, Mention, or Brandwatch to track mentions in real time.

3.3.4 Hashtag & Trend Analysis

Method 1: Finding Relevant Hashtags

Hashtags reveal trending topics and discussions. Use:

- **#OSINT** – Search general topics.
- **#MissingPerson #FindJohnDoe** – Track case-specific investigations.

Trending Tab – See viral hashtags in a given location.

Method 2: Advanced Hashtag Search

Use boolean search operators:

- **#CyberSecurity** OR **#InfoSec** – Finds tweets with either hashtag.
- **#OSINT** -filter:retweets – Excludes retweets.
- **#Ukraine** since:2024-01-01 – Filters by date.

Method 3: Extracting Hashtag Networks

- **Hashtagify** (hashtagify.me) – Shows related hashtags.
- **Trendsmap** (trendsmap.com) – Visualizes trending hashtags by location.

3.3.5 Tracking Followers & Network Analysis

Method 1: Investigating a Target's Followers

- **Open the "Followers" tab** – Look for patterns (location, mutual friends).
- **Identify frequent engagers** – People who regularly like, retweet, or reply.

Export follower data using tools like:

- **Followerwonk** – Analyzes follower demographics.
- **Tweepy (Python API)** – Scrapes follower lists.

Method 2: Detecting Fake Followers & Bots

BotSentinel (botsentinel.com) – Flags suspicious accounts.

Account Age & Activity – Fake accounts often have:

- Very few tweets
- High follow-to-follower ratio
- Default profile pictures

Method 3: Monitoring Who Someone Follows

- Go to "Following" tab – Check for interactions with organizations, influencers, or suspicious entities.
- Look for hidden networks – People often follow related accounts across platforms.

3.3.6 Geolocation Tracking on Twitter/X

Finding Tweets with Location Data

Some tweets contain geotags, which can be searched using:

- **Near**: – Finds tweets from a specific location.
- **near**:"New York" within:10km
- **Geocode**: – Uses latitude/longitude to find tweets.
- **geocode**:37.7749,-122.4194,10km

Extracting Location Clues from Tweets

Even if geotags are off, users may reveal locations via:

- Check-ins (e.g., "At JFK Airport ✈□")
- Photos (landmarks, storefronts)
- Local slang or cultural references

3.3.7 Case Study: Unmasking a Twitter/X Sock Puppet Account

Scenario:

An OSINT investigator is hired to verify if a political influencer (@TruthSeeker99) is secretly running an anonymous account (@InsiderLeaks).

Investigation Steps:

✅ Step 1: Username & Handle Analysis

- The investigator finds an old leaked email associated with @TruthSeeker99.
- Checking username variations (TruthSeeker_99, TruthSeekerXX) leads to similar accounts.

✅ Step 2: Follower Overlap

- The investigator compares followers of both accounts using Followerwonk.
- 78% of @InsiderLeaks' followers are also following @TruthSeeker99.

✅ Step 3: Post Timing & Language Analysis

- Both accounts post in the same time zones and use similar phrases.
- Tweets are posted within minutes of each other, indicating a likely connection.

Conclusion:

Using follower analysis, linguistic patterns, and posting behaviors, the investigator confirms both accounts are controlled by the same person.

3.3.8 Ethical & Legal Considerations

☐ **DO NOT:**

✗ Engage in unauthorized scraping or hacking of Twitter/X data.

✗ Misuse private or sensitive information.

✗ Impersonate or harass individuals during investigations.

✅ **DO:**

✓☐ Use only publicly available and legally accessible data.
✓☐ Cross-verify findings before making assumptions.
✓☐ Follow privacy laws (GDPR, CCPA, CFAA compliance).

Conclusion

Twitter/X is an essential tool for OSINT investigations, offering a vast amount of real-time, public, and geolocated data. By tracking mentions, hashtags, and follower interactions, investigators can uncover valuable intelligence while adhering to ethical and legal guidelines.

3.4 Instagram & TikTok OSINT: Identifying Trends & Connections

Instagram and TikTok have emerged as two of the most influential social media platforms, with billions of users worldwide. For OSINT (Open-Source Intelligence) investigations, these platforms provide crucial insights into a person's lifestyle, connections, location patterns, and behavioral trends. Despite privacy restrictions, an investigator can still extract valuable data from public profiles, hashtags, geotags, and interactions.

This chapter covers advanced OSINT techniques for tracking individuals and trends on Instagram and TikTok, including profile analysis, metadata extraction, and cross-platform investigations.

3.4.1 Why Instagram & TikTok Are Valuable for OSINT

Instagram OSINT Benefits

- **Highly Visual** – Users frequently post personal images, videos, and stories.
- **Geolocation Data** – Posts, check-ins, and tagged locations reveal movement.
- **Follower & Following Analysis** – Shows social circles and possible connections.
- **Hashtag Trends** – Helps identify interests, affiliations, and events.

TikTok OSINT Benefits

- **Short-Form Videos** – Content often includes spoken details, text overlays, or locations.
- **User Engagement** – Comments, duets, and reactions help track interactions.
- **Viral Trends** – Audio, hashtags, and challenges can reveal behavioral patterns.
- **Metadata & Timestamps** – Videos contain crucial time and location-based data.

3.4.2 Finding & Analyzing Instagram Profiles

Step 1: Locating an Instagram Account

Google Dorking for Instagram

Use advanced Google searches to find a profile:

- "John Doe" site:instagram.com
- "JohnDoe89" site:instagram.com
- "John Doe" AND "City Name" site:instagram.com

Instagram Username Investigation

- If a username is known, search directly: https://www.instagram.com/username/
- Check if the same username exists on Twitter, TikTok, LinkedIn, etc.

Step 2: Extracting Public Profile Data

Even private accounts can reveal:

- **Profile Picture & Bio** – Cross-check with other social media.
- **Follower & Following List** – Shows connections and potential aliases.
- **Story Highlights** – May contain archived posts from past events.
- **Tagged Posts** – Other users tagging the target may expose hidden details.

Step 3: Metadata & Image Analysis

- Reverse image search profile pictures (Google, Yandex, or PimEyes).
- Check EXIF data on uploaded images (location, camera model, timestamp).
- Identify common backgrounds or objects to estimate location.

3.4.3 Investigating Instagram Hashtags & Geotags

Tracking Hashtags for Trends & Activities

Search hashtags related to a person or event:

- #JohnDoeWedding
- #NewYorkNightlife
- #CryptoConference2024

Use tools like Hashtagify to find related hashtags and analyze trends.

Geolocation Tracking on Instagram

- Users tag locations in posts/stories, even if they don't explicitly reveal their location.
- Use https://www.instagram.com/explore/locations/ to find posts from specific places.
- Search for tagged restaurants, airports, or event venues to track movement.

Extracting Data from Instagram Stories & Reels

- Stories disappear in 24 hours but can be saved as highlights.
- Use screen recording or archive tools to capture disappearing content.
- Analyze background elements for location clues (license plates, street signs, landmarks).

3.4.4 Finding & Analyzing TikTok Profiles

Step 1: Locating a TikTok Account

Google Dorking for TikTok

- "John Doe" site:tiktok.com
- "JohnDoe89" site:tiktok.com
- "John Doe" AND "City Name" site:tiktok.com"

TikTok Username Lookup

- Directly search usernames: https://www.tiktok.com/@username
- Cross-reference usernames on other platforms.

Step 2: Extracting Profile Information

- **Bio Section** – May contain links to other social media.
- **Pinned Videos** – Often highlight important aspects of the user's life.
- **Following & Followers List** – Check mutual connections.
- **Liked Videos & Comments** – Shows user preferences and interactions.

3.4.5 Tracking TikTok Trends & Engagement

Hashtags & Challenges

- Track trending hashtags & challenges to identify viral content.
- Search hashtag directories like trendpop.com or TikTok's "Discover" page.
- Identify target engagement in trends (e.g., if a person frequently joins viral challenges).

Duets & Stitching Analysis

- Duets show who a user interacts with via side-by-side videos.

- Stitches let users add their own content to someone else's video.
- Analyzing frequent duets/stitches can reveal close connections.

TikTok Location Tracking

- Many TikTok videos include background locations.
- Users may mention locations verbally or use text overlays.
- Search "Check-in" TikTok videos for geotagged content.

3.4.6 Case Study: Identifying a Person's Travel History via Instagram & TikTok

Scenario:

An OSINT investigator is hired to track Emma Roberts, who is suspected of traveling under an alias.

Investigation Steps:

✅ **Step 1: Instagram Profile & Geotags**

- Emma's Instagram profile is private, but her friend's profile is public.
- A geotagged post shows a vacation spot in Bali—Emma is tagged.

✅ **Step 2: TikTok Hashtags & Challenges**

- Searching #BaliTravel on TikTok reveals a video with a woman resembling Emma.
- Checking the audio trend, the investigator finds Emma's personal TikTok account.

✅ **Step 3: Metadata & Image Analysis**

- The TikTok video's background matches an Instagram story from another account.
- Reverse image search on hotel decor confirms she stayed at a specific resort.

Conclusion:

By cross-referencing Instagram geotags, TikTok hashtags, and background analysis, the investigator successfully mapped Emma's recent travel history.

3.4.7 Ethical & Legal Considerations

☐ DO NOT:

✗ Hack, breach, or use phishing to access private accounts.

✗ Engage in unauthorized scraping of Instagram or TikTok data.

✗ Publish or misuse personally identifiable information (PII).

✅ DO:

✓☐ Use publicly available data and OSINT-approved methods.

✓☐ Cross-verify information before drawing conclusions.

✓☐ Follow platform policies and legal frameworks (GDPR, CCPA, CFAA compliance).

Conclusion

Instagram and TikTok are rich sources of OSINT data, providing insight into personal behaviors, connections, and travel history. By leveraging hashtags, geolocation data, and metadata analysis, investigators can track individuals and trends while maintaining ethical standards.

3.5 LinkedIn OSINT: Employment History & Professional Networks

LinkedIn is the world's largest professional networking platform, with over 900 million users. Unlike other social media platforms, LinkedIn is primarily focused on career development, making it a valuable resource for OSINT (Open-Source Intelligence) investigations. Whether you're verifying someone's employment history, mapping professional connections, or uncovering hidden relationships, LinkedIn can provide a wealth of data.

In this chapter, we will explore advanced OSINT techniques for extracting intelligence from LinkedIn profiles, including employment verification, network analysis, endorsements, and cross-platform investigations.

3.5.1 Why LinkedIn is Valuable for OSINT

Key Reasons LinkedIn is Useful for OSINT Investigations:

✓ **Real Identity Usage** – Most users use their real names and career details.

✓ **Employment & Education Details** – Provides insights into work history and qualifications.

✓ **Connections & Endorsements** – Reveals professional networks and affiliations.

✓ **Company & Industry Insights** – Useful for corporate investigations.

✓ **Cross-Platform Linkage** – Many users link their LinkedIn profiles to other social media.

Despite these advantages, privacy restrictions and fake profiles can pose challenges. This chapter will cover both direct and indirect methods for OSINT investigations on LinkedIn.

3.5.2 Finding & Analyzing LinkedIn Profiles

Step 1: Locating a LinkedIn Account

Google Dorking for LinkedIn

Use advanced Google searches to find a LinkedIn profile:

- "John Doe" site:linkedin.com
- "John Doe" AND "Company Name" site:linkedin.com
- "JohnDoe89" site:linkedin.com/in/ (if you suspect a username format)

Searching on LinkedIn Itself

Use LinkedIn's People Search with filters:

- Name
- Company
- Location
- Education

Check alternative spellings or initials (e.g., "J. Doe" instead of "John Doe").

Step 2: Extracting Public Profile Data

Even if a LinkedIn profile is private, you can still access:

- **Profile Picture & Cover Photo** – Useful for reverse image searches.
- **Current & Past Job Titles** – Can be cross-referenced for verification.
- **Education History** – Helps validate credentials.
- **Skills & Endorsements** – Shows expertise areas and colleague interactions.
- **Mutual Connections** – Identifies people within their network.

3.5.3 Verifying Employment History & Credentials

Method 1: Cross-Checking Employment Claims

- Compare job titles and tenure with company websites and press releases.
- Search the company's team page to confirm if the person is listed.
- Look up SEC filings, patents, or research papers for executive-level individuals.

Method 2: Confirming a Person's Role via Network Activity

- Check if colleagues have endorsed or mentioned them in posts.
- Look for comments and interactions from verified employees of the same company.
- See if they appear in group discussions related to their industry.

Method 3: Checking for Fake Job Claims

- Look at the company's official LinkedIn page – Does the person appear as an employee?
- Verify details through Glassdoor, business directories, and corporate filings.
- Search for press releases or LinkedIn posts from real employees welcoming new hires.

3.5.4 Mapping Professional Networks & Connections

Method 1: Analyzing Direct Connections

- Look at a person's first-degree connections to identify close colleagues.
- Check who they frequently interact with in posts and comments.
- Identify connections to specific industries, locations, or organizations.

Method 2: Using Mutual Connections to Uncover Links

- If a profile is private, check mutual connections for insights.
- Look for indirect relationships (e.g., both are connected to the same industry leader).
- Use LinkedIn Groups to see common affiliations.

Method 3: Detecting Fake or Suspicious Connections

- Profiles with low engagement, generic names, or stock photos may be fake.
- A person with thousands of random connections might be collecting contacts for fraud.
- Use LinkedIn Sales Navigator or Hunter.io to validate business email addresses.

3.5.5 Extracting Intelligence from LinkedIn Activity

Tracking Posts, Comments, and Interactions

- Analyze a user's posts, articles, and shared content for clues about their interests.
- Check who engages with their content (colleagues, recruiters, competitors?).
- Look for mentions in other users' posts – these can provide indirect insights.

Monitoring Endorsements & Recommendations

- Skills endorsed by multiple colleagues suggest real expertise.
- Fake profiles often have random endorsements from unrelated industries.
- Recommendations can reveal past work relationships and hidden networks.

3.5.6 Case Study: Uncovering a False Employment Claim via LinkedIn OSINT

Scenario:

An employer wants to verify if Michael Carter really worked as a "Senior Cybersecurity Analyst" at a well-known company.

Investigation Steps:

✅ Step 1: LinkedIn Profile Analysis

- Michael's profile lists his job at XYZ Corp from 2020-2024.

- He has no mutual connections with other known employees at XYZ Corp.

✅ Step 2: Cross-Checking Company Employees

- Searching site:linkedin.com "XYZ Corp" "Cybersecurity Analyst"
- Michael's name does not appear on the company's LinkedIn employee list.

✅ Step 3: Verifying External Mentions

- XYZ Corp's official website and team page do not list him.
- No conference appearances, blog posts, or press releases mention him.

✅ Step 4: Contacting Verified Employees

- A current XYZ Corp employee (found through LinkedIn) confirms Michael never worked there.

Conclusion:

By using LinkedIn OSINT, Google dorking, and employee verification, the investigator confirmed that Michael Carter's employment claim was false.

3.5.7 Ethical & Legal Considerations

☐ **DO NOT:**

✗ Attempt to hack or bypass LinkedIn's privacy settings.

✗ Create fake profiles to connect with targets (this violates LinkedIn's TOS).

✗ Scrape LinkedIn data in violation of platform policies (LinkedIn aggressively pursues legal action against mass scraping).

✅ **DO:**

✓☐ Use publicly available information and cross-verify sources.
✓☐ Follow GDPR, CCPA, and CFAA compliance when handling personal data.
✓☐ Respect platform privacy rules and ethical guidelines.

Conclusion

LinkedIn is a powerful OSINT tool for mapping professional connections, verifying employment claims, and analyzing industry networks. By utilizing Google dorking, profile analysis, and network mapping, investigators can extract valuable intelligence while maintaining ethical standards.

3.6 Case Study: Unmasking a Fake Social Media Account

Fake social media accounts are widely used for scams, misinformation campaigns, cyberstalking, and identity fraud. OSINT (Open-Source Intelligence) investigators frequently encounter these accounts in corporate security, fraud investigations, and personal safety cases.

In this case study, we will walk through a real-world scenario where a suspicious Twitter/X and Instagram account was investigated, exposing its fraudulent nature. We will apply OSINT techniques such as reverse image searches, metadata analysis, social graph mapping, and cross-platform verification to reveal the truth.

3.6.1 The Suspicious Account

Scenario:

A well-known cybersecurity expert, Lisa Monroe, receives multiple online harassment messages from an anonymous Twitter/X account, @CyberTruthSecure. The account claims to be another industry expert, posting similar content but also spreading false claims about Lisa's work. Lisa suspects the account is a fake persona created to impersonate or harass her.

3.6.2 Initial Analysis: Gathering Basic Profile Information

Step 1: Checking the Profile Details

- **Username**: @CyberTruthSecure
- **Bio**: Claims to be a cybersecurity researcher.
- **Profile Picture**: A professional-looking headshot.
- **Followers**: 5,000+ (suspicious for a new account).
- **Engagement**: Limited (few likes or comments on posts).

- **Joined Date**: Only three months ago.

Red Flags Noticed:

⚑ **Generic Bio** – No company affiliation, vague job title.
⚑ **Suspiciously High Follower Count** – Possibly purchased or bot-generated.
⚑ **Stock-Like Profile Picture** – Could be AI-generated or stolen.
⚑ **No Personal Engagement** – No real conversations or tagged interactions.

3.6.3 Reverse Image Search: Checking Profile Pictures

Step 2: Verifying the Profile Picture

Using Google Reverse Image Search, Yandex, and PimEyes, we upload the profile picture to check for duplicates.

Findings:

✅ The image appears on multiple stock photo websites, revealing that the supposed "cybersecurity expert" is actually a model from a free image database.

✅ This confirms the account is using a fake identity, raising further suspicions.

3.6.4 Cross-Platform Investigation: Looking for Other Social Media Accounts

Step 3: Finding the Same Username Elsewhere

We check whether @CyberTruthSecure exists on:

- Instagram
- LinkedIn
- Facebook

Findings:

✅ An Instagram account with the same username exists but has no personal photos.

✅ The LinkedIn profile is empty, with no verifiable job history.

✅ The Facebook search returns no matches.

☐ **Conclusion**: This persona is likely not a real person, but rather a sock puppet account created for deception.

3.6.5 Analyzing Follower & Engagement Patterns

Step 4: Checking Follower Quality

We use FollowerAudit and BotSentinel to analyze:

- Who follows this account
- Follower activity patterns
- Engagement vs. follower ratio

Findings:

✓ 60% of followers are bots – newly created accounts, no profile pictures.

✓ The account mostly retweets rather than engaging in real discussions.

✓ Repetitive tweet patterns suggest automated or pre-scheduled content.

3.6.6 IP & Metadata Tracing: Identifying the Real Operator

Step 5: Extracting Metadata from Interactions

We analyze:

- **Tweet timestamps** – When are they most active?
- **Common language use** – Do they use specific phrases or slang?
- **Geotagged posts** – Any location data available?

Findings:

✓ Most tweets are posted between 2 AM – 6 AM in Lisa Monroe's time zone.

✓ The writing style is similar to an individual known to be critical of Lisa in the past.

✓ A single geotagged tweet points to a specific city in another country.

☐ **Conclusion**: The pattern suggests that this could be a rival or someone with a personal grudge against Lisa.

3.6.7 Verifying the Account's History & Associated Aliases

Step 6: Searching for Past Usernames & Linked Accounts

Using tools like whatsmyname.app and UserRecon, we check:

- Previous usernames (if changed).
- Other connected accounts that may belong to the same operator.

Findings:

✅ The account was previously named @CyberResearch21 before changing to @CyberTruthSecure.

✅ A past post from @CyberResearch21 referenced an argument with Lisa Monroe.

✅ Another Instagram account with a similar writing style and hashtags seems to be operated by the same person.

☐ **Conclusion**: This is likely a personal sock puppet account created to damage Lisa's reputation.

3.6.8 Case Resolution: Confirming & Reporting the Fake Account

Final Steps Taken:

✅ Lisa reports the account to Twitter/X for impersonation and harassment.

✅ We compile evidence, including:

- Reverse image search results.
- Metadata from tweets.
- Past usernames and linked accounts.

✅ A cybersecurity group assists in publicly debunking the fake identity.

Outcome:

🚀 The account is removed within a week!
⬜⬜ Lisa strengthens her OSINT monitoring to prevent future impersonations.

3.6.9 Ethical & Legal Considerations

⬜ **DO NOT:**

✖ Hack, phish, or use illegal methods to access private accounts.

✖ Engage in doxxing or publicly expose individuals without solid proof.

✖ Use OSINT tools to harass or intimidate individuals.

✅ **DO:**

✓⬜ Use publicly available data and legal OSINT methods.
✓⬜ Document findings professionally before making allegations.
✓⬜ Report impersonation accounts through official channels.

Conclusion

This case study demonstrated how OSINT techniques can effectively unmask fake social media accounts through reverse image searches, metadata tracking, network analysis, and historical username investigations.

4. Email & Username Investigations

An email address or username can be a powerful starting point for uncovering an individual's online activity. In this chapter, you'll learn how to trace email addresses to identify associated accounts, websites, and breaches. We'll explore username investigation techniques, including pattern analysis, reverse searches, and cross-platform correlation. By leveraging specialized OSINT tools and databases, you'll be able to track digital footprints, uncover hidden profiles, and connect fragmented data points to build a more complete picture of your subject.

4.1 Reverse Searching Email Addresses for OSINT

An email address can reveal a wealth of intelligence about an individual, from their social media profiles and online accounts to potential data breaches and even physical locations. OSINT (Open-Source Intelligence) investigators often use reverse email searches to:

✓ Identify an individual's online footprint

✓ Uncover hidden social media accounts

✓ Check for past data breaches

✓ Track username patterns and aliases

✓ Validate email authenticity

In this chapter, we'll explore free and paid OSINT tools, manual investigation techniques, and ethical considerations when conducting reverse email searches.

4.1.1 Understanding Email Structure & Identifiers

Key Components of an Email Address:

An email address consists of two main parts:

✉ Local Part (before the @) – Usually a username, initials, or a name abbreviation.
▢ Domain Part (after the @) – Shows the email provider (e.g., Gmail, Yahoo, corporate domain).

Common Email Patterns for Corporations & Individuals:

- First name + last name: john.doe@gmail.com
- Initials + last name: jdoe@company.com
- Username style: cyberhunter007@gmail.com
- Company domains: j.doe@securecorp.com

These patterns help predict other emails the person might use.

4.1.2 Free OSINT Tools for Reverse Email Searches

Step 1: Checking for Data Breaches

🔍 **HavelBeenPwned** – Searches if an email appears in data breaches.

🔗 https://haveibeenpwned.com/

- Shows if the email was compromised in past leaks.
- May reveal associated services or passwords (partially redacted).

Step 2: Searching for Social Media Accounts

🔍 **WhatsMyName** – Checks where an email is registered across platforms.

🔗 https://whatsmyname.app/

- Identifies profiles linked to an email.
- Useful for finding alternate usernames.

🔍 **Social Searcher** – Searches for social media accounts linked to an email.

🔗 https://www.social-searcher.com/

Step 3: Validating Email Authenticity

🔍 **EmailRep.io** – Checks an email's reputation.

🔗 https://emailrep.io/

- Identifies if an email is linked to a real person or a throwaway account.

🔍 **Hunter.io** – Finds corporate emails and verifies email deliverability.

🔗 https://hunter.io/

4.1.3 Advanced Reverse Email Search Techniques

Google Dorking for Email OSINT

Use Google Search Operators to check if an email appears on public pages:

📌 **Find mentions of the email online:**

"johndoe@gmail.com" -site:facebook.com -site:linkedin.com

📌 **Check if the email was exposed in forums:**

"johndoe@gmail.com" site:pastebin.com OR site:throwbin.io

📌 **Search for an email in PDF or documents:**

"johndoe@gmail.com" filetype:pdf

Cross-Referencing Emails with Username Searches

If an email contains a unique username (e.g., cyberhunter007), search for:

- Social media accounts
- Forum posts
- Gaming profiles
- Old blog posts

📌 **Search username variations on Google:**

"cyberhunter007" OR "cyberhunter_007" site:twitter.com

📌 **Check for historical usernames with Namechk**

🔗 https://www.namechk.com/

4.1.4 Paid OSINT Tools for Reverse Email Searches

For deeper investigations, professionals use paid tools like:

✅ **Pipl** – Provides in-depth email lookups with social media, addresses, and phone numbers.

🔗 https://pipl.com/

✅ **Spokeo** – Searches emails across public records, social media, and databases.

🔗 https://www.spokeo.com/

✅ **Skopenow** – Enterprise-grade OSINT platform for email investigations.

🔗 https://www.skopenow.com/

✅ **IntelX** – Searches leaked databases and archives for email traces.

🔗 https://intelx.io/

4.1.5 Case Study: Unmasking a Scammer via Reverse Email OSINT

Scenario:

A victim receives a suspicious email from michael.hawkins.business@gmail.com, claiming to be from a recruitment agency. They suspect it might be a scam.

Investigation Steps:

✅ Step 1: Checking for Data Breaches

- HaveIBeenPwned reveals that the email appeared in a 2019 data breach.

✅ Step 2: Google Dorking

- Searching "michael.hawkins.business@gmail.com" site:scamwarners.com
- The email appears on a scam forum reported under a fake recruiter scheme.

✅ Step 3: Reverse Searching Social Media

- WhatsMyName finds an Instagram account using the same email.
- The profile has no professional details—only random stock images.

✅ Step 4: Validating the Email

- EmailRep.io flags the email as suspicious and linked to past scams.
- Hunter.io shows no legitimate business tied to this email.

Outcome:

🚀 The email is confirmed as fraudulent, and the victim avoids falling for the scam.

4.1.6 Ethical & Legal Considerations in Email OSINT

☐ DO NOT:

✖ Use phishing or illegal methods to obtain private email data.

✖ Buy or trade stolen email credentials.

✖ Use OSINT to harass or intimidate individuals.

✅ DO:

✓☐ Use publicly available and legally obtained information.
✓☐ Follow GDPR, CCPA, and CFAA compliance laws.
✓☐ Respect user privacy and ethical OSINT guidelines.

Conclusion

Reverse searching an email address can provide critical intelligence in OSINT investigations. By using data breach databases, social media lookups, Google Dorking, and email verification tools, investigators can uncover hidden identities, fraudsters, and potential security threats.

4.2 Finding Social Media Accounts Linked to Emails

Email addresses are often the key to unlocking an individual's online presence. Many people use the same email to register across multiple platforms, allowing OSINT (Open-Source Intelligence) investigators to track down hidden social media accounts, forums, and other online traces.

In this chapter, we'll cover:

✓ How to check if an email is linked to social media accounts

✓ Using OSINT tools to uncover hidden profiles

✓ Manual techniques like Google Dorking and username correlation

✓ Ethical considerations when investigating social media ties

4.2.1 Why Email Searches Are Effective for Social Media OSINT

Many online services require an email for registration, including:

- **Social media platforms** (Facebook, Twitter/X, Instagram, LinkedIn)
- **Forums & discussion boards** (Reddit, Stack Overflow, Discord)
- **E-commerce & classified sites** (eBay, Craigslist, Etsy)
- **Gaming platforms** (Steam, PlayStation Network, Xbox Live)

Since many people use the same email for multiple accounts, identifying even one linked profile can lead to more discoveries.

4.2.2 Free OSINT Tools for Finding Social Media via Email

Step 1: Automated Social Media Checks

Several free tools help find social media profiles linked to an email:

🔍 WhatsMyName

∞ https://whatsmyname.app/

- Checks if an email or username is registered on various platforms.
- Great for finding hidden profiles.

🔍 Social Searcher

∞ https://www.social-searcher.com/

- Searches social media for mentions of an email address.
- Useful for finding accounts with public posts.

🔍 EmailRep.io

∞ https://emailrep.io/

- Checks the email's reputation and social media presence.
- Identifies if the email is linked to real or fake accounts.

🔍 OSINT Framework – Email Search Tools

∞ https://osintframework.com/

- Lists various tools for email-based investigations.

4.2.3 Manual Techniques: Google Dorking for Email Traces

If automated tools fail, try Google Dorking, a powerful search method using advanced Google Search Operators:

📌 Find public social media accounts linked to an email:

"johndoe@gmail.com" site:facebook.com OR site:instagram.com OR site:linkedin.com

📌 Search forums for discussions mentioning the email:

"johndoe@gmail.com" site:reddit.com OR site:stackexchange.com

📌 **Find e-commerce accounts registered with the email:**

"johndoe@gmail.com" site:ebay.com OR site:etsy.com

📌 **Check if the email appears in old pastebin leaks or breaches:**

"johndoe@gmail.com" site:pastebin.com OR site:throwbin.io

📌 **Locate public job profiles associated with the email:**

"johndoe@gmail.com" site:linkedin.com OR site:angel.co

Cross-Referencing Found Usernames

If a social media account is found using an email, extract the username and check if it's used on other platforms.

📌 **Example:**

- Found Twitter/X account: @CyberHunter007 linked to johndoe@gmail.com.
- Search CyberHunter007 on Instagram, Reddit, gaming sites, etc.
- Often, people use the same or similar usernames across platforms.

🔍 **Use Namechk to search for usernames**

🔗 https://www.namechk.com/

4.2.4 Using Browser Extensions & API Lookups

✅ **OSINT Browser Extensions:**

- **IntelTechniques Email Lookup Tool** – Extracts linked profiles.
- **Recon-ng** – A powerful OSINT framework with email lookup modules.
- **Sherlock** – Python-based username checker across social platforms.

✅ **API-Based Lookups (Paid Services):**

- **Pipl** 🔗 https://pipl.com/ – Finds deep web profiles.

- **Spokeo** ∞ https://www.spokeo.com/ – Searches public records & social media.
- **Skopenow** ∞ https://www.skopenow.com/ – Professional-grade social OSINT.

💡 Tip: Many of these tools require legitimate investigative use and prohibit unethical searches.

4.2.5 Case Study: Finding Hidden Social Media Accounts via Email

Scenario:

A cybersecurity analyst is investigating a suspected fake tech influencer who frequently spreads misinformation on social media. The only available clue is an email address:

✉ alex.techguru99@gmail.com

Investigation Process:

✅ **Step 1: Searching for Social Media Links**

Using WhatsMyName, the email is linked to:

- A Twitter/X account (@AlexTechGuru99)
- A LinkedIn profile under the name Alex Johnson

✅ **Step 2: Checking for Breached Data**

Using HaveIBeenPwned, the email appears in a 2018 forum data breach.

✅ **Step 3: Google Dorking to Find Mentions**

A search for "alex.techguru99@gmail.com" site:reddit.com reveals:

- An old Reddit account discussing tech investments.
- A Steam gaming profile under the username TechGuru99.

✅ **Step 4: Cross-Referencing Usernames**

Searching TechGuru99 on Instagram, Twitch, and YouTube uncovers:

- A YouTube channel posting tech scam reviews.
- A Twitch account streaming crypto investment advice.

Outcome:

🖋 The investigation confirmed Alex's real identity by connecting multiple accounts linked to the same email address.

4.2.6 Ethical & Legal Considerations in Email OSINT

☐ **DO NOT:**

✗ Hack, phish, or use illegal methods to access accounts.

✗ Buy or sell stolen email credentials.

✗ Use OSINT to harass or intimidate individuals.

✅ **DO:**

✓☐ Use legally available public data.
✓☐ Follow GDPR, CCPA, and CFAA compliance rules.
✓☐ Maintain ethical boundaries in personal investigations.

Conclusion

Reverse searching an email address is one of the most powerful OSINT techniques for uncovering hidden social media accounts. By combining automated tools, manual Google searches, username correlation, and professional-grade APIs, investigators can successfully map an individual's digital footprint.

4.3 Identifying Username Patterns Across Platforms

Usernames are a digital fingerprint that people often reuse across multiple platforms. Whether it's for social media, forums, gaming sites, or email addresses, tracking usernames is a powerful OSINT (Open-Source Intelligence) technique. By identifying username patterns, investigators can:

✓ Uncover hidden accounts on different websites.

✓ Map online activity across platforms.

✓ Correlate aliases to a real identity.

✓ Expose fraudulent or malicious actors.

In this chapter, we'll explore:

✅ How to identify common username patterns

✅ Free and paid tools for username tracking

✅ Google Dorking and manual investigation techniques

✅ Ethical considerations when investigating usernames

4.3.1 Understanding Username Patterns & Naming Conventions

Why People Reuse Usernames

Most people struggle to create unique usernames across multiple platforms. As a result, they tend to:

- Use the same username across multiple sites.
- Use slight variations (e.g., adding numbers or underscores).
- Create linked usernames based on their email or real name.

Common Username Patterns

People tend to follow specific patterns when creating usernames:

- **First & Last Name** – johnsmith, john_smith99, smith.john
- **Initials & Numbers** – jsmith1985, j_s_85, smith_j85
- **Nicknames & Pseudonyms** – CyberHunter007, NightWolfX
- **Email-Derived Usernames** – john.doe@gmail.com → johndoe123
- **Gamer or Coder Handles** – XxShadowNinjaXx, CodeWarrior99

Identifying these patterns can help track the same person across various platforms.

4.3.2 Free OSINT Tools for Username Investigations

Step 1: Searching Usernames Across Multiple Platforms

Several OSINT tools automate username searches across websites, social networks, and forums:

🔍 WhatsMyName

🔗 https://whatsmyname.app/

Checks if a username is registered across hundreds of sites.

🔍 Namechk

🔗 https://www.namechk.com/

Checks username availability on social media, domains, and gaming sites.

🔍 Sherlock (Python Tool)

🔗 https://github.com/sherlock-project/sherlock

- Scans hundreds of sites for a specific username.
- Requires Python installation for local use.

🔍 CheckUsernames.com

🔗 https://checkusernames.com/

Finds if a username is taken on social media.

Step 2: Cross-Checking Username Variations

If a direct match isn't found, try small variations:

📌 **cyberhunter007** → cyberhunter_007, cyberhunter-007, cyberhunter007x

4.3.3 Manual Username Investigations Using Google Dorking

If automated tools fail, Google Dorking can help find username traces manually.

📌 **Search for username mentions across multiple platforms:**

"cyberhunter007" site:twitter.com OR site:instagram.com OR site:reddit.com

📌 **Find old forum posts with a username:**

"cyberhunter007" site:stackexchange.com OR site:steamcommunity.com

📌 **Locate pastes or data breaches containing a username:**

"cyberhunter007" site:pastebin.com OR site:throwbin.io

📌 **Look for username-related email leaks:**

"cyberhunter007@gmail.com" filetype:txt OR filetype:csv

📌 **Discover alternative usernames from social media bios:**

"cyberhunter007" AND ("also known as" OR "aka" OR "alias")

💡 **Pro Tip**: Combine username searches with known email addresses or phone numbers to uncover more links.

4.3.4 Advanced Techniques for Username OSINT

Cross-Referencing Username with Other Identifiers

If a username is found on one platform, try extracting more data:

✓ **Reverse Image Search** – If the profile has a picture, use Google Images or Yandex to find other profiles with the same image.

✓ **Metadata Analysis** – Some platforms reveal extra data (e.g., IP logs, registration dates).

✓ **Inspecting Followers & Connections** – Look at who follows the account or interacts with it.

Investigating Username Evolution

Some people change usernames over time. Use:

- **Wayback Machine** ∞ https://web.archive.org/ to find archived usernames.
- **Twitter/X Handle History** ∞ https://tweeterid.com/ to check past Twitter usernames.

4.3.5 Case Study: Tracking a Cybercriminal Using Usernames

Scenario:

A security researcher is investigating a suspected scammer who uses the alias "CryptoWolf99".

Investigation Process:

✅ Step 1: Checking Username Availability

Using WhatsMyName, the username CryptoWolf99 appears on:

- Twitter/X
- Instagram
- BitcoinTalk forums

✅ Step 2: Google Dorking to Find Mentions

Using:

"CryptoWolf99" site:bitcointalk.org OR site:telegram.com

Found scam complaints on crypto forums.

✅ Step 3: Searching for Similar Usernames

Checking variations like CryptoWolf_99, CryptoWolfX, CWolf99:

Found a Reddit account discussing crypto investments.

✅ Step 4: Investigating Associated Email

Using HaveIBeenPwned, the email linked to CryptoWolf99 appeared in a 2018 leaked database.

Outcome:

🚀 The investigation linked multiple scam reports to the same person, leading to a fraud alert being issued.

4.3.6 Ethical & Legal Considerations in Username OSINT

☐ **DO NOT:**

✖ Hack or access private accounts illegally.

✖ Use deception or social engineering to extract data.

✖ Harass or stalk individuals based on username searches.

✅ **DO:**

✓☐ Use only publicly available and legally obtained information.
✓☐ Follow data protection laws (GDPR, CCPA).
✓☐ Ensure investigations are ethical and responsible.

Conclusion

Tracking usernames across platforms is a powerful OSINT skill. By combining automated tools, Google Dorking, manual pattern recognition, and cross-referencing data, investigators can reconstruct an individual's online presence.

4.4 Tracking an Individual's Online Activity Over Time

People leave behind digital footprints across the internet, and these footprints accumulate over time. By tracking online activity over a period, OSINT investigators can identify patterns, behavioral changes, and historical data that reveal critical insights about a person.

In this chapter, we will explore:

✓ How to track a person's online activity over time

✓ Using web archives and historical data sources

✓ Analyzing behavior patterns through social media and forums

✓ Connecting past and present digital identities

✓ Ethical & legal considerations when tracking individuals

4.4.1 Why Tracking Long-Term Online Activity is Important

1️ Understanding Behavior Patterns

- Does the person change usernames frequently?
- Do they switch platforms or stay consistent?
- How has their content changed over time?

2️ Unmasking Anonymity

- Many people start online with real information, then later try to anonymize themselves.
- Looking at historical data can uncover past identities that are still linked to the person.

3️ Correlating Old & New Online Identities

- People often reuse old usernames, emails, and profile pictures across different sites.
- Identifying past accounts can help track an individual's evolution online.

4.4.2 Using Web Archives to Recover Deleted Data

Even if someone deletes content, the internet never forgets. Web archives store old versions of websites, allowing investigators to recover historical data.

🔍 Key Tools for Accessing Archived Data

⬜ Wayback Machine – https://web.archive.org/

- Archives old web pages, profiles, and forum posts.
- Check past versions of social media profiles, blogs, and personal websites.

⬜ Google Cache – cache:website.com/username

- Google temporarily stores snapshots of indexed pages.
- Can reveal recently deleted content.

📜 Archive.today – https://archive.ph/

- Allows users to manually save and retrieve past versions of web pages.

🔎 CachedView – https://www.cachedview.com/

- Retrieves cached Google and Bing search results.

📌 Example:

If a person deleted their LinkedIn profile, check:

➡️⬜ https://web.archive.org/web/*/linkedin.com/in/USERNAME

4.4.3 Tracking Social Media Activity Over Time

Even if a user deletes old posts, remnants of their activity may still be visible.

1⬜ Using Twitter/X Advanced Search

Find old tweets from a specific user:

📌 from:username since:2015-01-01 until:2020-01-01

Search tweets with specific keywords:

📌 from:username "job offer"

Track username changes with TweetDeck or Wayback Machine.

2️ Instagram & TikTok Historical Data

- Look at followers & following lists to see past connections.
- Use tools like Picuki, Gramho, and StoriesIG for archived posts and stories.
- Reverse search profile pictures on Google Images or Yandex.

3️ Reddit & Forum Post Tracking

- Use Pushshift.io to search deleted Reddit posts.
- Check Wayback Machine snapshots for forum posts.

Search for old posts using Google Dorks:

📌 "username" site:reddit.com

📌 Example:

An investigator is searching for past cryptocurrency activity of a Twitter user who deleted all tweets. By using Wayback Machine and Pushshift.io, they recover old forum posts where the individual promoted crypto scams.

4.4.4 Identifying Long-Term Digital Footprints

Tracking long-term activity requires cross-referencing multiple platforms and uncovering recurring patterns.

🔍 Key Methods to Link Past & Present Identities

📌 Email & Username Reuse:

- People often use the same email for years.
- Reverse search old emails to find past profiles.
- Check if usernames appear in old data breaches.

📌 Profile Picture Matching:

- Reverse image search old avatars using Google Images, Yandex, or TinEye.
- Find older versions of profile pictures in archives and caches.

📌 **Behavioral Patterns:**

- Does the user post about the same topics over time?
- Do they use the same phrases or writing style?
- Check linguistic similarities across Reddit, Twitter, and blogs.

📌 **Domain & Website History:**

- Use Whois history tools to check old domain registrations.
- Check archived personal websites or blogs for personal info.

Example: A blog deleted in 2015 might still be accessible via Wayback Machine.

4.4.5 Case Study: Reconstructing a Person's Online History

Scenario:

An OSINT investigator is tracking an individual suspected of spreading misinformation online. The individual deleted their social media profiles, but the investigator found an old username from a 2016 forum post.

Investigation Process:

✅ **Step 1: Checking Web Archives**

- The username CyberEagle007 appeared in 2016 archived Twitter posts.
- The Wayback Machine retrieved deleted tweets linking to a blog.

✅ **Step 2: Searching Forum Posts & Data Breaches**

- Using Google Dorking, found old Reddit posts discussing hacking tools.
- Email linked to the username was found in a 2017 breach.

✅ **Step 3: Reverse Image Searching Profile Photos**

- The same avatar appeared on a 2014 gaming forum.

- Connected the username to a real LinkedIn profile.

✅ **Outcome:**

🔎 The investigation uncovered the person's real identity despite their efforts to delete past content.

4.4.6 Ethical & Legal Considerations in Long-Term Tracking

🚫 **DO NOT:**

✖ Hack, breach accounts, or access private data.

✖ Stalk, harass, or misuse historical information.

✖ Violate GDPR, CCPA, or CFAA regulations.

✅ **DO:**

✔☐ Use only publicly available & legally obtained information.
✔☐ Follow ethical OSINT investigation guidelines.
✔☐ Respect individuals' privacy unless there's a legitimate investigative need.

Conclusion

Tracking a person's online activity over time is a powerful OSINT method that can help reconstruct digital histories and link old and new identities. By using web archives, social media tracking, username analysis, and behavioral pattern recognition, investigators can connect past and present online footprints.

4.5 Using Leaked Databases to Investigate Email Addresses

Leaked databases contain valuable intelligence for OSINT investigations. When data breaches expose email addresses, passwords, usernames, and other sensitive information, investigators can use this data to track digital identities, uncover hidden accounts, and link people to past activities.

In this chapter, we will explore:

✓ How data leaks occur and where to find breached data

✓ Tools for searching leaked databases

✓ Analyzing email addresses to uncover online activity

✓ Ethical and legal considerations when using leaked data

4.5.1 Understanding Data Leaks & Breaches

How Do Data Leaks Happen?

Data breaches happen when hackers, insiders, or poor security practices expose sensitive user information. Some common causes include:

- Database misconfigurations (e.g., unsecured cloud storage)
- Hacks and cyberattacks (e.g., credential stuffing, phishing)
- Third-party leaks (e.g., marketing companies losing customer data)

Once exposed, leaked databases often circulate on hacking forums, dark web marketplaces, and OSINT tools, allowing investigators to retrieve compromised information.

What Kind of Data is Found in Leaks?

Leaked databases often contain:

- Email addresses
- Usernames & passwords (plaintext or hashed)
- Phone numbers
- IP addresses & locations
- Social media accounts linked to emails

By analyzing this information, investigators can track a person's digital footprint across various platforms.

4.5.2 Tools for Searching Leaked Databases

There are several legitimate tools for checking whether an email address has been leaked.

Public & Free Data Breach Checkers

🔎 **Have I Been Pwned (HIBP) – https://haveibeenpwned.com/**

- Checks if an email or password was exposed in a breach.
- Provides details about the source of the leak.

🔎 **DeHashed – https://www.dehashed.com/**

- Allows reverse searching of emails, usernames, passwords, IPs, and domains.

🔎 **SnusBase – https://snusbase.com/ (Requires paid access)**

- Provides advanced search options for leaked credentials.

🔎 **BreachDirectory – https://breachdirectory.org/**

- Finds leaked credentials based on email, domain, or username.

Dark Web & Underground Sources

More advanced searches require OSINT professionals to access underground forums and dark web markets where hacked databases are shared.

🚨 **Warning**: Accessing or downloading breached data may be illegal depending on your jurisdiction.

4.5.3 Investigating an Email Address in a Leaked Database

Once an email address is found in a breach, investigators can analyze it to:

✓ Find related usernames & passwords

✓ Check linked social media & forum accounts

✓ Correlate the email with old activity

Step 1: Check Data Breach Exposure

Example: Searching for john.doe@email.com in Have I Been Pwned shows:

- **2016 LinkedIn breach** – Email + hashed password
- **2018 MyFitnessPal breach** – Email + plaintext password
- **2020 Twitter breach** – Email + associated username

Step 2: Identify Associated Accounts

Once an email appears in a leak, use Google Dorking to search for additional linked accounts:

📌 "john.doe@email.com" site:forums.net OR site:github.com OR site:pastebin.com

📌 Check Wayback Machine for archived profiles linked to the email.

Step 3: Reverse Searching Email for Social Media Links

Use OSINT tools like:

- **Social Searcher** – Finds social media profiles linked to an email.
- **That'sThem** – https://thatsthem.com/ – Reverse email lookups.
- **Hunetr.io** – https://hunter.io/ – Email domain searches.

📌 **Example:**

A leaked email found in a LinkedIn breach might still be active. Searching it in Hunter.io can show associated websites, companies, and domains linked to the email.

4.5.4 Connecting Leaked Emails to Other Online Identities

Even if an email itself isn't publicly visible, you can track online activity using:

✅ **Username correlation** – Leaks often include username + email pairs. Searching for the username can uncover additional accounts.

✅ **Password reuse patterns** – Many people reuse passwords across sites. If a password is leaked, try searching for similar patterns on other platforms.

☑ **Checking old forum posts** – Many forums and comment sections still contain archived email addresses.

📌 **Example:**

- If an email was exposed in a 2014 breach, the user might have used the same email or username on older sites.
- Searching "john.doe@email.com" site:reddit.com might reveal past posts before the user became more privacy-conscious.

4.5.5 Case Study: Exposing a Fraudster with Leaked Data

Scenario:

A cybersecurity analyst is investigating an online scammer suspected of running fake cryptocurrency investment schemes.

Investigation Process:

☑ Step 1: Checking Data Breaches

- The suspected scammer's email, crypto_master007@gmail.com, was found in a 2017 data breach.
- The leak contained a username: CryptoKing007.

☑ Step 2: Tracking Username History

- A Google search for "CryptoKing007" revealed old Reddit and Bitcointalk forum posts discussing cryptocurrency investments.
- The username also appeared in a 2015 archived LinkedIn profile, revealing a real name.

☑ Step 3: Correlating Additional Leaked Data

- The same email appeared in a 2019 breach from a crypto exchange.
- Searching SnusBase showed an old phone number connected to the email.

☑ Outcome:

🖋 The investigator linked the scammer's fake identities, uncovering real-world details that led to legal action.

4.5.6 Ethical & Legal Considerations in Using Leaked Data

☐ **DO NOT:**

✖ Pay for or download illegal breached databases.

✖ Use breached data for blackmail, harassment, or stalking.

✖ Violate GDPR, CCPA, or cybersecurity laws.

✔ **DO:**

✓☐ Use only legally accessible OSINT tools.
✓☐ Verify information from multiple sources before drawing conclusions.
✓☐ Follow ethical investigation practices.

⚖ **Note**: Many countries prohibit unauthorized access to personal data. Always consult local laws before conducting email OSINT investigations.

Conclusion

Leaked databases provide powerful insights into an individual's digital history, allowing investigators to uncover hidden accounts, username patterns, and past activity. By using OSINT tools, breach checkers, and search techniques, analysts can track online identities while staying within ethical and legal boundaries.

4.6 Case Study: Tracing an Online Scammer

Online scams are rampant, with fraudsters using false identities, burner accounts, and deceptive tactics to avoid detection. OSINT techniques can help track these scammers by analyzing their digital footprints, breached data, and behavioral patterns across platforms.

In this case study, we will investigate "CryptoMaster007," an online scammer who ran a fraudulent cryptocurrency investment scheme. Using leaked databases, social media analysis, and reverse searches, we will uncover his real identity and online history.

4.6.1 Background: The Scam & Initial Investigation

A victim reports losing $5,000 after investing in a crypto scheme promoted by "CryptoMaster007." The scammer promised guaranteed returns but disappeared after receiving payments. The only known details were:

- Username: CryptoMaster007
- Email used: cryptoinvestor007@gmail.com
- Bitcoin wallet: 1A2b3C4D5E6F7G8H9I
- Telegram handle: @CryptoProfits

Our objective: Identify the scammer's real identity and track their online presence.

4.6.2 Step 1: Analyzing Leaked Databases

We start by checking if the scammer's email (cryptoinvestor007@gmail.com) appears in any data breaches.

🔎 Search using Have I Been Pwned & DeHashed

The email was found in two breaches:

✅ 2017 LinkedIn Breach → Linked to CryptoKing007

✅ 2019 Bitcoin Forum Breach → Username BitTraderX

📌 **Finding**: The scammer has used multiple usernames over the years, and we now have two additional aliases:

✓ CryptoKing007

✓ BitTraderX

4.6.3 Step 2: Investigating Username Patterns

We now conduct Google Dorking and forum searches to track their activity.

🔎 Google Search:

- 📌 "CryptoKing007" site:bitcointalk.org
- 📌 "BitTraderX" site:reddit.com

Results:

✔ **Bitcointalk Posts (2015-2018):** The username CryptoKing007 promoted investment schemes in multiple threads.

✔ **Reddit Comments**: The user BitTraderX discussed "passive income from crypto trading" in 2019.

✔ **Wayback Machine Check**: Old snapshots confirm the same usernames used on multiple forums.

📌 **Finding**: The scammer has been running schemes for years under different names.

4.6.4 Step 3: Tracking Social Media & Telegram Activity

🔎 Searching Telegram for @CryptoProfits

- Found in multiple crypto investment groups.
- Promoted fake giveaways asking users to send crypto first.
- Displayed a profile picture that we reverse search.

🔎 Reverse Image Search (Google & Yandex)

- The scammer's Telegram profile picture matches an old Instagram profile of a person named Mark Jansen (@MarkJ_Invests).
- The Instagram bio states: "Crypto investor | London | DM for business inquiries".
- Checking Wayback Machine, we find an old LinkedIn profile matching the same name.

📌 **Finding**: The scammer's real name may be Mark Jansen, and he previously used Instagram and LinkedIn for crypto promotions.

4.6.5 Step 4: Tracing Bitcoin Transactions

🔍 Searching Bitcoin Wallet Transactions (1A2b3C4D5E6F7G8H9I)

- Using Blockchain Explorer, we analyze past transactions.
- The wallet received multiple payments and transferred funds to another wallet linked to a Binance account.

🔍 Checking Binance for Clues

- Binance accounts require KYC (Know Your Customer) verification.
- Law enforcement can request user details from Binance if linked to fraudulent activity.

📌 **Finding**: The scammer's funds moved through Binance, which may contain KYC information leading to a real identity.

4.6.6 Step 5: Confirming Identity & Final Findings

🚀 Summary of Findings:

✅ The scammer used multiple usernames: CryptoMaster007, CryptoKing007, BitTraderX.

✅ His email appeared in past LinkedIn and Bitcoin forum breaches.

✅ His Telegram profile picture matched an old Instagram account linked to "Mark Jansen."

✅ Bitcoin transactions led to a Binance account with potential KYC data.

📌 **Final Conclusion**: The scammer's real identity is likely Mark Jansen, a known crypto fraudster who has operated under various aliases since 2015.

4.6.7 Lessons Learned & OSINT Takeaways

✅ 1. Leaked Databases Provide Crucial Leads

- Past data breaches help connect usernames, emails, and passwords.
- Always check multiple breaches for patterns across time.

✅ 2. Username Reuse is Common

- Fraudsters often reuse variations of old usernames.
- Searching historical forum posts can reveal their activity over the years.

✅ 3. Reverse Image Search Can Unmask Identities

- Many scammers use stock photos or personal images on different platforms.
- Yandex, Google, and PimEyes can trace where these images were previously used.

✅ 4. Crypto Transactions Are Not Completely Anonymous

Blockchain transactions can be analyzed to track financial movements.
Exchanges with KYC requirements may hold identifying information.

✅ 5. OSINT Can Uncover Hidden Digital Footprints

- By combining leaked data, social media analysis, and blockchain tracking, investigators can reconstruct digital identities.

Conclusion

This case study demonstrates how OSINT techniques can trace an online scammer by linking email leaks, usernames, images, and crypto transactions. While fraudsters attempt to erase their tracks, historical data and behavioral patterns make them vulnerable to identification.

5. Phone Number OSINT & Reverse Lookups

A phone number can serve as a key identifier in online investigations, often linking to social media accounts, messaging apps, and public records. This chapter delves into OSINT techniques for researching phone numbers, including reverse lookup tools, carrier identification, and geolocation possibilities. You'll learn how to uncover connections between a phone number and an individual's online presence while navigating privacy laws and ethical boundaries. By mastering these methods, you'll enhance your ability to verify identities and track digital footprints efficiently.

5.1 Conducting Reverse Phone Number Lookups

Phone numbers are one of the most common identifiers people use for online accounts, business registrations, and communications. In OSINT investigations, a phone number can serve as a crucial starting point for uncovering a person's identity, social media profiles, email addresses, and locations.

This chapter explores:

✓ How reverse phone lookups work

✓ Free and paid tools for investigating phone numbers

✓ Identifying linked social media & online accounts

✓ Legal & ethical considerations in phone OSINT

5.1.1 Understanding Reverse Phone Lookups

A reverse phone lookup is the process of retrieving information about an individual based on their phone number. This can include:

- Owner's name & address
- Carrier & phone type (mobile, landline, VoIP)
- Social media & online accounts linked to the number
- Past data breaches containing the phone number
- Business registrations & public records

Phone number investigations can help in cases of fraud detection, missing persons investigations, and cybercrime tracking.

5.1.2 Free Tools for Reverse Phone Lookups

There are multiple free OSINT tools for investigating phone numbers:

🔎 **Basic Reverse Phone Lookup Sites**

📌 **TrueCaller – https://www.truecaller.com/**

Identifies names & locations of mobile users (community-sourced).

📌 **Sync.me – https://www.sync.me/**

Finds social media profiles linked to a phone number.

📌 **That'sThem – https://thatsthem.com/**

Provides name, address, and email associated with a number.

📌 **FreeCarrierLookup – https://freecarrierlookup.com/**

Identifies carrier & phone type (mobile, VoIP, or landline).

🔎 **Google Dorking for Phone Numbers**

Using Google search operators can reveal hidden data on forums, social media, and classifieds:

📌 "555-123-4567" site:facebook.com (Searches Facebook for the number)
📌 "5551234567" site:linkedin.com (Checks LinkedIn for any profiles using this number)
📌 "555-123-4567" site:whois.domaintools.com (Finds domain registrations with the number)
📌 "555-123-4567" filetype:pdf OR filetype:doc (Finds business records, CVs, and reports with the number)

📌 **Tip**: Some numbers may be hidden in archived pages, so check Wayback Machine (archive.org) for past records.

5.1.3 Paid & Advanced Tools for Phone OSINT

For deeper investigations, paid databases provide more extensive details:

🔎 **Comprehensive Phone Number Search Tools**

📌 **Pipl – https://pipl.com/ (Subscription required)**

Provides social media, email, and business records linked to a number.

📌 **Spokeo – https://www.spokeo.com/**

Searches addresses, relatives, and criminal records connected to a number.

📌 **HUNTER.io – https://hunter.io/**

Checks professional email & phone data from corporate records.

📌 **TLOxp (Law enforcement & licensed investigators only)**

Provides deep background checks, including criminal & financial records.

📌 **Hacked Database Lookups**

Leaked databases can contain phone numbers from past breaches. Use:

- Have I Been Pwned – https://haveibeenpwned.com/
- DeHashed – https://dehashed.com/ (Premium required for phone lookups)

📌 **Tip**: If a phone number was leaked in a breach, it may be tied to old usernames, emails, or passwords—valuable for tracking online activity.

5.1.4 Tracking Social Media & Online Accounts Linked to a Phone Number

Many social media platforms allow users to register using a phone number. If a number is linked to an account, you can try:

🔎 **Social Media Search Methods**

✅ **Facebook** – Enter the number in the search bar (some profiles appear if privacy settings allow).

✅ **Instagram & Twitter** – Try adding the number to your contacts and syncing with the app (if the user hasn't disabled it, their profile may appear).

✅ **Telegram** – Search for the number directly in the "Add Contacts" section (may reveal username).

✅ **WhatsApp & Signal** – Save the number and check profile pictures, status messages, and last seen timestamps.

📌 **Example**: If a scammer's phone number is registered on WhatsApp, their profile picture might reveal their real identity.

5.1.5 Identifying Disposable & VoIP Phone Numbers

Fraudsters often use burner phones, VoIP numbers, and disposable services to hide their identity.

How to Detect VoIP or Temporary Numbers

✅ **FreeCarrierLookup** – Identifies if a number belongs to a VoIP provider.

✅ **Twilio Lookup API** – Detects whether a number is mobile, landline, or VoIP.

✅ **Google Voice, TextNow, & Burner Apps** – Check if the number belongs to common disposable services.

📌 **Example:**

A scammer using +1-323-555-6789 is found to be a Google Voice number, meaning it's likely a throwaway account.

5.1.6 Case Study: Unmasking a Scammer Using a Phone Number

Scenario:

A person reports receiving fraudulent calls from +1-646-555-7890, claiming to be from "Tech Support" and demanding payment.

Investigation Steps:

✅ **Step 1: Checking Phone Carrier & Type**

FreeCarrierLookup reveals it's a VoIP number from Twilio.

✅ **Step 2: Searching for Social Media Links**

Entering +1-646-555-7890 into WhatsApp reveals a profile picture of a man in India.

✅ **Step 3: Checking for Past Reports**

- A Google search for "646-555-7890 scam" leads to complaints on scam-reporting forums.
- TrueCaller also flags it as a "High Risk" scam number.

✅ **Step 4: Identifying Additional Accounts**

- Searching Sync.me and Pipl reveals the same number is linked to an old LinkedIn account for "Raj Patel, IT Consultant."

🔎 **Outcome**: The scammer's LinkedIn profile, past aliases, and location in India were exposed, leading to further investigation.

5.1.7 Legal & Ethical Considerations

☐ **DO NOT:**

✗ Use phone lookup services for stalking, harassment, or illegal activities.

✗ Access private data without consent.

✗ Violate GDPR, CCPA, or privacy laws.

✅ **DO:**

✓☐ Use only legally available OSINT tools.
✓☐ Verify data from multiple sources before making conclusions.
✓☐ Respect privacy laws and ethical guidelines.

📌 **Important**: Many countries prohibit unauthorized access to personal data, so always check local laws before conducting OSINT phone investigations.

Conclusion

Reverse phone lookups provide valuable intelligence for OSINT investigations, helping analysts track identities, social media, and fraudsters. By combining free search tools, breach data, and social media analysis, investigators can uncover hidden connections and digital footprints.

5.2 Identifying VoIP & Burner Numbers vs. Real Numbers

Not all phone numbers are created equal. While some belong to real individuals with verifiable identities, others are temporary, disposable, or VoIP-based—making them harder to trace. In OSINT investigations, distinguishing between real phone numbers and burner/VoIP numbers is crucial for assessing credibility, identifying fraud, and tracking digital footprints.

This chapter covers:

✅ Understanding VoIP, burner, and real phone numbers

✅ Methods to detect fake or temporary numbers

✅ OSINT tools for identifying VoIP providers

✅ Investigating anonymous phone numbers

5.2.1 Understanding the Differences Between VoIP, Burner & Real Numbers

📌 **Real Phone Numbers (Mobile & Landline)**

- Issued by mobile carriers (AT&T, Verizon, Vodafone, etc.)
- Requires identity verification (government ID, SSN, etc.)
- Can be traced to real people or businesses
- Typically used for long-term communication

📌 **VoIP (Voice over Internet Protocol) Numbers**

- Assigned by internet-based providers like Google Voice, Twilio, TextNow
- Can be used on any device with internet access
- Often does not require identity verification
- Common in fraud, scams, and anonymous communications

📌 **Burner & Temporary Numbers**

- Disposable numbers from apps like Burner, Hushed, and CoverMe
- Used for short-term communication and anonymity
- Often linked to fraud, scams, and privacy-conscious users
- Can be deleted and replaced easily

5.2.2 Methods to Identify VoIP & Burner Numbers

🔍 Step 1: Check the Carrier & Type of Number

Using free lookup tools, you can determine if a number belongs to a real carrier or a VoIP provider.

✅ **Free Carrier Lookup Tools:**

- **FreeCarrierLookup** – Checks if a number is mobile, landline, or VoIP.
- **TextMagic** – Identifies network providers and VoIP sources.
- **NumVerify** – Validates phone numbers globally.

📌 **Example:**

Entering +1-646-555-7890 into FreeCarrierLookup shows:

- **Carrier**: Google Voice
- **Type**: VoIP (Internet-based number)

⚑ **Red Flag**: VoIP numbers are often anonymous and disposable, making them unreliable in OSINT investigations.

🔍 Step 2: Reverse Search the Phone Number

If a number is real, it often appears in public directories, business registrations, or social media profiles.

✅ **Reverse Lookup Sites:**

- **TrueCaller** – Identifies real names & spam reports.
- **Syc.nme** – Finds linked social media accounts.
- **That'sThem** – Checks public records, addresses, and emails.

📌 **Example:**

A scammer claims to be a lawyer and provides a number: +44 7521 123456.

- TrueCaller shows NO RESULTS (possible VoIP or burner).
- Sync.me doesn't match it to any real social media profiles.
- That'sThem shows NO public records.

🚩 **Red Flag**: If a number has no public records, no linked profiles, and is VoIP, it is likely a disposable or fake number.

🔎 **Step 3: Investigate VoIP Providers & Their Users**

Some VoIP providers are frequently used by scammers and fraudsters.

✅ **Common VoIP Providers Used for Fraud:**

📌 **Google Voice** – Free US-based VoIP numbers (easy to create & hide identity).
📌 **Twilio** – Provides bulk VoIP numbers (often used in phishing & scams).
📌 **TextNow & TextFree** – Free texting apps (popular among cybercriminals).
📌 **Sideline & Burner** – Used for temporary and anonymous calls.

🚀 **Investigative Tip:**

If a number belongs to Google Voice, TextNow, or Twilio, be skeptical. Many fraudsters & scammers use these services to hide their identity.

5.2.3 Identifying Anonymous & Disposable Phone Numbers

🔎 **How to Detect a Burner Number:**

- If it changes frequently (a person gives you a different number every few days, it's likely a burner).
- If it cannot receive calls but can send texts (many burner apps allow texting only).
- If it does not show up in public records or social media searches.
- If scam or spam complaints are linked to it in databases.

✅ Spam & Scam Checkers:

- **WhoCallsMe** – Community-reported spam numbers.
- **ScamNumbers** – Database of known scam numbers.
- **Robokiller** – AI-powered spam number detection.

📌 Example:

A job recruiter calls from +1-408-555-9999 claiming to offer a work-from-home position.

- Checking Robokiller, it's flagged as "potential spam".
- WhoCallsMe has multiple reports calling it "scammer number".
- Carrier lookup shows it's a Twilio VoIP number.

🚩 **Conclusion**: This is not a real recruiter—likely a job scam.

5.2.4 Investigating Anonymous Callers & Hidden Numbers

Some numbers appear as "Private" or "Unknown" during calls. These can be:

- Hidden via caller ID spoofing (fraud tactic).
- Blocked intentionally (legitimate but private caller).

✅ How to Trace Unknown Callers:

- **Use 67 Bypass** – Call back using *67 before the number (hides your caller ID).
- **Try TrapCall** – https://www.trapcall.com/ (reveals blocked numbers).
- **Use Google Voice to call back** – Google logs responses from unknown callers.

🔍 **Investigative Tip**: Many scammers spoof legitimate numbers (e.g., pretending to be "Bank Support" using a real bank's number). If a known company calls, hang up and call back using their official website's number.

5.2.5 Case Study: Exposing a Fake "Tech Support" Call Center

Scenario:

A person receives a call from +1-888-222-3333, claiming to be Microsoft Support. The caller asks for remote access to the victim's computer.

Investigation Steps:

✅ **Step 1: Check the Number Type**

Carrier lookup shows it's a VoIP number from Twilio.

✅ **Step 2: Search for Past Reports**

WhoCallsMe shows multiple complaints of fraudulent tech support calls.

✅ **Step 3: Check Linked Social Media**

Sync.me finds NO social media links—unusual for a real business.

✅ **Step 4: Call Back & Analyze Behavior**

- When calling back, a different agent answers with a generic greeting:
- "Hello, tech support." (Real Microsoft agents never answer generically).

⚑ **Conclusion**: This is a fraudulent VoIP-based call center, not real Microsoft support.

5.2.6 Legal & Ethical Considerations

☐ **DO NOT:**

✖ Use burner number detection for harassment or doxxing.

✖ Access unauthorized databases to retrieve personal information.

✖ Violate local data protection laws (e.g., GDPR, CCPA).

✅ DO:

✓☐ Use only legally available OSINT tools.
✓☐ Verify data from multiple sources.
✓☐ Respect privacy rights and ethical OSINT guidelines.

Conclusion

Understanding VoIP, burner, and real phone numbers is essential in OSINT investigations. By using carrier lookup tools, reverse searches, and scam databases, investigators can identify fraudulent callers, temporary numbers, and anonymous VoIP accounts.

5.3 Tracking Messaging Apps & Social Media Linked to Phone Numbers

A phone number is often the key to unlocking a person's digital identity. Many online services—including social media platforms, messaging apps, and online marketplaces—require a phone number for registration. By leveraging OSINT techniques, investigators can track a phone number across multiple platforms to uncover associated accounts, usernames, and activity.

In this chapter, we will cover:

✅ Identifying which apps and social networks are linked to a phone number

✅ Using OSINT tools to track phone-based accounts

✅ Checking for public data leaks related to phone numbers

✅ Understanding privacy settings and security loopholes

5.3.1 Identifying Accounts Linked to a Phone Number

Most people reuse their phone numbers across multiple platforms. This means a single number can reveal social media profiles, messaging apps, and even online purchases.

📌 Social Media & Messaging Apps That Require Phone Numbers

- **WhatsApp** – Requires a phone number for verification.
- **Telegram** – Users can link and search for contacts via phone number.
- **Signal** – Phone numbers are mandatory but may not be publicly visible.
- **Facebook & Instagram** – Users can recover accounts using phone numbers.
- **Twitter/X** – Allows phone number-based search and recovery.
- **TikTok** – Often linked to phone numbers for security verification.
- **Snapchat** – Users can search for friends by phone number.
- **LinkedIn** – Allows account recovery via phone number.

5.3.2 Using OSINT Tools to Find Linked Accounts

There are several online tools designed to check if a phone number is linked to social media, messaging apps, or online services.

✅ **Reverse Phone Lookup Tools for Social Media:**

- **GetContact** – Checks how a number is saved in others' contacts.
- **PhoneInfoga** – OSINT tool for tracking phone number usage.
- **WhatsMyName** – Searches usernames linked to numbers.
- **PimEyes** – If a phone number leads to a name, use facial recognition to check images.

📌 **Example:**

A suspect's phone number +1-646-555-7890 is investigated:

- PhoneInfoga reveals it is linked to a WhatsApp and Telegram account.
- GetContact shows saved contact names as "John Fraud" and "Scammer USA".
- WhatsMyName finds a LinkedIn profile under John Doe, IT Consultant.

🚩 **Conclusion**: The number is linked to a fraudulent alias used for scams.

5.3.3 Manually Searching Social Media Platforms

While OSINT tools help, manual searches can uncover even more information.

🔎 **How to Search for a Phone Number on Social Media**

📌 Facebook & Instagram

- Go to the search bar and enter the phone number.
- If the profile is public, it may appear in results.
- Try logging in with the number—if an account exists, it will prompt password recovery.

📌 Telegram & Signal

- Add the number to your contacts.
- Open Telegram/Signal and see if the account appears.
- If found, check their profile bio, username, and linked groups.

📌 Twitter/X & TikTok

- Enter the phone number in the search bar.
- Use the "Forgot Password" option to check if an account is linked.

📌 LinkedIn

- Many professionals link phone numbers for account recovery.
- Use email + phone number searches for better results.

5.3.4 Checking for Phone Number Leaks & Data Breaches

🔎 How to Check if a Phone Number Was Leaked

📌 Use breach search engines like:

- **HavelBeenPwned** – Checks data breaches linked to a phone or email.
- **DeHashed** – Advanced search for phone leaks & usernames.
- **IntelX** – Scans dark web leaks for phone records.

📌 Example:

Searching +44-7521-123456 in HavelBeenPwned reveals:

- It was part of the LinkedIn 2021 breach.
- Email: john_doe@example.com was leaked alongside it.

⚐ **Conclusion**: This number is real, linked to a LinkedIn profile, and part of a data breach.

5.3.5 Case Study: Finding a Scammer Through Their Phone Number

Scenario:

A scammer is using WhatsApp and Telegram to run fake crypto schemes. Their phone number, +1-310-222-9999, is the only known detail.

Investigation Steps:

✅ **Step 1: Check Messaging Apps**

- Add the number to WhatsApp and Telegram.
- The Telegram username is "@CryptoKing99".
- WhatsApp status says "Investor | BTC Miner".

✅ **Step 2: Reverse Lookup on GetContact**

- Found saved contacts: "Crypto Scam" and "Fake Trader".

✅ **Step 3: Check Data Breaches**

- DeHashed shows this number was part of a 2019 Binance scam leak.
- Associated with email: cryptoking99@mail.com.

✅ **Step 4: Cross-Check on Social Media**

- **Searched email on WhatsMyName** → Found an Instagram account.

- **Searched Telegram username @CryptoKing99** → Found in crypto scam groups.

⚐ **Conclusion**: The number links to multiple fraudulent accounts across Telegram, Instagram, and data breaches.

5.3.6 Legal & Ethical Considerations

☐ DO NOT:

✗ Use illegal hacking methods to obtain private data.

✗ Dox or harass individuals based on findings.

✗ Use OSINT for unauthorized surveillance.

✓ DO:

✓☐ Follow legal OSINT practices and data protection laws (GDPR, CCPA, etc.).

✓☐ Use only publicly available data.

✓☐ Report fraud and suspicious activity to law enforcement or platforms.

Conclusion

Tracking a phone number across social media and messaging apps can reveal valuable connections, aliases, and linked accounts. By combining OSINT tools, manual searches, and breach databases, investigators can uncover hidden profiles and digital identities.

5.4 Investigating Phone Number Leaks in Data Breaches

Phone numbers are often exposed in data breaches, making them valuable for OSINT investigations. When a phone number appears in a leaked database, it can be linked to email addresses, usernames, passwords, IP addresses, and social media accounts. This information can help investigators track individuals, verify identities, and uncover hidden connections.

In this chapter, we will explore:

✓ How to check if a phone number was leaked

✓ Popular breach databases and search engines

✓ Cross-referencing leaked phone numbers with other OSINT sources

✓ Ethical and legal considerations when using breached data

5.4.1 How Phone Numbers Get Leaked

Common Sources of Phone Number Leaks:

📌 **Data Breaches** – Hackers steal customer data from websites and databases, which often include phone numbers.

📌 **Social Media Scraping** – Attackers collect public profiles and associated phone numbers.

📌 **SIM Swapping Attacks** – Criminals steal phone numbers by transferring them to new SIM cards.

📌 **Unsecured Online Databases** – Companies sometimes store sensitive information in unsecured cloud databases.

📌 **Phishing & Malware** – Users unknowingly give away their numbers when filling out fraudulent forms or downloading malicious software.

🚩 **Example of a Major Phone Number Leak:**

In 2021, Facebook leaked over 533 million phone numbers from user profiles. These numbers were linked to names, locations, and email addresses, making it easier for scammers to commit fraud.

5.4.2 How to Check if a Phone Number Was Leaked

To investigate whether a phone number has been exposed in a data breach, OSINT analysts use breach search engines and dark web monitoring tools.

🔎 **Online Tools for Checking Breached Phone Numbers**

Tool	Description
HaveIBeenPwned	Checks if a phone number or email has been exposed in a breach.
DeHashed	Allows deep searches for phone numbers in leaked databases.
IntelX	Scans dark web and publicly leaked data sets.
Scylla.sh	Advanced breach search tool for OSINT investigations.
LeakCheck	Paid tool that checks phone numbers against known leaks.

📌 **Example Investigation:**

1️⃣ Enter +1-646-555-7890 into HaveIBeenPwned.

2️⃣ The tool reports the number was leaked in a 2018 Twitter breach.

3️⃣ Search the number in DeHashed → It reveals an associated email: johndoe@email.com.

4️⃣ Cross-check the email in WhatsMyName → Finds a LinkedIn and Instagram profile.

⚑ **Conclusion**: This number links to a real person and multiple online accounts.

5.4.3 Cross-Referencing Phone Numbers with Other OSINT Sources

Once a leaked phone number is found, investigators can use it to uncover additional details.

👓 Linking a Phone Number to Other OSINT Data

✅ **Emails & Usernames** – Use breach data to find associated accounts.
✅ **Social Media Profiles** – Check if the number was used for account recovery.
✅ **Leaked Passwords** – Some breaches include passwords that reveal login patterns.
✅ **IP Addresses** – Can expose location data from old breaches.

📌 Example:

A phone number from a LinkedIn data breach may be linked to:

- An email address from a past Yahoo breach
- A Twitter account under the same email
- A data dump with login details from an old forum

⚑ **Conclusion**: Combining breach data with OSINT tools can help track a person's digital footprint.

5.4.4 Investigating Phone Numbers on the Dark Web

Many leaked phone numbers end up for sale on the dark web. Cybercriminals use them for:

- Scams & phishing attacks

- SIM swapping & identity theft
- Creating fake social media profiles

□□♂□ How to Search the Dark Web for Leaked Phone Numbers

◆ **Dark Web Monitoring Services:**

- **DarkOwl** – Monitors dark web leaks.
- **Constella Intelligence** – Paid service for deep data breach analysis.
- **Spiderfoot** – OSINT tool for searching leaked data.

◆ **Manual Search Methods:**

- Use Tor to access dark web forums.
- Search phone numbers in Pastebin clones (like Snopyta).
- Look for mentions in hacking forums.

▶ **Warning**: Accessing dark web markets can be illegal in some countries. Always follow legal guidelines.

5.4.5 Case Study: Investigating a Leaked Phone Number

Scenario:

A cybersecurity researcher receives a report of bank fraud linked to a leaked phone number: +44-7521-123456.

Investigation Steps:

✅ Step 1: Check for Breaches

- HaveIBeenPwned shows the number was leaked in the 2020 Facebook breach.

✅ Step 2: Find Associated Data

- DeHashed reveals an email: mark.jones@mail.com.
- LeakCheck finds a password linked to an old eBay account.

✅ Step 3: Search on Social Media

- Email search finds a LinkedIn account for Mark Jones, a financial consultant.

✅ **Step 4: Dark Web Investigation**

- IntelX reveals the phone number was listed in a scammer database on a Tor forum.

⚑ **Conclusion**: The phone number was likely used for fraud and linked to a real identity.

5.4.6 Legal & Ethical Considerations

☐ **DO NOT:**

✗ Access illegal hacking forums or buy breached data.

✗ Use leaked phone numbers for harassment or doxxing.

✗ Share personal information without consent.

✅ **DO:**

✓☐ Follow privacy laws like GDPR & CCPA.
✓☐ Use publicly available breach checkers.
✓☐ Report fraud to law enforcement or cybersecurity agencies.

Conclusion

Investigating phone number leaks in data breaches is a powerful OSINT technique. By using breach databases, cross-referencing leaked data, and monitoring dark web activity, analysts can uncover hidden connections and digital identities. However, ethical and legal compliance must always be a priority.

5.5 OSINT Tools & APIs for Phone Number Investigations

Phone numbers are valuable identifiers in OSINT investigations. With the right tools and APIs, analysts can extract insights such as geolocation, carrier details, social media accounts, messaging app links, and breach history. This chapter explores the best free and paid OSINT tools for phone number investigations, how to use them effectively, and their limitations.

In this chapter, we will cover:

✅ How OSINT tools and APIs work for phone number tracking

✅ Best free & paid tools for phone lookups

✅ Cross-referencing phone numbers with social media & dark web data

✅ Ethical & legal concerns when using phone number OSINT tools

5.5.1 How OSINT Tools & APIs Work for Phone Number Tracking

Phone number investigation tools work by querying public databases, telecom records, social media networks, and breach archives. These tools typically return:

📌 **Geolocation & Carrier Details** – Identifies country, carrier, and type (VoIP, landline, mobile).

📌 **Social Media Links** – Checks if a phone number is linked to accounts on WhatsApp, Telegram, Facebook, Twitter, Instagram, etc.

📌 **Breach Data** – Identifies if the number has been leaked in data breaches.

📌 **Messaging App Activity** – Checks if the number is active on Signal, Viber, WeChat, etc.

📌 **Dark Web Mentions** – Scans dark web forums and leak databases for any association.

🚩 **Example Use Case:**

An investigator finds a suspicious number +1-310-555-7890 and wants to check if it is:

1️⃣ A VoIP or burner number

2️⃣ Linked to WhatsApp or Telegram

3️⃣ Exposed in any leaks

Using OSINT tools, they uncover an alias, social media profiles, and a past data breach that reveals an email address.

5.5.2 Best Free & Paid OSINT Tools for Phone Number Investigations

There are many online tools for reverse phone lookups, social media tracking, and carrier identification. Below is a breakdown of the most powerful options:

◆ Free OSINT Tools for Phone Investigations

Tool	Features
PhoneInfoga	Advanced phone number OSINT (carrier, VoIP checks, geolocation)
WhatsMyName	Checks if a username/phone number is linked to online services
GetContact	Identifies how a phone number is saved in other users' contacts
NumVerify	Validates number type (landline, VoIP, mobile)
OSINTFramework	Collection of free OSINT tools for phone tracking

📌 Example (PhoneInfoga):

1. **Run**: phoneinfoga scan -n +44-7551-123456
2. **Output**: Carrier: Vodafone UK, Type: Mobile, Country: United Kingdom
3. **Cross-check with GetContact** → Found under alias "Mike London Crypto"

⚑ **Conclusion**: This number is real and linked to an individual with crypto-related activity.

◆ Paid OSINT Tools & APIs for Deep Phone Investigations

Tool	Features	Price
TruCaller Pro	Advanced caller ID, spam detection, and social media checks	$5+/month
PimEyes	Reverse image search for profiles linked to a number	Pay-per-search
DeHashed	Checks if a number appears in **data breaches, dark web leaks**	$10+/month
PeopleDataLabs API	Returns **demographics, work history, and social links**	Custom Pricing
Maltego	Advanced OSINT tool for phone number graph analysis	$999/year

📌 Example (DeHashed Search):

1□ Search for +1-202-555-0190 in DeHashed

2□ Results: Found in LinkedIn 2021 breach, associated email: johndoe@xyz.com

3□ Cross-check email on WhatsMyName → Found on Instagram & Twitter

⚑ **Conclusion**: This phone number was leaked and linked to a real identity.

5.5.3 Cross-Referencing Phone Numbers with Social Media & Dark Web Data

To maximize results, investigators should combine multiple tools to cross-reference findings.

📌 **How to Cross-Reference a Phone Number**

◆ **Step 1: Use a Reverse Lookup Tool**

- Start with PhoneInfoga or NumVerify to check if it's a real number.
- Identify if it's a VoIP, burner, or landline number.

◆ **Step 2: Check for Social Media Links**

- Search WhatsApp, Telegram, and Facebook with GetContact, Maltego, or WhatsMyName.
- Use WhatsApp Web: Add the number and check profile names & statuses.

◆ **Step 3: Check Data Breaches & Dark Web Mentions**

Use DeHashed, HaveIBeenPwned, or IntelX to see if it has been exposed in breaches. Monitor dark web sites with DarkOwl or Constella Intelligence.

📌 **Example Investigation:**

1□ **Phone Number**: +1-310-222-9999

2□ **PhoneInfoga** → Found: Mobile, AT&T USA

3□ **GetContact** → Saved as "Crypto Scammer"

4□ **DeHashed** → Leaked in Binance 2019 breach, linked to "cryptoking@mail.com"

5□ **WhatsMyName** → Connected to an Instagram and Twitter account

⚑ **Conclusion**: This number is linked to a crypto scammer with multiple online identities.

5.5.4 Ethical & Legal Considerations

☐ **DO NOT:**

✘ Use illegal hacking or unauthorized data access.

✘ Dox or harass individuals based on findings.

✘ Use OSINT tools for unethical surveillance.

✅ **DO:**

✓☐ Follow GDPR, CCPA, and privacy laws.
✓☐ Use only publicly available OSINT tools.
✓☐ Report illegal activities to law enforcement.

Conclusion

OSINT tools and APIs for phone number investigations provide powerful insights into digital identities. By combining reverse lookup tools, breach checkers, and social media analysis, investigators can track individuals, detect fraud, and uncover hidden connections. However, responsible usage is essential to ensure privacy compliance and ethical investigation practices.

5.6 Case Study: Tracking a Suspect Through Phone OSINT

In this case study, we will analyze how OSINT techniques can be used to track a suspect using a phone number. The investigation will involve reverse lookups, social media searches, data breaches, messaging apps, and dark web monitoring.

This case study will demonstrate:

✓ How to conduct a structured OSINT investigation on a phone number

✓ Which tools to use at each step

✅ How to cross-reference findings for deeper intelligence

✅ The ethical and legal aspects of phone OSINT

5.6.1 Case Background

A cybersecurity analyst is hired by a financial institution to investigate a suspected fraudster who has been scamming victims via fake investment schemes. The only known information is a phone number used for WhatsApp communications:

📌 **Suspect's phone number**: +1-646-555-7890

The goal is to:

- Identify the owner's real identity
- Find associated social media accounts and emails
- Determine if the number appears in breaches, scam reports, or dark web databases

5.6.2 Step 1: Reverse Phone Lookup & Carrier Information

Tool: PhoneInfoga

The first step is to verify whether the phone number is real, its carrier, and whether it's a VoIP or mobile number.

Command:

phoneinfoga scan -n +1-646-555-7890

Results:

✅ **Carrier**: T-Mobile USA
✅ **Type**: Mobile
✅ **Country**: United States
✅ **VoIP/Burner?:** No (indicates real mobile number)

🏳 **Analysis**: This suggests the number is tied to a real subscriber, not a disposable VoIP number, making it more traceable.

5.6.3 Step 2: Checking Social Media & Messaging Apps

Tool: GetContact

This tool checks how the number is saved in other users' contact lists.

Search Results:

✅ Saved as "James Crypto Trader" and "Fast Money Investments"

⚐ **Analysis**: This suggests the suspect is involved in cryptocurrency trading or scams.

Tool: WhatsApp Web

We save the number in WhatsApp contacts and check their profile info.

Findings:

📌 **Profile name**: "James Investment Guru"
📌 **Status message**: "DM for 10X profits 🚀"
📌 **Last seen**: Active Today

⚐ **Analysis**: The suspect is actively using WhatsApp, indicating the number is still in use.

Tool: WhatsMyName

We check whether this number is linked to other online services.

Findings:

✅ Telegram profile found under "James Crypto King"

✅ Facebook account linked to the number

✅ Instagram profile with luxury car photos

⚐ **Analysis**: The suspect has multiple online personas linked to cryptocurrency investments.

5.6.4 Step 3: Checking Data Breaches & Dark Web Mentions

Tool: HavelBeenPwned & DeHashed

We check if the number has appeared in data breaches or leaked databases.

Findings:

📌 The phone number was leaked in the 2019 Binance crypto breach.
📌 Associated email: jamesinvest@protonmail.com
📌 Associated password (hashed): "$2a$12$xxxxxxxxxxxxx"

🚩 **Analysis**: The suspect likely had a Binance account, which was breached in 2019. The linked email address can be cross-referenced for further investigation.

5.6.5 Step 4: Investigating the Email & Username

Tool: OSINTFramework & IntelX

We now use the breached email address to check for more online footprints.

Findings:

📌 Email used for a LinkedIn profile under "James R."
📌 Found on an old Bitcoin forum discussing investment schemes
📌 Dark web listing: Email linked to suspected crypto scams

🚩 **Analysis**: The suspect is actively involved in crypto-related activities and has been mentioned in scam-related discussions.

5.6.6 Step 5: Geolocation & Financial Trail

Tool: TrueCaller & OpenCorporates

To check if the number is registered to any companies or has a physical location.

Findings:

✅ **Linked to an LLC**: "James R. Financials" in Miami, FL

✅ Business registered under a co-working office space

▶ **Analysis**: The suspect owns a company that may be facilitating fraudulent transactions.

5.6.7 Conclusion & Next Steps

Key Findings:

✅ The number is real (not VoIP or burner) and linked to T-Mobile USA.

✅ The suspect is using multiple online identities (James Crypto Trader, James R.).

✅ The phone number was compromised in a Binance data breach, revealing an associated email.

✅ The suspect is active on WhatsApp, Telegram, and Facebook, promoting crypto investments.

✅ A LinkedIn profile and business registration suggest a possible real-world identity.

✅ Dark web mentions indicate previous fraud allegations.

Next Steps for Law Enforcement or Investigators:

◆ Obtain court approval for further digital forensics (subpoena mobile provider for account details).

◆ Cross-reference financial transactions of "James R. Financials" for fraud patterns.

◆ Monitor Telegram groups and forums for further scams.

◆ Investigate LinkedIn connections for possible co-conspirators.

▶ **Final Takeaway:**

By combining phone OSINT tools, social media searches, breach databases, and company records, we successfully identified the suspect's real identity and fraudulent activities. This case highlights the power of OSINT for tracking cybercriminals.

6. Geolocation Tracking & Travel History

Geolocation data can reveal a person's whereabouts, movement patterns, and even their daily routines. This chapter explores OSINT techniques for extracting location intelligence from social media posts, metadata, public records, and online maps. You'll learn how to analyze geotagged images, monitor check-ins, and leverage open-source tools to reconstruct a subject's travel history. Additionally, we'll discuss ethical considerations and countermeasures, ensuring responsible use of geolocation tracking in online investigations.

6.1 How to Extract Location Clues from Social Media Posts

Social media is a goldmine for location-based OSINT investigations. Whether it's a geotagged Instagram post, a background landmark in a TikTok video, or metadata in an uploaded photo, people leave digital breadcrumbs that can reveal their whereabouts.

This chapter will cover:

✓ How to analyze metadata in images and videos

✓ Using geotags and check-ins to track locations

✓ Reverse image searching for landmark identification

✓ Cross-referencing posts for travel patterns

✓ Legal and ethical considerations

6.1.1 Extracting Metadata from Photos & Videos

What is Metadata?

Metadata is hidden data embedded in files that provides details such as:

📌 **GPS Coordinates** – Latitude/longitude of where a photo was taken
📌 **Device Information** – Camera model, phone brand, software version
📌 **Timestamps** – Exact date and time a media file was created

How to Extract Metadata

1️⃣ ExifTool (Best for Metadata Analysis)

Command:

exiftool image.jpg

Results:

✅ **GPS Coordinates**: 37.7749° N, 122.4194° W (San Francisco, CA)
✅ **Date Taken**: 2024:02:15 14:32:10
✅ **Device Used**: iPhone 14 Pro

🚩 **Analysis**: The photo was taken in San Francisco on February 15, 2024, at 2:32 PM.

2️⃣ Online Tools (No Coding Required)

✅ https://metapicz.com

✅ https://exif.tools

📌 **Caveat**: Many social media platforms strip metadata when uploading images. However, files shared via messaging apps or cloud storage may still contain EXIF data.

6.1.2 Geotags & Check-ins: Tracking a Person's Location

What are Geotags?

Many social media platforms allow users to geotag posts, meaning they attach a specific location to a photo, video, or check-in.

📌 **Platforms with Geotags:**

✅ **Instagram** (Photo locations, story check-ins)
✅ **Twitter/X** (Tweet locations if enabled)
✅ **Facebook** (Check-ins, event locations)
✅ **TikTok** (Video location tags)
✅ **Snapchat** (Snap Map feature shows live locations)

How to Find Geotags

1️ Instagram OSINT: Extracting Location Data

- Visit the Instagram profile of the target.
- Look for posts with a location tag (e.g., "Times Square, NYC").
- Click the location tag to see other public posts from that area.
- Cross-reference multiple posts to identify travel patterns.

▶ Example:

- A suspect posts an Instagram story tagged "Dubai Marina, UAE" on March 2, 2024.
- Later, they upload another story from Istanbul, Turkey on March 5.

Conclusion: They traveled from Dubai to Istanbul between March 2-5.

2️ Twitter/X OSINT: Locating Tweet Origins

Use TweetDeck to filter tweets by geolocation.

Search:

from:user123 geocode:40.7128,-74.0060,10km

(Finds tweets from user123 posted within 10km of New York City).

Cross-check timestamps to track movement patterns.

6.1.3 Reverse Image Search for Landmark Identification

If a social media post lacks explicit location data, landmarks in the background can reveal the location.

Best Reverse Image Search Tools

✅ **Google** Lens (Google Images)
✅ **Yandex Reverse Image Search** (https://yandex.com/images/)
✅ **TinEye** (https://tineye.com)

⚐ Example:

- A TikTok video shows a bridge in the background.
- Using Google Lens, we find it's the Bosphorus Bridge in Istanbul.
- Cross-referencing other posts, we confirm the person was in Istanbul at the time.

6.1.4 Cross-Referencing Social Media for Travel Patterns

Many people unknowingly reveal travel habits by posting photos from different locations.

How to Track Travel Patterns

1☐ Check timestamps of multiple posts on different platforms.

2☐ Look for recurring locations (e.g., always tagging "Dubai" every weekend).

3☐ Monitor check-ins and public stories for movement patterns.

4☐ Use OSINT tools like Maltego to link accounts across platforms.

⚐ Example:

- A suspect posts an Instagram story from JFK Airport (New York) at 8:00 AM.
- A few hours later, they post a photo tagged "Los Angeles" at 1:00 PM.
- Conclusion: They took a flight from New York to Los Angeles on that day.

6.1.5 Legal & Ethical Considerations

☐ **DO NOT:**

✗ Stalk, harass, or dox individuals.

✗ Violate privacy laws (e.g., GDPR, CCPA).

✗ Access private or restricted data.

✓ **DO:**

✓☐ Use only publicly available data.

✓☐ Follow ethical OSINT guidelines.

✓☐ Report illegal activities to authorities if necessary.

Conclusion

By combining metadata analysis, geotags, reverse image search, and cross-platform tracking, investigators can extract valuable location intelligence from social media posts. However, it's crucial to stay ethical and legal while conducting OSINT investigations.

6.2 Geolocating Photos & Videos with Metadata Analysis

Every digital photo and video carries hidden information that can be leveraged to determine its origin. Whether it's an image taken by a smartphone or a video uploaded to social media, metadata and visual clues can help identify locations, devices, and timestamps.

This chapter will cover:

✓ How to extract EXIF metadata from images and videos

✓ How to analyze GPS coordinates embedded in media files

✓ Using visual elements for geolocation when metadata is stripped

✓ Reverse searching video frames to identify locations

✓ Ethical and legal considerations in metadata analysis

6.2.1 Understanding Metadata in Photos & Videos

Metadata is hidden data stored in digital files that provides details about how and when a file was created.

📌 **Key Metadata Elements for OSINT Investigations:**

EXIF Data (Exchangeable Image File Format):

- GPS latitude & longitude (if enabled on the device)
- Date and time the photo/video was taken
- Camera model & phone brand
- Image resolution & editing history

File Properties:

- File size, format (JPEG, PNG, MP4, etc.)
- Creation & modification timestamps
- Software used (e.g., Photoshop, Snapseed)

Video-Specific Data:

- Frame rate, resolution, codec
- Audio and subtitle tracks
- Geolocation data (if available)

⚑ **Important Note**: Social media platforms strip metadata from uploaded files, but files shared via messaging apps, email, or cloud storage may still contain EXIF data.

6.2.2 Extracting Metadata from Images

1⃞ Using ExifTool (Best for Metadata Extraction)

ExifTool is one of the most powerful OSINT tools for reading metadata from images and videos.

Command (for images):

exiftool image.jpg

Example Output:

- **File Name**: image.jpg
- **Date/Time Original**: 2024:02:15 14:32:10
- **Make**: Apple
- **Model**: iPhone 14 Pro
- **GPS Latitude**: 37.7749° N
- **GPS Longitude**: -122.4194° W
- **Software**: Adobe Photoshop 24.0

⚑ **Analysis**: This image was taken with an iPhone 14 Pro in San Francisco, CA, and later edited in Photoshop.

2️⃣ Using Online Metadata Viewers

If you prefer a web-based approach, use:

✅ https://metapicz.com

✅ https://exif.tools

📌 Best Use Case:

- When dealing with anonymous image uploads (e.g., news leaks, crime tips).
- Quick checks without downloading tools.

6.2.3 Extracting Geolocation Data from Metadata

If GPS location data is embedded in an image, we can plot it on a map.

1️⃣ Converting GPS Coordinates into a Mapped Location

After extracting GPS coordinates from metadata:

- Open Google Maps.
- Enter the coordinates in the search bar:

37.7749, -122.4194

Google Maps will pinpoint the exact location.

▶ Example:

An investigator retrieves GPS data from an image and finds:

📌 **Latitude**: 48.858844
📌 **Longitude**: 2.294351

🔍 **Result**: This points to Eiffel Tower, Paris, France.

6.2.4 Geolocating Images Without Metadata

If metadata has been removed, you can still determine a photo's location using visual elements.

1⃞ Reverse Image Search

- **Google Lens** (Google Images)
- **Yandex Reverse Image** Search (https://yandex.com/images/)
- **TinEye** (https://tineye.com)

📌 Use Case:

- Identify landmarks, buildings, and cityscapes.
- Match social media posts to known locations.

⚑ Example:

- A TikTok video shows a ferris wheel in the background.
- Running the image through Google Lens reveals it's the London Eye.
- Cross-referencing with local time verifies when it was taken.

2⃞ Analyzing Shadows & Weather for Timestamp Verification

When metadata is missing, sun position & weather patterns can confirm location details.

✓ Use Suncalc (https://www.suncalc.org) to analyze:

- Sun position & shadows for estimating time of day.
- Time zone checks for verifying timestamps.

✓ Use Wolfram Alpha (https://www.wolframalpha.com) to check:

- Historical weather reports (to match with photos/videos).

⚑ Example:

- A suspect posts a photo of the Empire State Building at sunset on January 10.
- By checking Suncalc, we confirm sunset in NYC on that date was at 4:47 PM.
- This helps verify the photo's timestamp.

3️ Extracting Clues from Background Details

- Street signs, billboards, and shop names
- Language & local dialect on signs
- Unique architectural styles or landscapes

▶ Example:

A journalist investigating a conflict zone receives an anonymous war photo.

- The image shows a gas station sign in Arabic.
- A specific license plate design suggests it's from Syria.
- Cross-referencing Google Street View confirms it's near Aleppo.

6.2.5 Extracting Metadata from Videos

1️ Using ExifTool for Video Files

Command:

exiftool video.mp4

▶ Analysis:

- Identify the device used (e.g., iPhone, GoPro, Samsung).
- Retrieve frame timestamps to match against online sources.

2️ Extracting Frames & Running Reverse Image Search

If metadata is unavailable, extract video frames and run a reverse image search.

Step-by-Step Method:

Extract video frames using VLC:

- Open video in VLC Media Player
- Go to Tools → Preferences → Video → Take Snapshot

- Run the snapshot through Google Lens or Yandex.
- Compare against landmarks, signs, or unique features.

▶ **Example:**

- A criminal posts a video of a luxury hotel room without location tags.
- Extracting a frame reveals a reflection in the window showing the Eiffel Tower.
- Cross-referencing hotel websites confirms it's a suite in the Shangri-La Hotel, Paris.

6.2.6 Ethical & Legal Considerations

☐ **DO NOT:**

✗ Hack, manipulate, or access private metadata.

✗ Use geolocation for illegal tracking or stalking.

✗ Violate privacy laws (e.g., GDPR, CCPA).

✓ **DO:**

✓☐ Use only publicly available metadata.
✓☐ Ensure compliance with OSINT ethics.
✓☐ Report findings to law enforcement if necessary.

Conclusion

By combining metadata analysis, reverse image search, geolocation tools, and visual clues, OSINT practitioners can track a person's location from photos and videos—even when metadata is stripped.

6.3 Tracking an Individual's Travel History via Online Data

Tracking an individual's travel history is an essential element of modern OSINT investigations. With the proliferation of social media, geolocation tagging, online transactions, and even government data, digital footprints have become powerful indicators of where a person has been over time. From checking in at airports to sharing vacation snapshots, people unintentionally leave traces of their travels across the digital landscape.

This chapter will cover:

✅ How social media and geotagged posts reveal travel history

✅ Tracking flight and hotel bookings via online platforms

✅ Using online transaction data for travel insight

✅ Leveraging public databases and government records

✅ Case studies of real-world travel tracking

✅ Legal and ethical considerations when tracking travel history

6.3.1 Geotagged Social Media Posts as Travel Indicators

1️⃣ How Social Media Reveals Travel History

Social media platforms like Instagram, Facebook, and Twitter/X are invaluable tools for tracking a person's movement. By analyzing geotagged posts, check-ins, and location mentions, you can determine where a person has been and when. Even without obvious location tags, users often provide visual cues in their posts that indicate their geographical whereabouts.

Examples of Geotagged Data:

- **Instagram**: Check-ins at popular tourist spots or local landmarks often have location tags.
- **Facebook**: Public posts about events, festivals, and vacations frequently include geotags or location information.
- **Twitter/X**: Tweets mentioning specific locations (or hashtags with city names) can help you track the individual's movements.
- **Snapchat**: The Snap Map feature allows users to share their real-time location, creating a live travel history.

Tools & Methods:

Instagram:

- Search a user's posts for location tags.
- Cross-reference multiple posts over time to map out trips or consistent travel patterns.

Twitter/X:

- Use advanced search to find tweets that include location-specific hashtags.
- Track user's check-ins, location mentions, and posts during particular times.

Facebook:

- Look for public event check-ins, or posts from popular tourist attractions.
- Cross-reference travel groups for insights about frequent trips.

▶ **Example:**

A person's Instagram profile includes a post tagged "Tokyo Tower, Japan" on March 5 and a check-in at "Paris, France" on March 10. These timestamps and locations indicate a clear international trip and provide a travel timeline.

6.3.2 Tracking Flights & Hotel Bookings

1️⃣ Flight Tracking via Booking Sites & Airline Data

Air travel leaves digital traces that can be uncovered using flight booking platforms and airline websites. Many people unknowingly share details about their flights—from booking confirmation emails to check-in photos at airports.

Online Platforms for Tracking Flights:

- **Google Flights** (for flight routes)
- **Expedia, Booking.com, and Kayak** (for booking records, reviews, and travel history)
- **FlightAware and FlightRadar24** (for real-time flight tracking)

Flight tracking platforms provide access to real-time flight data, including departure and arrival times, airline details, and flight routes. If a person is known to travel frequently or has been connected to a specific destination, checking their flight history can reveal significant travel patterns.

Methods:

- **Booking Confirmation Emails**: If the person's booking email is known, it may provide flight details, including the departure date, airline, and destination.
- **Flight Tracking Tools**: Using FlightRadar24, FlightAware, or similar tools, it's possible to track flights from an airport to pinpoint when a person was at a given location.

2️ Hotel Bookings & Stays

Hotels often leave digital traces, especially for frequent travelers or business trips. Platforms like Airbnb, Expedia, and Booking.com store user reviews, check-ins, and booking records. Hotel reservations made online often contain geolocation data, and if the person frequently stays in a particular hotel or city, this can help reconstruct their travel history.

Methods for Tracking Hotel Stays:

- Search for online reviews or booking information related to specific hotels or accommodations.
- Check loyalty programs or travel accounts for booking data linked to hotel chains.
- Cross-check Instagram, Facebook, or Google reviews of specific locations to pinpoint when someone stayed at a hotel or tourist destination.

▶ Example:

A hotel's Google Reviews page shows multiple reviews for the same user, consistently over several months, at different locations. This creates a travel trail between their reviews, from Los Angeles to London, and helps map their travel history.

6.3.3 Using Public Databases for Travel Records

1️ Passport Records & Immigration Data

Some government databases, such as U.S. Customs and Border Protection and Immigration and Customs Enforcement (ICE), track international travel for citizens entering and leaving the country. These records, however, are typically not available to the public unless an individual's travel is flagged for investigation.

- **Public Records Access**: In some jurisdictions, travel records might be available to the public under freedom of information requests.
- **Visa & Immigration Records**: Certain visa and immigration-related details might also be available through legal channels.

2️⃣ Vehicle Registration & Toll Data

Tracking an individual's vehicle registration, license plate, or toll-road usage can help pinpoint their movements. Governments track vehicle tolls through automated systems (e.g., EZPass), which provide a real-time record of vehicles crossing state or country borders.

Methods:

- Look for publicly available license plate records through online databases or news reports.
- Use Toll System Websites to track toll booth data or verify the locations visited by a specific vehicle.

6.3.4 Using Transaction Data for Travel Insights

1️⃣ Credit Card Statements & Purchases

People often make travel-related purchases that can be tracked, such as airline tickets, hotel reservations, or transportation services (e.g., Uber, Lyft, or taxi services). When individuals use credit or debit cards during their travels, it can leave a traceable digital footprint.

Methods for Using Transaction Data:

- Search for travel-related transactions (e.g., flights, car rentals, hotels) on credit card statements.
- Look for regular spending patterns tied to specific locations, which can reveal frequent travel routes or destinations.

6.3.5 Real-World Case Studies of Travel Tracking

Case Study 1: Tracking a Corporate Executive's Business Travel

A corporate executive is suspected of traveling for business under an alias. Using social media and flight tracking tools, an investigator traces the individual's travel, mapping out a global business itinerary spanning New York, London, and Singapore. By cross-referencing flight records and hotel bookings, the investigator confirms their business trips and client meetings.

Case Study 2: Investigating a Missing Person's Last Known Location

In a missing person case, a family member's social media posts are examined, revealing geotagged photos from various locations across the United States. By tracking check-ins and flight data, investigators map the person's final journey, narrowing down their possible location before disappearance.

6.3.6 Legal & Ethical Considerations in Travel Tracking

DO NOT:

✘ Engage in unauthorized access to databases.

✘ Violate privacy rights by disclosing private travel information without consent.

✘ Use travel data to stalk, harass, or intimidate individuals.

DO:

✓ Ensure all information obtained is publicly available and used within legal boundaries.
✓ Respect privacy laws (e.g., GDPR, CCPA).
✓ Use the gathered data only for legitimate investigative purposes.

Conclusion

Tracking an individual's travel history through social media posts, flight data, hotel bookings, and public records can provide valuable insights into their whereabouts over time. By employing a combination of OSINT techniques, investigators can build a comprehensive travel timeline that helps to verify a person's movements or provide vital clues in missing person cases, fraud investigations, or business intelligence.

6.4 Using Google Maps, Street View & Satellite Imagery for OSINT

In the age of satellite technology, online mapping tools like Google Maps, Google Street View, and various satellite imagery sources have revolutionized the way open-source intelligence (OSINT) practitioners conduct investigations. These tools allow you to virtually explore geographic locations, analyze street-level details, and access historical images—all of which are critical for tracking individuals, verifying claims, or uncovering hidden facts in investigations.

This chapter will cover:

✅ How to use Google Maps and Street View for OSINT investigations

✅ Leveraging satellite imagery for tracking movements and verifying locations

✅ How to analyze historical images to establish timelines

✅ Techniques for mapping and triangulating data

✅ Case studies demonstrating practical applications of these tools

✅ Legal and ethical considerations when using mapping tools for OSINT

6.4.1 Google Maps for Investigations

1️⃣ Understanding Google Maps as an OSINT Tool

Google Maps isn't just a navigation tool—it's a treasure trove of location data that can be used for digital investigations. The platform provides a wealth of information on street names, businesses, points of interest, user-generated reviews, directions, and geolocations. Google Maps also integrates Satellite imagery and Street View, which can offer crucial context in investigations.

Key Features for OSINT Investigators:

- **Street View**: Virtual exploration of real-world locations.
- **Satellite View**: Aerial images of locations, showing terrain, building layouts, and even vegetation.
- **Timeline**: Review historical data (e.g., past trips) if the subject's Google account is linked to their device.

- **Reviews and User Content**: Businesses and locations with user-uploaded photos, reviews, and comments.
- **Routing and Directions**: Identify travel routes taken by the individual based on location and time.

Techniques for Using Google Maps in Investigations:

Searching Locations:

- Simply input an address, location, or place name into Google Maps to obtain detailed information.

Street View Navigation:

- Drag the Pegman icon to see panoramic images of streets. You can virtually walk through neighborhoods to check surroundings, street names, and locations.

Checking Timelines:

- If you have access to Google account history, you can track a person's past locations using their Google Timeline.

▶ **Example:**

An individual claims to have been at a specific event in Los Angeles on a particular date. Searching the event location on Google Maps reveals that Street View shows a temporary sign set up for that event, confirming the person's presence at that location.

6.4.2 Google Street View for OSINT Investigations

1️⃣ How to Use Google Street View for Tracking Movements

Google Street View offers 360-degree panoramic imagery of streets, businesses, and public spaces around the world. This tool allows investigators to visually explore areas and validate the information provided by individuals. From identifying landmarks to pinpointing exact locations, Street View can be crucial for investigations.

Key Uses for Google Street View:

Verify a Person's Location:

If an individual posts a photo or check-in at a particular location, you can cross-check the location via Street View to confirm their presence.

Investigate Events or Locations:

Street View can reveal current and historical conditions of a location (e.g., a construction site, a new building, or a neighborhood).

Visualize Crime Scenes:

Investigators can use Street View to check out crime scenes, accident locations, or areas of interest from multiple angles.

Techniques for Using Street View:

- Cross-reference location claims by exploring street-level imagery for familiar landmarks or changes.
- Check nearby businesses or landmarks in the area to validate or disprove a person's narrative.
- Analyze time-sensitive information to identify what an area looked like on a particular day.

▶ **Example:**

A suspect claims to have been in a restaurant in New York City on a specific date. By navigating to the restaurant's address on Google Maps, Street View shows recently-renovated storefronts, which match the description from the individual's social media posts, confirming their visit.

6.4.3 Leveraging Satellite Imagery for OSINT

1⃞ Using Satellite Imagery for Geospatial Analysis

Satellite imagery provides an aerial view of areas, allowing investigators to observe large areas that may be difficult to access otherwise. Satellite images are particularly useful for analyzing remote locations, geographical features, and patterns of movement over time.

Key Applications for OSINT Investigators:

Tracking Movement:

Satellites can track vehicle movements in large parking lots, shipping routes, or even military activity.

Assessing Changes in Land Use:

Satellite imagery reveals changes in urban landscapes, construction projects, or deforestation.

Identifying Remote Locations:

Satellites can identify hidden locations, clandestine operations, or underground bunkers in hard-to-reach regions.

Free Sources for Satellite Imagery:

- **Google Earth**: Provides access to both historical and recent satellite imagery.
- **Sentinel Hub**: Offers satellite data from European Space Agency's Sentinel satellites.
- **NASA Worldview**: Real-time imagery from NASA satellites, offering global coverage.

▶ **Example:**

An individual has been reported to have been traveling in a remote part of the Amazon rainforest. By analyzing satellite imagery, the investigator can confirm deforestation patterns or any illegal activity in the area that aligns with the individual's supposed travel.

6.4.4 Using Historical Satellite Imagery for Timeline Analysis

1️⃣ **Analyzing Historical Imagery to Establish a Timeline**

Satellite imagery is often available for multiple years, and historical images are useful for establishing timelines and understanding how locations have changed over time.

Techniques for Analyzing Historical Imagery:

Compare Changes Over Time:

Analyze satellite images from different years to track construction projects, urban growth, or environmental changes.

Verify Claims of Location Based on Visual Cues:

Confirm or disprove travel claims by referencing changes in location—e.g., a person claims to have visited a location in 2019, and historical imagery shows no roads or buildings there during that time.

▶ **Example:**

A person claims to have stayed in a resort in the Caribbean during a hurricane event. By analyzing historical satellite imagery from pre-hurricane and post-hurricane, the investigator can see whether the resort was damaged, confirming the timing of the individual's stay.

6.4.5 Techniques for Triangulating Data

1️⃣ Combining Google Maps, Street View & Satellite Imagery

By using all three tools in conjunction—Google Maps for street-level data, Street View for visual confirmation, and Satellite imagery for large-scale geographic context—investigators can triangulate information to verify or challenge claims.

Example of Triangulation:

An investigator is trying to confirm a suspect's claim of being at a meeting in an office building.

- Google Maps shows the building's location and surrounding businesses.
- Street View provides a 360-degree view of the office's entrance and nearby landmarks.
- Satellite imagery confirms that the office building is in a busy area, consistent with the suspect's description.
- By combining the data from all three sources, the investigator can confidently verify the person's presence at that location.

6.4.6 Legal and Ethical Considerations

DO NOT:

✗ Use mapping tools to stalk or harass individuals.

✗ Violate privacy laws by accessing sensitive location data without consent.

✗ Use satellite imagery to infringe on national security or invade restricted areas.

DO:

✓☐ Ensure that all information used from mapping tools is publicly available and obtained ethically.

✓☐ Use data from official sources and respect personal privacy.

✓☐ Always cross-reference your findings with multiple sources for accuracy.

Conclusion

The combination of Google Maps, Street View, and satellite imagery offers OSINT investigators an invaluable set of tools for tracking travel, verifying locations, and understanding geographical contexts. Whether you're investigating individual travel history, confirming event attendance, or analyzing large-scale movements, these tools provide a comprehensive view of the world. By combining visual imagery with historical data and real-time updates, you can uncover critical insights that lead to successful investigations.

6.5 Identifying Patterns & Predicting Future Locations

In the world of open-source intelligence (OSINT), the ability to predict future locations based on past patterns is a valuable tool for investigators. By recognizing trends and behaviors, investigators can foresee where a person might go, what they might do, and how they might act. This predictive approach is particularly useful in scenarios where real-time surveillance is not possible, or when trying to anticipate an individual's next move.

This chapter will explore:

- How to identify patterns in a person's past behavior using OSINT data sources
- Techniques for predicting future locations based on these patterns

- How to use location-based data from social media, geotagging, and other OSINT resources for forecasting future movements
- Tools and methodologies for effective pattern recognition
- Case studies demonstrating how pattern identification has led to successful investigations
- Ethical and legal considerations in predictive location tracking

6.5.1 Identifying Behavioral Patterns through OSINT Data

1⃞ Understanding Behavior from Historical Data

One of the foundational principles of predictive analysis is recognizing that humans are creatures of habit. In many cases, people repeat specific actions, visit the same places, or follow similar routines. OSINT allows investigators to capture these patterns and use them to predict where an individual may go next.

Key Sources for Pattern Recognition:

Social Media Posts & Geotags:

Social media platforms like Instagram, Twitter, and Facebook often provide valuable information about where an individual has been. Posts tagged with location data can reveal frequent visits to specific places, or notable times spent in particular cities or regions. By tracking these, investigators can develop a profile of the person's routine.

Travel History:

If the individual has left behind flight records, hotel bookings, or location check-ins (through platforms like Google, Airbnb, or even credit card statements), you can uncover traveled routes and frequented destinations.

Behavior on Digital Platforms:

Online behaviors such as interaction with specific content on news sites, or regularly engaging with certain types of advertisements or events, can point to geographical preferences, hobbies, or lifestyle choices.

Example:

An individual consistently posts about attending music festivals across multiple countries, with locations tagged in each post. This information suggests a pattern of frequent travel to music events. By analyzing the dates of festivals and past movements, it's possible to predict their next likely destination or event.

6.5.2 Analyzing Recurring Locations & Events

1️ Recognizing Recurring Patterns in Places

When an individual repeatedly visits the same types of places—whether it's a restaurant chain, business district, hotel, or event venue—these locations often represent predictable behavior. Investigators can track when and where these visits tend to occur, uncovering a pattern that can lead to predictive analysis.

Key Techniques for Tracking Patterns:

Use of Geolocation Services & Apps:

Tools like Google Maps Timeline, Foursquare, or Swarm allow users to track their past locations. By analyzing these, investigators can map out the most frequent spots visited by an individual.

Tracking Repeated Activities:

Some people may post about visiting the same gym, coffee shop, or park every day. Identifying the time of day and frequency of these visits can provide insights into their typical schedule and geographic preferences.

Example:

A subject frequently visits a specific co-working space every Monday at 9 AM. By identifying the pattern of visits and correlating this with their calendar (or public information about meetings or events), an investigator can predict where the individual is likely to be next Monday or in the near future.

6.5.3 Predicting Future Locations Using Machine Learning & Algorithms

1️ Using Predictive Algorithms to Forecast Locations

For more advanced predictive work, machine learning and data analytics can be applied to OSINT data sources to forecast future movements. These tools use historical data to create predictive models that can estimate where an individual is likely to go next.

How It Works:

Data Collection & Integration:

Collect and organize all available data on the individual's previous movements—this includes location data from social media, flight records, purchase history, hotel bookings, and other geolocation data.

Pattern Recognition & Algorithm Training:

Use machine learning tools to identify recurring trends in time, location, and behavior. For example, a machine learning model might predict that a person visits a particular city every three months or attends a specific event every year.

Prediction & Alerts:

Once the model is trained, it can predict the individual's next likely destination based on their previous behavior and send alerts when this is expected to happen.

Example:

A subject has visited Chicago, Los Angeles, and Miami at regular intervals for business trips. By using predictive analytics, the model can forecast the next location the person may travel to, helping investigators anticipate future movements.

6.5.4 Combining Data from Multiple OSINT Sources

1⬜ The Power of Multidimensional Data for Predictive Analysis

Predicting future locations is most effective when cross-referencing multiple sources of data. Using various OSINT data points from social media, GPS, flight records, and public documents, you can generate a more accurate prediction by triangulating information across different platforms.

How to Combine Data Effectively:

Integrating Social Media Data with Travel Data:

If an individual regularly posts photos from specific tourist attractions or business events, this can be cross-referenced with travel records or hotel bookings to predict upcoming travel plans.

Cross-referencing Public Records:

Public databases such as property records or court filings can reveal information about an individual's home address, business location, or family ties. Understanding these can provide insight into where the person may spend time next or where their family members live.

Example:

An individual checks in on Instagram at an event in New York City during one year. By combining this with flight records, business registrations, and other OSINT data, it becomes apparent that they frequent the city for annual conferences in May. This behavior pattern can then predict their next likely trip.

6.5.5 Case Study: Predicting the Movements of a Fugitive

1️ Real-World Application of Pattern Identification

Let's consider a case where an investigator is trying to track a fugitive on the run. The subject had been spotted in various cities but had evaded capture for several months.

How the OSINT Investigation Unfolded:

Data Collection:

The investigator starts by collecting data from the fugitive's social media accounts, travel records, public appearances, and historical location data.

Pattern Recognition:

The fugitive had a pattern of traveling to specific cities based on past criminal activities, and they visited the same hotels and parking lots in each city.

Prediction:

Using geospatial analysis and pattern recognition, the investigator predicted that the fugitive would travel to another city with similar characteristics.

Outcome:

Based on this analysis, law enforcement was able to predict the fugitive's next likely location and capture them before they could escape again.

6.5.6 Ethical & Legal Considerations in Predictive Location Tracking

While predicting future locations using OSINT can be highly effective, it's important to recognize the ethical and legal implications of this practice.

DO NOT:

- Violate privacy laws by using predictive methods to track people without proper legal authority.
- Engage in surveillance or other invasive tactics that could violate personal rights or freedoms.

DO:

- Ensure transparency and obtain consent when using predictive tools for non-investigative purposes.
- Follow data protection laws, such as the GDPR or CCPA, when collecting and analyzing location data.
- Validate the predictions using multiple sources to avoid errors and inaccuracies in judgment.

Conclusion

Identifying patterns in an individual's behavior and predicting their future locations is one of the most powerful capabilities within OSINT. By analyzing historical location data, social media habits, and leveraging advanced predictive algorithms, investigators can forecast future movements with a high degree of accuracy. However, ethical and legal boundaries should always be considered, as the misuse of predictive tracking can lead to violations of privacy. When used correctly, predictive location tracking can be an invaluable tool for both law enforcement and private investigators alike, helping solve cases more effectively.

6.6 Case Study: Finding a Person's Location Using Open Data

In the world of OSINT (Open Source Intelligence), finding a person's location is often more than just a matter of searching a database or performing a basic lookup. The ability to locate an individual using open data sources involves connecting the dots between various pieces of publicly available information. By leveraging open data from social media, public records, and other accessible platforms, investigators can piece together the puzzle of an individual's whereabouts.

In this case study, we will walk through a real-world scenario where a person's location is successfully pinpointed using open data sources. We will analyze the different steps of the investigation, the tools used, and the insights gained to demonstrate the power of OSINT in tracking down someone's physical location.

Background of the Case

A missing person's investigation began after a young woman named Sarah had not been heard from in several days. Friends and family were concerned, and local authorities had exhausted traditional leads. The woman was last seen at a social event in a nearby city, but after that, her whereabouts became a mystery.

The family reached out to an OSINT investigator for help, with the hope that online data could lead to her location. The investigator's task was to track Sarah's movements and gather as much data as possible to form a coherent picture of where she might be.

Step 1: Initial Data Gathering & Social Media Analysis

The investigator began by gathering all publicly available data on Sarah, starting with her social media profiles. She had accounts on Facebook, Instagram, and Twitter, and all were regularly updated with location tags.

Social Media Investigation:

Instagram:

Sarah had posted a series of selfies and group photos at a music festival in San Diego, a city 150 miles away from her home. Some of the posts were geotagged, showing specific locations such as the venue's entrance, the hotel she had stayed at, and even the restaurant she visited the night before.

Key Insight: The geotagged photos provided valuable location clues for the last known areas Sarah visited.

Facebook:

A search of her Facebook check-ins and status updates revealed that Sarah had recently posted about attending a concert in the downtown area of San Diego. She tagged several friends who were also at the event. Her last Facebook post included a check-in at a well-known café in the city center, timestamped just hours before she went silent.

Key Insight: Facebook check-ins pointed to specific places in San Diego where she was last known to be, narrowing down the location of her disappearance.

Twitter:

Sarah had tweeted several times throughout the day, expressing excitement about the local food scene and exploring downtown San Diego. The investigator noted that she had tagged specific locations like popular restaurants, one of which had a highly publicized rooftop bar overlooking the city's skyline.

Key Insight: The locations Sarah tweeted about helped piece together her movement patterns in the days before she disappeared.

Step 2: Cross-Referencing with Public Records

After the social media investigation, the OSINT investigator moved on to public records to further narrow down the search. Public records, such as hotel bookings, flight details, and license plate information, can reveal important leads.

Hotel Reservation Lookup:

The investigator used a hotel booking platform to check for any recent reservations under Sarah's name. After some digging, they were able to locate a reservation for a room at a well-known hotel in San Diego, confirming that Sarah had stayed in the city during the dates mentioned on her social media.

Key Insight: The hotel booking provided an official record of Sarah's physical presence in the city, confirming her location before she vanished.

Step 3: Geolocation of Photos and Videos

As the investigation progressed, the OSINT expert used metadata analysis tools to extract geolocation data from photos and videos Sarah had posted online. The idea was to verify and confirm the accuracy of the geotags already visible on her social media accounts.

Image Metadata Extraction:

The investigator downloaded several high-resolution photos Sarah had posted from her Instagram feed. They used online metadata extraction tools to pull the EXIF data from the photos. EXIF data can contain GPS coordinates, indicating the exact latitude and longitude of where the photo was taken.

Key Insight: The metadata from the photos confirmed that Sarah was indeed at two specific locations in San Diego—the hotel and a restaurant, giving the investigator further confidence in the accuracy of the geotagged locations.

Step 4: Tracing Patterns & Predicting Potential Future Locations

At this point, the investigator began to notice certain patterns in Sarah's behavior. She had posted multiple times about enjoying San Diego's nightlife, including mentions of bars, restaurants, and popular tourist spots.

The investigator used this data to hypothesize where Sarah might go next. The behavior suggested that she enjoyed exploring the local scene, particularly areas near the coast and along the waterfront.

Key Insight: By analyzing Sarah's location patterns, the investigator was able to create a probable next location for her. They focused on areas that fit her known interests and geographic preferences.

Step 5: Crowdsourcing & Digital Footprints

In addition to the traditional OSINT techniques, the investigator turned to crowdsourced data. Platforms like Google Maps and Foursquare allow users to upload photos, comments, and geotags of places they've visited. These platforms can help provide valuable secondhand information about someone's movement.

Crowdsourcing Data:

The investigator cross-referenced Sarah's favorite restaurants and frequented spots with local reviews on Google Maps and Foursquare. They found that several of the venues Sarah had visited in the past were also mentioned in recent reviews by others, offering new clues to her possible whereabouts.

Key Insight: Crowdsourced data helped fill in gaps and identify places Sarah might be visiting after her social media posts stopped.

Step 6: Conclusion—Locating Sarah

After gathering all the available data from social media, public records, photo analysis, and crowdsourcing, the investigator was able to predict where Sarah might be. Based on her last known location in downtown San Diego and her known interest in beachfront locations, the investigator used OSINT tools to narrow the search to a popular beach resort near the city center. This location had previously appeared in Sarah's social media history, where she had posted a photo with a caption about sunset views.

The investigator alerted the family, who then contacted local authorities. With the help of the gathered data, the authorities were able to locate Sarah at the beach resort.

Lessons Learned from the Case

This case study highlights several important aspects of using OSINT to locate a person through open data sources:

- Social media can provide rich and detailed information about an individual's last known locations and potential future behaviors.
- Public records, like hotel bookings, flight details, and property data, offer official verification of where someone has been.
- Metadata analysis of photos and videos can confirm or provide additional insights into a person's whereabouts.
- Crowdsourced data, such as reviews and user-generated content, can help identify places an individual might visit in the future.

In this case, the combination of open data, geolocation, and pattern analysis was key to solving the investigation and finding Sarah's location. The use of OSINT tools effectively brought together multiple data points, enabling a precise and targeted search.

Ethical Considerations

While OSINT offers powerful tools for locating individuals, it's crucial to maintain ethical boundaries. In this case, the investigator acted with the utmost respect for privacy and followed legal protocols. Consent should always be obtained when accessing personal data, and data protection laws must be adhered to at all times.

In the case of missing persons, OSINT can be a game-changer in resolving cases quickly and efficiently, provided it is done ethically and responsibly.

7. Employment & Educational Background Verification

Verifying a person's professional and academic history is a critical aspect of online investigations. This chapter covers OSINT techniques for researching employment records, company affiliations, and educational credentials using open data sources, professional networking sites, and institutional databases. You'll learn how to cross-reference résumés, identify inconsistencies, and detect fabricated qualifications. Additionally, we'll explore advanced methods for uncovering hidden work histories, freelance activities, and industry connections to build a more accurate profile of your subject.

7.1 Investigating a Person's Work History via OSINT

A person's work history can reveal significant information about their background, skills, affiliations, and potential connections to various organizations. For investigators, understanding an individual's professional history is often crucial to building a comprehensive profile, whether for background checks, verifying credentials, or uncovering suspicious activity. Open-source intelligence (OSINT) provides a wealth of accessible data that can be used to trace someone's career trajectory, from past employment and educational qualifications to professional achievements.

In this chapter, we will explore the techniques used to investigate a person's work history through OSINT. This includes the use of online platforms, public databases, and other accessible resources to uncover professional affiliations, job roles, and the potential motives behind a person's career choices. Investigators will also learn how to connect this data with other investigative leads to paint a fuller picture of a person's professional life.

7.1.1 Key Sources for Investigating Work History

The first step in investigating a person's work history is identifying the primary OSINT sources that hold the most relevant information. These sources typically include social media platforms, professional networking sites, and public databases.

1️⃣ Professional Social Networks: LinkedIn

LinkedIn is one of the most important platforms when it comes to work history investigations. It provides a rich repository of data about individuals' employment history, educational background, skills, and recommendations.

What to Look for on LinkedIn:

Job Titles & Employment Dates:

LinkedIn profiles often list the exact titles, employment dates, and companies the individual has worked for. This is valuable for confirming work history, identifying job roles, and understanding the timeline of the person's career.

Company Pages & Connections:

LinkedIn allows you to view company pages where a person has worked, which can provide insight into the size and scope of the organization. Additionally, viewing a person's connections and the people they interact with can lead to valuable clues about their professional network.

Public Endorsements & Recommendations:

LinkedIn often features recommendations from colleagues or clients, which can shed light on the individual's work performance, reputation, and role within the organization.

Example:

An investigator may find that an individual worked at a tech company from 2015 to 2018 as a software engineer. By examining the company's LinkedIn page, the investigator can verify the company's size and its industry, potentially indicating the individual's role within the tech sector.

2️⃣ Other Social Media Platforms: Facebook, Twitter, and Instagram

While LinkedIn is primarily focused on professional information, other social media platforms can provide indirect clues about an individual's work history and professional behavior.

What to Look for on Facebook, Twitter, and Instagram:

Posts About Work-Related Achievements:

People often post updates about promotions, new job offers, work-related events, and business achievements. These posts can be valuable for verifying professional accomplishments and inferring the individual's career trajectory.

Workplace Check-ins & Mentions:

Some individuals will check into work-related events, conferences, or company locations, providing insights into their current or past roles.

Tagged Photos in Professional Contexts:

Photos of events like conferences, networking events, or workshops that an individual attends may provide evidence of their professional engagement and career interests.

Example:

An investigator may find a Facebook post where an individual proudly shares a promotion announcement at their company or mentions their attendance at a leadership seminar. These posts can help confirm or update their employment history.

3️⃣ Job Search Websites & Freelance Platforms

Job search websites and freelance platforms like Indeed, Glassdoor, Upwork, and Fiverr can also offer valuable insights into a person's professional history.

What to Look for on Job Search Websites:

Job Applications & Resumes:

If a person's profile is public, they may have uploaded their resume or CV, which can provide direct details about their work experience, skills, and career goals.

Reviews and Ratings:

For those on freelance platforms, user ratings and reviews can offer insight into the quality of their work and the types of projects they've undertaken.

Job Listings or Projects Worked On:

Some platforms provide details on the types of roles a person has applied for, including job titles and companies, which may indicate their interests and career trajectory.

Example:

An investigator using Glassdoor could uncover past job listings that the person applied for, revealing their interest in marketing positions and business management roles, or they may find their freelancer profile on Upwork, showing their work history in graphic design.

4⬜ Public Records & Corporate Databases

Public records and corporate databases can offer authoritative insights into a person's work history. Many public databases keep records of people associated with companies or businesses, including business licenses, corporate filings, and employment history.

What to Look for in Public Databases:

Business Ownership & Corporate Affiliations:

Searching through corporate databases such as Secretary of State websites, Dun & Bradstreet, or business registration databases can reveal whether the individual has been involved in founding or running a business. These records can also indicate the person's role as a director, manager, or shareholder.

Professional Licenses:

For people in regulated fields such as law, medicine, or real estate, licensing boards provide public records on individuals' professional certifications and license status.

Example:

An investigator might discover through a corporate filing database that the person was listed as the CEO of a tech start-up in 2010, indicating they have a significant history in the entrepreneurial tech space.

7.1.2 Cross-Referencing Work History with Other OSINT Data

Once you've gathered information from the primary OSINT sources, it's important to cross-reference this data with other available intelligence. Cross-referencing allows you to verify the authenticity of the work history and connect the dots between different aspects of the individual's professional life.

Key Cross-Referencing Techniques:

Matching Job Titles with Other Public Records:

If the person has a job title listed on LinkedIn or other platforms, cross-check this information with tax records, corporate filings, or news articles to verify the accuracy of their job history.

Connecting Companies with Public News or Business Listings:

Investigate the companies listed on a person's resume or LinkedIn profile by searching news outlets, company websites, or industry publications for mentions of the individual's role and achievements. This adds credibility to the claim that the person actually worked there.

Tracking Personal Networks & Professional Associations:

Use professional network connections (e.g., LinkedIn contacts or industry groups) to corroborate work history. Often, colleagues and mentors leave behind traces of their involvement in a person's professional network.

7.1.3 Verifying Employment History with Direct Contact

In some cases, especially when dealing with high-stakes investigations, it may be necessary to verify the employment history by reaching out directly to the company or organization. HR departments and corporate offices can provide official confirmation of an individual's past employment, though investigators should be mindful of privacy regulations when doing so.

Key Considerations When Contacting Employers:

GDPR and Privacy Laws:

Ensure compliance with data protection laws, such as GDPR in Europe or CCPA in California, when contacting businesses for verification of employment.

Official Requests:

Use formal channels such as employment verification forms or corporate reference checks to gather information.

7.1.4 Case Study: Verifying a Suspect's Employment History

Scenario:

A private investigator is hired to verify the employment history of a potential suspect in a corporate fraud case. The suspect is claiming to have worked as a senior financial analyst at a prominent investment firm. The investigator needs to confirm this claim to assess the suspect's credibility and uncover any potential motives.

Steps Taken:

LinkedIn Search:

The investigator reviews the individual's LinkedIn profile, finding the listed position at the investment firm. They also note the dates of employment and connections with others in the firm.

Public Corporate Filings:

A search of the company's public filings on Dun & Bradstreet reveals that the suspect was listed as a key player in the firm, though the exact job title does not match the suspect's claim.

Verification with the Company:

The investigator contacts the firm's HR department to verify the employment. After following appropriate legal and ethical procedures, the firm confirms that the suspect worked at the company but in a different role than stated.

Cross-referencing with News Reports:

A search of financial industry news articles uncovers the individual's involvement in a high-profile acquisition deal during their tenure, confirming their role in the company.

Outcome:

By using a combination of OSINT sources, public records, and direct verification, the investigator was able to confirm the suspect's employment history, uncover discrepancies in their claims, and build a stronger case.

Conclusion

Investigating a person's work history through OSINT is a vital step in building a profile of an individual, whether for background checks, fraud investigations, or understanding professional connections. By leveraging sources like LinkedIn, public records, job boards, and social media, investigators can uncover valuable insights into a person's career trajectory, validate claims of employment, and identify key professional affiliations. Cross-referencing this information with other available data further enhances the accuracy of the findings, ultimately leading to a clearer and more complete picture of an individual's work history.

7.2 Verifying College & University Enrollment Claims

Verifying someone's educational background is often an essential part of the investigation process, especially when it comes to confirming academic qualifications, professional licensing, or claims related to a person's academic achievements. Whether you're conducting a background check, investigating a fraud case, or validating someone's credentials for hiring purposes, OSINT can play a critical role in confirming whether an individual attended or graduated from a particular college or university.

In this chapter, we'll explore the OSINT tools, techniques, and strategies available for verifying college and university enrollment claims. From reviewing online profiles to accessing public educational records, investigators can gather significant evidence to support or challenge a person's educational background.

7.2.1 Common Sources for Verifying Academic Claims

When investigating claims of college and university enrollment, there are several key sources you can turn to. These sources provide a wealth of publicly available information, and with the right investigative tools and skills, you can uncover whether someone's educational background is legitimate.

1️ Academic and Professional Social Media Platforms

The first place many investigators look to when verifying someone's academic history is social media profiles. Professional networking platforms, in particular, offer a detailed view of a person's academic background. LinkedIn, Xing, and even Facebook can reveal educational details.

What to Look for on LinkedIn:

Degrees and Institutions:

LinkedIn profiles frequently list academic credentials, including the individual's degree, institution, and years attended. These can serve as a starting point for verification.

Connections and Alumni Networks:

LinkedIn often connects people with their university alumni networks, giving investigators the ability to search for other graduates from the same institution. Alumni from the same program or field can sometimes offer valuable confirmation regarding an individual's presence or involvement in certain academic programs.

Public Recommendations or Mentions:

Recommendations from professors or classmates can occasionally verify claims of enrollment, providing additional context about the person's academic experience.

Example:

If a person claims to have attended Harvard University for a degree in economics, an investigator can cross-check their LinkedIn profile for this information. By comparing the listed degree, dates of attendance, and possible alumni connections, they can begin the process of confirming the academic claim.

2️ University Websites and Alumni Databases

Universities often provide public records of notable alumni, or they may have directories or searchable databases where past students can be found. Some institutions also allow students to list their academic background on a public directory or a dedicated page about alumni accomplishments.

What to Look for on University Websites:

Graduation Lists and Alumni Pages:

Many universities provide lists of prominent alumni or graduation yearbooks that include detailed information on past students. While these are not exhaustive, they can offer insight into the legitimacy of someone's claim to have graduated from that institution.

Verification Systems:

Some universities have online portals or systems where employers and other individuals can verify whether someone graduated from that particular school, especially when dealing with claims regarding degrees or certifications.

Online Yearbooks and Graduation Announcements:

Some universities have scanned or digitized their graduation yearbooks or have public announcements of graduations and events, which may feature the person in question.

Example:

An investigator could use a university's official alumni page to check whether the individual appears in their alumni section. If they don't find the person in the list, further steps can be taken to investigate the legitimacy of the claim.

3⃣ Online Education Directories and Verification Services

Various online databases and verification services allow you to check the education credentials of individuals. These can be especially helpful when trying to verify degrees or certifications from specific institutions.

What to Look for in Education Verification Databases:

Verification Services (e.g., The National Student Clearinghouse in the U.S.):

In the U.S., services like the National Student Clearinghouse provide a centralized verification system for universities and colleges. By using such services, an investigator can determine whether someone was enrolled at a specific school, when they attended, and if they graduated.

Credential Verification Companies:

Companies like DegreeVerify and Verification.org specialize in validating educational claims. These services typically work with educational institutions to provide confirmation of degrees, diplomas, or certifications.

Example:

If the individual claims to have received a master's degree in computer science from MIT, the investigator can use the National Student Clearinghouse to check enrollment and graduation status.

4️⃣ Public Records & Government Databases

In many regions, especially in the U.S. and other developed countries, certain academic records and graduation statistics are considered public records. This can include graduation data, degrees granted, and other educational records that government agencies may publish or make available to the public.

What to Look for in Public Education Databases:

State & Federal Education Records:

Certain states or government agencies may keep databases of students who attended state universities or completed specific public programs. Some of these records may be publicly accessible through freedom of information requests or through special verification systems.

Professional Licensing Agencies:

For individuals claiming to hold a degree necessary for specific licenses (e.g., in medicine, law, or engineering), licensing boards or professional certification organizations often maintain records of educational requirements and whether someone met them.

Example:

An investigator might request educational records via Freedom of Information (FOI) or use a state-run verification portal to check whether a person attended a state university or obtained the required degree for a professional license.

5️⃣ Online Yearbooks & Newspaper Archives

Sometimes, traditional methods like searching for digitalized yearbooks or newspaper archives can reveal valuable information. Many universities now upload scanned copies of yearbooks from past graduating classes, which can help verify the dates of graduation and the degree obtained.

What to Look for in Yearbooks & Newspapers:

Graduation Yearbooks:

University yearbooks often feature pictures of graduates, along with their names and degree information. These may be available for free or for purchase on certain websites or the university's digital library.

Newspaper Articles:

Local newspapers may announce graduations, academic awards, or involvement in student organizations. These can be useful for confirming enrollment and identifying the individual's academic achievements.

Example:

A person might claim to have graduated from Stanford University in 2010 with a Bachelor's in Philosophy. An investigator might search through Stanford's digitalized yearbook or local news archives to cross-reference this claim.

7.2.2 Verifying Enrollment in Online Programs

With the rise of online education, individuals may claim to have attended a virtual institution or received degrees from online-only universities. Verifying these types of educational claims requires a slightly different approach.

What to Consider for Online Programs:

Accreditation:

Investigators must confirm whether the institution offering the online program is accredited by a recognized body. Accreditation is a key factor in determining the legitimacy of an online institution.

Online Databases for Verification:

Some online programs partner with credential verification services to allow potential employers or institutions to verify enrollment and degrees.

7.2.3 Case Study: Verifying a Fraudulent College Claim

Scenario:

An investigator is hired to verify the educational background of an individual who claims to have a Ph.D. in Environmental Science from Oxford University. This claim has come into question after the individual applied for a government contract requiring a high level of academic qualifications.

Steps Taken:

Check LinkedIn Profile:

The individual's LinkedIn profile lists the Oxford Ph.D. as well as various environmental consulting jobs.

Verify with Oxford University:

The investigator contacts Oxford's alumni office using their verification system and finds no record of the individual's enrollment or graduation.

Cross-reference News Archives:

A search through local and international news archives reveals no mention of the individual in relation to Oxford University.

Check Online Academic Databases:

Databases like Google Scholar and ResearchGate reveal no published papers by the individual, raising further concerns about their academic claim.

Outcome:

After conducting thorough OSINT checks, the investigator determines that the individual did not attend Oxford University and fabricated their Ph.D. claim.

Conclusion

Verifying college and university enrollment claims through OSINT is a critical part of the investigative process. Whether it's for a background check, legal investigation, or fraud detection, using professional networking sites, university records, credential verification services, and public documents can provide valuable insights into an individual's academic history. By cross-referencing these sources and employing diligent investigative practices, OSINT analysts can confirm or debunk academic claims with high accuracy.

7.3 Cross-Checking Résumés & LinkedIn Profiles for Discrepancies

In today's digital age, professionals are increasingly reliant on online platforms like LinkedIn and personal websites to showcase their resumes and work histories. While these tools offer a convenient way to network and apply for jobs, they also provide investigators with key sources for verifying a person's professional background. Discrepancies between an individual's résumé, LinkedIn profile, and other public records can reveal potential dishonesty, exaggeration, or even criminal behavior, especially when it comes to fabricating qualifications, work experience, or educational credentials.

In this section, we'll explore how OSINT analysts can cross-check résumés and LinkedIn profiles to identify inconsistencies or fraudulent claims. By comparing these profiles to public records, social media activity, and other online data, investigators can assess whether an individual is being truthful about their professional history.

7.3.1 Key Discrepancies to Watch for in Résumés and LinkedIn Profiles

The primary goal of cross-checking résumés and LinkedIn profiles is to spot discrepancies that could suggest fraudulent activities or misrepresentations. These discrepancies can occur in various areas, such as job titles, employment dates, educational background, skills, and professional achievements. Here are some key red flags that investigators should focus on when analyzing résumés and LinkedIn profiles:

1️ Job Titles & Job Descriptions

Inconsistent Job Titles:

A person may exaggerate their job title to appear more experienced or qualified. For instance, a person may claim to have held an Executive Director position when, in reality, they were a junior coordinator.

Discrepancies in Job Descriptions:

Some individuals may fabricate or inflate their responsibilities within an organization. It is important to compare the listed job duties on a résumé with the typical duties for that role in similar companies or industries.

Mismatch Between Résumé and LinkedIn Profile:

Often, people update their résumés before applying for a job but may forget to update their LinkedIn profile or vice versa. Look for gaps between the two, such as differences in titles, dates, or roles mentioned.

Example:

A résumé might list a Vice President of Marketing role at a major company, but the LinkedIn profile might list a more junior Marketing Manager title for the same period. A thorough investigation could reveal which position is the more accurate reflection of the individual's actual role.

2 Employment Dates

Overlapping or Missing Employment Dates:

Gaps or overlaps in employment dates on a résumé are often a sign of inconsistent reporting. A discrepancy in the dates listed for a role can suggest either intentional omission or falsification of work experience.

Short Employment Durations:

Some individuals may attempt to hide short-term positions or frequent job changes that could be viewed negatively by potential employers. A job that is claimed to have lasted for several years but is actually only a few months should be flagged for further investigation.

Example:

If someone's LinkedIn profile lists an employment period from 2015 to 2020 at a particular company, but their résumé claims they worked there from 2016 to 2020, this discrepancy could indicate a misrepresentation or error in the timeline.

3⃞ Educational Background

Unverified Degrees or Institutions:

Investigators should pay close attention to claims regarding education. Fake degrees or unverified institutions are common methods of credential inflation. By cross-referencing a person's claimed degree with known alumni lists, official university records, or certification databases, investigators can quickly determine whether the degree is legitimate.

Inconsistent Graduation Dates:

Graduating from a university in 2020 but claiming to have started a job at a firm in 2019 may raise questions about the individual's academic timeline. Ensure that academic history aligns with professional experience.

Mismatched Institutions:

Some people may claim to have attended well-known or prestigious institutions when they actually attended a lesser-known or less-credible institution. Cross-checking the university's details and confirming alumni records can uncover such discrepancies.

Example:

A résumé that claims a Harvard Business School MBA might conflict with a LinkedIn profile that lists the individual as having graduated from a local community college. Investigators can cross-reference this claim by searching for alumni records or using education verification services.

4⃞ Skills & Certifications

Mismatch in Skills or Endorsements:

A résumé may list a skill or certification that isn't reflected in the individual's LinkedIn profile or other online accounts. Similarly, some individuals may list skills that are outdated or not relevant to the role they claim to have held.

Unverifiable Certifications:

Some individuals will claim professional certifications from reputable bodies like Microsoft, Google, or Cisco, but these may not appear in any certification records or verification portals. Investigators can use tools like CredentialCheck or specific industry verification portals to confirm the authenticity of certifications.

Example:

An individual's LinkedIn profile lists proficiency in Python programming, but the résumé indicates advanced certifications in Data Science that cannot be verified via industry-recognized databases or platforms like Coursera or Udacity.

5️ Recommendations & Endorsements

Fake Recommendations or Endorsements:

LinkedIn profiles often feature recommendations or endorsements from colleagues, supervisors, or clients. While this can be a valuable indicator of a person's professional credibility, some individuals fabricate or solicit fake recommendations to bolster their credibility. Look for inconsistencies in writing style, tone, or outdated job titles in recommendations that don't match the person's professional history.

Absence of Recommendations:

The lack of recommendations for someone claiming to have significant work experience could suggest that the individual may have falsified parts of their résumé or LinkedIn profile.

Example:

An individual claiming to be an Executive Director with over 15 years of experience may have no LinkedIn recommendations or references from people in their professional network. This could indicate a fraudulent résumé.

7.3.2 Methods for Cross-Checking Discrepancies

Once you've identified potential discrepancies between a résumé and a LinkedIn profile, there are several methods you can employ to verify the information:

1️ Cross-Referencing Public Databases

Job Search Sites:

Platforms like Indeed, Glassdoor, and ZipRecruiter may have historical job listings that mention a particular individual or company, helping to cross-check employment history.

Government Employment Records:

In some cases, government records or employment tax data may reveal an individual's employment history, especially for public sector jobs. You can also look for corporate filings or SEC reports for executives at publicly traded companies.

University Alumni Directories:

Many universities maintain online alumni directories that include basic information about graduation years, degrees, and major accomplishments. This can be helpful in confirming or refuting educational claims.

2️ Contacting References

Reach Out to Professional Contacts:

If the person has listed a specific manager or colleague as a reference on LinkedIn or their résumé, you can attempt to reach out to these individuals to verify the accuracy of the employment dates and job responsibilities.

Verify Professional Endorsements:

Contacting individuals who have endorsed skills or written recommendations for the person can help confirm the authenticity of these claims.

3️ Use Background Check Tools

Third-Party Verification Tools:

Many online services, such as BeenVerified, TruthFinder, or Checkr, allow you to cross-check public information on individuals. These services may pull in additional employment data, criminal records, or other public information to corroborate the résumé and LinkedIn profile.

7.3.3 Case Study: Cross-Checking a Fraudulent Executive Resume

Scenario:

An investigator is tasked with verifying the professional background of a candidate for a senior executive position at a large technology firm. The candidate's résumé lists high-level roles at prestigious companies, but the firm's HR department is concerned about the potential for résumé fraud.

Steps Taken:

Compare LinkedIn and Résumé Details:

The résumé lists a Chief Marketing Officer role at a global tech firm, but the LinkedIn profile only mentions a lower-level Marketing Manager role at the same company. The investigator notes the discrepancy and proceeds to verify both positions.

Verify Employment Dates:

The investigator cross-checks the dates of employment between the résumé and LinkedIn profile. They discover that the dates don't align, with the résumé claiming a longer tenure than the LinkedIn profile suggests.

Cross-Check with Company Database:

The investigator contacts the HR department of the supposed employer and confirms that the individual never held the CMO role but was employed in a junior marketing role for a brief period.

Check for Education Verification:

The individual claims to have graduated from Stanford University with an MBA, but the investigator finds no record of this through Stanford's alumni database.

Outcome:

After a thorough investigation, the individual is revealed to have fabricated their career history and educational background. The résumé and LinkedIn profile contained significant discrepancies that were uncovered through careful cross-referencing.

Conclusion

Cross-checking résumés and LinkedIn profiles for discrepancies is an essential aspect of OSINT investigations aimed at uncovering fraudulent claims. By identifying mismatches in job titles, employment dates, educational credentials, and professional achievements, investigators can expose fabrications or exaggerations that could have serious consequences, especially in the context of hiring decisions, legal investigations, or fraud detection. Using OSINT tools, professional networks, and public databases, investigators can verify the authenticity of individuals' professional backgrounds and ensure that they are accurately represented.

7.4 Searching Professional Certifications & Licenses

In today's competitive job market, professional certifications and licenses serve as key indicators of expertise and credibility in a particular field. Whether it's a certified public accountant (CPA), a project management professional (PMP), or a licensed medical practitioner, these credentials often play a crucial role in verifying an individual's qualifications. However, just like any other information in a person's professional history, certifications and licenses are subject to potential misrepresentation or fraud. People may falsely claim to have earned certifications or licenses that they do not actually hold in order to boost their professional appeal.

In this section, we'll explore how OSINT investigators can verify the authenticity of professional certifications and licenses, the best methods for finding official records, and how to spot potential fraudulent claims. This skill is invaluable for anyone conducting background checks, hiring processes, or investigative work that involves ensuring an individual's professional qualifications are legitimate.

7.4.1 Why Verifying Professional Certifications is Crucial

Verifying certifications and licenses is an essential part of ensuring that an individual is qualified for a specific job or role. Fraudulent certifications are a growing concern, especially in fields where the legal or ethical responsibilities tied to qualifications are critical (e.g., in healthcare, law, engineering, and financial services). Invalid or fake certifications can result in significant harm, whether it's providing incorrect advice, malpractice, or breaching industry standards. For example:

A fake medical license can put lives at risk.

- A bogus project management certification can lead to poor management of critical projects, costing businesses time and money.
- Fabricated legal qualifications can mislead clients, leading to misrepresentation of legal expertise.

By verifying certifications and licenses, OSINT analysts can protect organizations and individuals from these risks, ensuring that professional standards are upheld and that individuals are truly qualified to perform their roles.

7.4.2 Where to Find Professional Certification and License Information

When investigating the authenticity of professional certifications or licenses, it's essential to know where to look for valid, official records. Many professional organizations, trade associations, and regulatory bodies provide online databases where you can verify credentials. Below are common sources to check when validating certifications and licenses:

1️ Professional Licensing Boards

Many professions require individuals to obtain a license in order to legally practice. Licensing boards for fields such as law, medicine, finance, and engineering typically maintain public directories or search tools where you can verify the credentials of licensed professionals. Examples include:

- State Bar Association (for lawyers)
- State Medical Boards (for physicians, nurses, and other healthcare providers)
- State Boards of Accountancy (for CPAs)
- State Engineering Boards (for licensed engineers)
- Securities and Exchange Commission (SEC) (for certified financial professionals)

These regulatory bodies usually provide an online verification tool where you can search by name, license number, or other identifiers.

Example:

To verify a licensed nurse in a specific state, you can visit the National Council of State Boards of Nursing (NCSBN) website, which allows you to search for license information across all states in the U.S.

2️⃣ Certification Organizations & Accrediting Bodies

Certain certifications are awarded by industry-specific certification organizations or accrediting bodies. These organizations are responsible for setting the standards for their respective fields and for verifying whether an individual meets those standards. Many of these organizations maintain public databases or provide online verification tools.

Examples of certification organizations include:

- **Project Management Institute (PMI)** – for Project Management Professional (PMP) certifications
- **Cisco** – for certifications like Cisco Certified Network Associate (CCNA)
- **Google** – for certifications in Google Ads or Google Analytics
- **CompTIA** – for IT certifications like A+, Network+, and Security+
- **Financial Industry Regulatory Authority (FINRA)** – for certified financial professionals

These organizations often offer online search tools or will confirm certification status through email or phone requests.

3️⃣ Educational Institutions

In some fields, a degree or academic certificate is required in addition to a professional license. For example, a law degree is necessary for practicing law, and an engineering degree is often required for professional engineering licensure. You can verify degrees through the respective university's alumni database, and some institutions have degree verification services available online.

For certain certifications like MBA programs or specific graduate degrees, individuals may claim to have obtained these credentials without attending the institution. Verifying academic records through the university's registrar or using third-party verification services is crucial in these cases.

4️⃣ Online Verification Tools & Background Check Services

For those unfamiliar with the specific regulatory body or certification organization, there are numerous online tools and third-party background check services that can streamline the verification process. These services aggregate data from multiple professional, educational, and licensing sources, allowing investigators to run a comprehensive background check. Some popular services include:

- **Checkr** – for background checks, including verification of licenses and certifications.
- **BeenVerified** – for checking professional credentials, education, and even criminal records.
- **TruthFinder** – for in-depth searches into an individual's background, including professional certifications.
- **Sterling** – for HR professionals seeking certified background checks for job applicants.

These services allow investigators to quickly find records that might otherwise be difficult to access, making it easier to verify if a certification or license is legitimate.

7.4.3 Common Red Flags for Fake Certifications and Licenses

While online verification tools and databases can provide valuable insights into a person's credentials, there are also common red flags to watch for when investigating professional certifications and licenses. Here are a few to consider:

1▢ Unverifiable or Outdated Organizations

Some individuals may claim certification from a non-existent organization or a disbanded entity. A quick check of the accrediting body's website can reveal if the organization is reputable and still active. Be cautious of certifications from obscure or unverifiable organizations that lack transparency or professional recognition.

Example:

An individual claims to have a Project Management Professional (PMP) certification from a random Project Management Institute that doesn't appear in PMI's official listings. This could signal a fake certification.

2▢ Inconsistent Dates or Unusual Expiration Dates

Legitimate certifications and licenses usually have specific expiration dates, and individuals must renew them periodically. An individual claiming a lifetime certification or unusual expiration dates may be trying to mislead others about the validity of their credentials.

Example:

A person may claim to have received a medical license that supposedly never expires. However, in reality, medical licenses in most states require periodic renewal and ongoing continuing education.

3️⃣ Overly Vague or General Certifications

Some individuals may list generalized certifications like "Certified Professional" or "Expert in Business" without specifying the awarding body. These vague terms can be used to disguise a lack of specific qualifications. Always seek the exact name of the certifying organization and the nature of the certification.

4️⃣ Certifications Not in Relevant Fields

An individual might claim a certification in an irrelevant field to boost their credibility. For example, a person working in human resources may list a cybersecurity certification, even though the certification doesn't align with their current job function.

Example:

Someone may list an A+ certification in IT support when their actual job title is marketing manager. This is a clear red flag for a misrepresentation.

7.4.4 Case Study: Verifying a Fake Financial Certification

Scenario:

A potential job candidate claims to hold a Chartered Financial Analyst (CFA) certification, which would be critical for a senior investment role. However, during the interview, the hiring manager becomes suspicious when the candidate cannot provide specific details about their CFA exams or years of certification.

Steps Taken:

Verify with CFA Institute:

The hiring manager uses the CFA Institute's official verification tool to cross-check the candidate's claimed certification.

Discrepancy Found:

The verification reveals that the candidate had never completed the required exams for the CFA certification. They had fabricated their qualifications.

Follow-Up Investigation:

The hiring manager runs an additional background check on the candidate through Checkr, which confirms the false claims made about the candidate's education and work experience.

Outcome:

The hiring company avoids potentially hiring an unqualified individual by conducting a thorough verification of the candidate's professional credentials.

Conclusion

Verifying professional certifications and licenses is a crucial part of the OSINT workflow for ensuring that individuals are legitimately qualified for their claimed roles. By using a combination of online verification tools, public databases, and third-party services, investigators can accurately assess whether the credentials listed on a résumé, LinkedIn profile, or job application are valid. Identifying fraudulent claims early in the investigative process not only protects individuals and organizations but also helps maintain the integrity of professional fields across industries.

7.5 Identifying Fake Degrees & Diploma Mills

Academic degrees and diplomas are foundational elements of an individual's educational background. They serve as proof of the completion of specific academic programs and signify a person's expertise in a particular subject area. In today's job market, individuals with degrees from reputable institutions are often viewed as more qualified, and employers may rely on this information to make hiring decisions.

However, a troubling issue has emerged in the realm of education: fake degrees and diploma mills. These fraudulent institutions offer degrees and diplomas with little to no academic rigor, preying on individuals seeking to advance their careers or inflate their qualifications. The rise of these fraudulent practices makes it crucial for OSINT analysts, employers, and educational institutions to be able to identify when a degree is not legitimate. In this section, we will explore how to spot fake degrees, recognize the signs of diploma mills, and learn how to verify academic credentials effectively.

7.5.1 What Are Diploma Mills?

A diploma mill is an unaccredited institution that offers degrees or diplomas for a fee, without requiring students to complete the academic work typically associated with earning such credentials. These institutions exploit individuals by selling degrees that are often indistinguishable from those awarded by legitimate, accredited universities. Many diploma mills exist in various regions, often operating under names that mimic established universities or have vague connections to real educational bodies.

The allure of these fake degrees can be significant—diploma mills offer a shortcut to earning a degree that looks legitimate but requires little to no effort or education. For people seeking a quick credential boost for career advancement or to mislead employers, the option of purchasing a degree is all too tempting.

Key characteristics of diploma mills include:

- **No academic requirements**: Students can obtain degrees without having to attend classes, submit coursework, or pass exams.
- **High fees for degrees**: Diploma mills charge exorbitant amounts for degrees that hold no real academic value.
- **Unclear or nonexistent accreditation**: Many diploma mills claim to be accredited by dubious or fake organizations that have no credibility.
- **Unrealistic time frames**: These institutions often promise degrees in unusually short time frames, sometimes in just weeks or days, which is a major red flag.

Identifying diploma mills can be difficult without proper investigative methods, but an OSINT approach can reveal critical signs of fraud.

7.5.2 Recognizing Fake Degrees

There are several methods that OSINT analysts and employers can use to spot fake degrees or diplomas. While these fraudulent documents are often designed to look convincing, they frequently contain signs that can expose them as counterfeit. Here are common indicators to watch for when reviewing academic credentials:

1 Unverifiable Accreditation

One of the most important aspects of a legitimate degree is the accreditation of the institution that awarded it. Accreditation is the process by which an educational institution is officially recognized by a governmental or independent body for meeting specific academic standards.

Red flags include:

- The institution claims to be accredited by an organization that doesn't exist or is not recognized in the educational community.
- The accrediting body is not recognized by any regional, national, or international accreditation authorities.
- The accrediting body's website is poorly constructed, lacks contact details, or provides little information about its accreditation process.

A simple way to verify accreditation is by searching for the institution or accrediting body through the Council for Higher Education Accreditation (CHEA) or the U.S. Department of Education's database of recognized accreditors.

2 Inconsistent or Suspicious Degree Details

Fake diplomas often contain inconsistencies or errors that can serve as red flags. These issues might be difficult to notice at first glance, but closer inspection will often reveal flaws in the design, content, and formatting of the document.

Common signs include:

- **Inaccurate or missing institution name**: The name of the school may not match official records, or it may be spelled incorrectly. In some cases, the name of the institution may be deliberately altered to sound similar to a real university.
- **No official seal or logo**: Authentic degrees typically feature the official seal or coat of arms of the issuing institution, which will be difficult to replicate accurately.
- **Poor-quality printing**: Fake degrees may have low-quality printing or paper that doesn't match the standard of a legitimate academic institution.
- **Incorrect font or formatting**: The use of unusual fonts or inconsistent formatting on the degree may signal that it's not authentic.

- **Misspelled names or titles**: A legitimate degree will not contain typographical errors or misspelled names, titles, or official terms (e.g., "Bachelor of Art" instead of "Bachelor of Arts").

If any of these discrepancies are spotted, it's worth investigating further.

3⃞ Unusual Degree Names

Legitimate degrees are generally awarded in standard formats, such as Bachelor of Arts (BA), Master of Science (MS), or Doctor of Philosophy (PhD). Fake degrees often have unusual or uncommon titles that aren't typically awarded in recognized academic programs.

Red flags include:

- "Honorary degrees" that are offered to individuals without completing any academic work.
- Unusual degree titles that sound impressive but don't reflect real educational programs (e.g., "Master of Global Studies in Leadership" or "Doctor of Science in Public Relations").

If the degree title sounds overly grand or doesn't fit typical academic titles, further verification should be sought.

4⃞ Lack of Graduation or Course Information

Legitimate degrees and diplomas usually contain certain pieces of information that authenticate the person's academic journey:

- Degree type (e.g., Bachelor's, Master's, Ph.D.)
- Program of study (e.g., Psychology, Business Administration, Engineering)
- Graduation date
- Coursework or academic program information

Fake degrees may lack these details, or they may contain vague and uninformative descriptions of coursework or program requirements.

7.5.3 Verifying Degrees and Diplomas

Now that you know the signs of a fake degree, it's time to explore how to verify degrees and confirm the legitimacy of academic credentials. Here are several methods to check the authenticity of a degree:

1 Contacting the Issuing Institution

One of the most effective ways to verify a degree is to contact the school directly. Legitimate universities and colleges keep records of graduates and can confirm whether an individual graduated from their program.

Steps to verify:

- Search the institution's official website to find their alumni or registrar office.
- Use official contact methods (email or phone) to request verification of the individual's degree.
- Provide all available information (name, graduation year, degree program, etc.) to facilitate the verification process.

2 Using Online Degree Verification Services

There are various online services available to verify academic credentials. Many institutions provide direct access to degree verification via their website or third-party services. Examples of services include:

- National Student Clearinghouse (for U.S.-based institutions)
- DegreeVerify
- My eQuals (for universities in Australia and New Zealand)

These services allow employers and investigators to verify an individual's academic records quickly and securely.

3 Cross-Checking Academic Records

If the degree is from a specific foreign institution, use resources like the World Higher Education Database (WHED) or UNESCO's International Network for Higher Education to confirm the legitimacy of the institution. Many foreign schools will be listed in these directories, and you can compare them to any degree claims.

7.5.4 Red Flags for Online Degrees and Fake Accreditation

With the rise of online education, it's important to distinguish between legitimate online programs and fraudulent diploma mills. Many legitimate universities now offer fully accredited online degrees, but diploma mills often exploit the flexibility of online education by offering subpar credentials.

Signs of a Fake Online Degree:

- **Non-accredited or poorly accredited institutions**: Always verify the institution's accreditation before accepting any online degree.
- **Lack of physical campus**: While some online programs are legitimate, some diploma mills don't have any physical facilities or campuses, which can be a sign of fraud.
- **No actual coursework or interaction**: Legitimate online degree programs will involve some form of real coursework or testing. Diploma mills often provide instant degrees without requiring academic work.

Conclusion

Fake degrees and diploma mills pose a significant threat to the integrity of educational credentials. By understanding the common signs of fraudulent degrees, utilizing accreditation verification, and checking with official registries and institutions, OSINT analysts and employers can safeguard against the dangers of hiring unqualified individuals or accepting fake qualifications. In a world where academic credentials are increasingly important, it's essential to remain vigilant and use proper verification techniques to ensure that the qualifications claimed by an individual are legitimate.

7.6 Case Study: Exposing a Fake Job Candidate

In the world of recruitment, employers and hiring managers are tasked with carefully vetting candidates to ensure they possess the skills, experience, and qualifications that match the position in question. Unfortunately, some candidates resort to falsifying their academic credentials or professional experience to secure employment. In this case study, we will walk through the process of identifying a fake job candidate who attempted to deceive a company with fabricated credentials, using open-source intelligence (OSINT) techniques to uncover the truth.

The candidate in this case was applying for a high-level management position at a well-established company. The application was impressive on paper, boasting an outstanding resume and a series of prestigious academic qualifications and past job experiences. However, the hiring manager had a suspicion that not everything was as it seemed. This is where OSINT tools and investigative techniques came into play, uncovering inconsistencies and exposing the candidate's deception.

7.6.1 The Candidate's Resume & Claims

The candidate's resume listed the following highlights:

- **Education**: Master of Business Administration (MBA) from a prestigious university, and a Bachelor's degree in Economics from another well-known institution.
- **Work Experience**: Director of Operations at a global tech firm, followed by a Senior Management role at a high-profile startup.
- **Professional Certifications**: PMP (Project Management Professional) and Six Sigma Black Belt.
- **Volunteer Work**: Board member for a charitable organization in the healthcare industry.

The resume looked very polished, but it raised a few red flags. A number of the organizations listed on the resume were incredibly high-profile, and the qualifications seemed almost too impressive. The hiring manager, though impressed, was experienced enough to know that a little due diligence could prevent a potential hiring disaster. This case study shows how the hiring manager leveraged OSINT to verify the candidate's claims and uncover the truth.

7.6.2 Step 1: Verifying Academic Qualifications

The first area that the hiring manager chose to investigate was the candidate's educational background. The candidate had claimed to have earned an MBA from a renowned business school, as well as a Bachelor's degree from a reputable university.

Education Verification:

The hiring manager started by verifying the existence of the institutions listed. One institution appeared to be legitimate, but the other raised suspicion. The "Bachelor's degree in Economics" from a university that claimed to have been founded in the 1950s seemed dubious—no significant information could be found regarding the university's accreditation or its standing in academic circles.

OSINT Techniques Used:

- **University Database Search**: The hiring manager used online databases such as the World Higher Education Database (WHED) and UNESCO to cross-check the university's accreditation status.
- **Google Search & University Website Analysis**: Further scrutiny revealed that the university did not have an official website, and the social media presence was sparse. A few forums mentioned the institution, but many referred to it in the context of being a degree mill offering online degrees with no academic rigor.
- **Alumni Profiles on LinkedIn**: The hiring manager searched LinkedIn for alumni from the claimed university. Interestingly, none of the profiles from the university seemed to hold degrees in Economics, despite the large number of individuals listed. This was a glaring discrepancy.

The conclusion was clear: the Bachelor's degree claim was fabricated, as the institution had no real academic presence or accreditation.

7.6.3 Step 2: Checking Work Experience and Job Roles

Next, the hiring manager turned their attention to the candidate's work history, which appeared to be well-established and reflected high-level managerial experience. The candidate had listed positions at reputable global companies and described significant accomplishments, such as overseeing multi-million-dollar projects and increasing company revenues.

Work History Verification:

While the job titles themselves sounded legitimate, the details of the companies listed were less clear. The first company, which was claimed to be a global tech firm, could not be found in any credible business directories. The second organization, a high-profile startup, appeared to have limited online presence.

OSINT Techniques Used:

- **Company Research**: The hiring manager cross-checked the companies listed on websites such as Crunchbase, LinkedIn, and business registries to see if the candidate's work experience could be corroborated.
- **Company Profiles**: Searching LinkedIn for the company name, the hiring manager found profiles of employees who had listed the company on their resumes. Interestingly, none of the current or past employees mentioned the candidate's name in their profiles, which was unusual for a director-level position.

- **News Articles and Press Releases**: A search of news outlets and press releases revealed no major references to the candidate's achievements at these organizations, despite their claimed seniority. Moreover, the company did not have significant news mentions for projects the candidate had purportedly led.

The investigation revealed that the work experience described was mostly fabricated. The two companies were real, but the candidate's involvement with them was nonexistent. This reinforced the suspicion that the resume was not truthful.

7.6.4 Step 3: Investigating Professional Certifications and Volunteer Work

The candidate also claimed to hold various professional certifications, including a Project Management Professional (PMP) certification and a Six Sigma Black Belt. Furthermore, the candidate stated they were actively involved with a non-profit organization focused on healthcare initiatives.

Certification Verification:

Professional certifications like PMP and Six Sigma are issued by respected organizations. These credentials can be easily verified through the respective professional bodies.

OSINT Techniques Used:

- **Certifying Body Verification**: The hiring manager contacted the certifying organizations for both certifications. After providing the candidate's name, it was confirmed that the candidate did not hold a PMP or Six Sigma Black Belt certification. The certifications had been fabricated.
- **Non-Profit Organization Search**: The charitable organization listed on the resume appeared to have a genuine presence online. However, after searching LinkedIn profiles and publicly available records, the hiring manager discovered that the candidate had never been a board member or held any position with the organization.

It became clear that the certifications and volunteer work were fabricated as well.

7.6.5 Conclusion: Exposing the Fake Candidate

After a thorough investigation using OSINT techniques, the hiring manager uncovered that the candidate had provided a series of false qualifications, including fabricated degrees, non-existent work experience, and fake professional certifications. The key to exposing the deception was cross-referencing the candidate's claims with reputable online databases, professional networks like LinkedIn, and public records.

In the end, the hiring manager was able to prevent a costly hiring mistake by using OSINT to verify the candidate's background. This case study illustrates the power of open-source intelligence in modern hiring practices and the importance of due diligence during the recruitment process.

7.6.6 Key Takeaways

- Cross-check academic credentials through official accreditation organizations and educational databases.
- Verify work experience by researching company profiles and connecting with current or former employees.
- Professional certifications can be validated through the issuing body or certification platforms.
- Social media and professional networks like LinkedIn are valuable tools for corroborating claims of employment and academic history.
- Use online databases and reputable sources to check for discrepancies in a candidate's history.

By utilizing these OSINT methods, employers can ensure that they are hiring qualified candidates and reduce the risk of fraudulent hires.

8. Facial Recognition & Biometric OSINT

Facial recognition technology has revolutionized online investigations, enabling analysts to identify individuals across multiple platforms with just an image. This chapter explores how to leverage open-source facial recognition tools, reverse image searches, and biometric databases to uncover hidden profiles and digital footprints. You'll learn techniques for analyzing facial features, detecting manipulated images, and correlating photos with social media, public records, and surveillance footage. Additionally, we'll discuss ethical concerns, privacy implications, and countermeasures to ensure responsible and legal use of biometric OSINT.

8.1 How Reverse Image Searching Helps in OSINT

In the digital age, images play a significant role in online interactions, serving as visual representations of individuals, events, products, and places. When conducting open-source intelligence (OSINT) investigations, images often offer a wealth of information—if you know how to analyze them effectively. One of the most powerful tools in image analysis is reverse image searching, a technique that allows investigators to trace the origin, history, and use of an image across the internet.

Reverse image searching involves uploading an image or entering its URL into a search engine or dedicated tool, which then provides links to web pages that feature the same or similar images. This method helps identify where an image first appeared, where it has been used, and how it relates to specific individuals or events. It can be instrumental in confirming a person's identity, verifying the authenticity of images, or uncovering additional leads in a case.

In this section, we will explore how reverse image searching can be applied in OSINT investigations, providing concrete examples of its utility in uncovering key information and solving complex cases.

8.1.1 The Basics of Reverse Image Searching

The core function of reverse image searching is to allow investigators to track the provenance of an image. When you conduct a reverse image search, the search engine scans the internet for matching or similar images and returns a list of results. The process works through algorithms that compare visual features—such as shapes, patterns, and textures—of the image you're querying with other images across the web.

Popular reverse image search tools include:

- **Google Reverse Image Search**: This tool allows you to upload an image or paste the image URL into Google's search bar. Google then returns results with similar or identical images found online.
- **TinEye**: TinEye is a specialized reverse image search engine that uses image recognition technology to match images across the internet. It is known for its precise image matching, even detecting slight alterations or crops.
- **Yandex**: A popular Russian search engine that also offers a reverse image search feature, capable of finding similar images and relevant content from websites across Russia and the global internet.

These tools can be accessed for free, with some offering advanced features for more thorough searching.

8.1.2 Applications of Reverse Image Searching in OSINT

Reverse image searching can be applied in various aspects of OSINT investigations. Here are several key areas where this technique can provide valuable insights:

1. Identifying People & Verifying Identities

One of the primary uses of reverse image searching in OSINT is to identify individuals by analyzing photographs and images associated with them. By running a reverse image search on a person's photo, investigators can cross-check their identity across different platforms and sources, verifying if the image is authentic or connected to other individuals.

Example: If a suspect or person of interest has a social media profile with a single profile picture, a reverse image search may reveal that the photo appears elsewhere on the internet, perhaps associated with a different name or identity. This can help uncover fraudulent or misrepresented identities. For instance, a common tactic for scammers is to use stolen photos from other people's social media profiles to create fake accounts or fake dating profiles.

2. Verifying the Authenticity of Images

In today's world, image manipulation is a common practice, whether for the purposes of art, advertisement, or disinformation. Reverse image searching can help OSINT analysts verify if an image is original or if it has been altered or taken from a different context.

Example: A viral image depicting a news event could be manipulated, taken out of context, or misattributed to a different location or event. Reverse image searching allows investigators to track the image's first occurrence and see how it has been used, helping them assess whether it's genuine or part of a disinformation campaign. If the image has been reused in various contexts, this could indicate that it is being falsely presented as evidence for a different narrative.

3. Investigating Image Origins & Context

In cases of criminal investigations or fraud, reverse image searches can track the origins of certain images that may be critical to the case. This technique helps identify where the image first appeared, allowing investigators to uncover the truth about how the image has been used over time.

Example: If an investigator is looking into a suspect's online activities, they may come across a specific image linked to the person in question. By running the image through a reverse search, they might discover that the image was first posted on a different website years ago, which could provide clues about the suspect's previous online behavior or activities.

4. Uncovering Image Sources & Associated Metadata

Reverse image searching can also uncover associated metadata, such as the website or page where the image was originally uploaded, or related social media profiles. This is helpful for understanding the context in which the image was shared and how it has evolved over time.

Example: An image of a suspect at a protest or crime scene may surface online. By performing a reverse image search, investigators can trace the image back to specific sources, such as news outlets, eyewitnesses, or social media posts, allowing them to understand the full context and possibly identify witnesses or other key details. This may also reveal timestamps or location markers attached to the photo, which could aid in identifying the exact time and place of the event.

8.1.3 Benefits of Reverse Image Searching in OSINT Investigations

1. Uncovering Hidden Information

A single image can often provide multiple insights when used in an OSINT investigation. Reverse image searching allows investigators to explore how an image has been used across different platforms, uncovering hidden or overlooked connections and patterns that might not be immediately obvious.

2. Verifying Online Content

Reverse image searching helps to determine if the image has been manipulated or used in a misleading manner. This is particularly useful when investigating online scams, fraud, or disinformation, where images are often altered to deceive or mislead people.

3. Tracking Historical Use

By identifying the first appearance of an image, reverse image searching can help trace the history of a photo or graphic. This is valuable when looking for evidence in criminal investigations, uncovering fraudulent claims, or verifying whether an image is current or outdated.

8.1.4 Challenges of Reverse Image Searching

While reverse image searching is an invaluable tool in the OSINT toolkit, it does come with certain limitations:

1. Limited Results for Low-Quality or Unique Images

Images that are particularly low-quality, highly unique, or heavily edited may not yield relevant results. The search algorithms used by image recognition tools are designed to match key features in the image, and unusual images may not be recognized as easily.

2. Privacy Concerns

Some reverse image search engines, particularly those that focus on social media, may raise privacy concerns for individuals. While these tools can help expose fraud or verify identities, they can also lead to unintentional privacy breaches by revealing personal or private images without consent.

3. False Positives

Reverse image searches may sometimes return results that are irrelevant or unrelated to the image being analyzed. This can occur when an image is used in many contexts or if it is a common image shared by multiple sources.

8.1.5 Conclusion

Reverse image searching is an essential tool in the arsenal of any OSINT investigator, enabling them to trace the origins of images, uncover hidden associations, verify claims, and identify fraudulent activities. By leveraging reverse image search engines like Google, TinEye, and Yandex, investigators can gain valuable insights into the authenticity and context of visual content, often uncovering leads that would otherwise remain hidden.

Whether you are verifying the identity of a suspect, assessing the credibility of an image in a news story, or tracking an individual's online footprint, reverse image searching provides powerful capabilities for identifying connections, verifying details, and protecting against disinformation. In the world of OSINT, where every piece of information counts, the ability to effectively track and analyze images is an indispensable skill.

8.2 AI & Facial Recognition Tools for Identifying People

In the realm of Open Source Intelligence (OSINT), the power of artificial intelligence (AI) and facial recognition technologies has revolutionized how investigators track and identify individuals online. While traditional OSINT methods, such as social media searches and data scraping, have proven invaluable, AI-driven tools now allow investigators to go a step further by automating the process of identifying and analyzing facial features from images and videos. These technologies can match faces across vast databases, helping analysts identify unknown individuals or confirm identities in a fraction of the time it would take using manual methods.

Facial recognition tools powered by AI have found widespread application in security, law enforcement, and intelligence work. However, these technologies also present challenges and ethical concerns, particularly regarding privacy rights and the potential for misuse. In this section, we will explore how AI and facial recognition tools are used in OSINT, the technology behind them, their practical applications, and the potential ethical considerations when using such tools in investigations.

8.2.1 How AI-Powered Facial Recognition Works

AI-driven facial recognition systems operate on the principle of analyzing specific features of a person's face to create a unique facial signature. These systems use machine learning and neural networks to identify and compare key facial features, such as:

- **Facial landmarks**: The distance between key points on the face, such as the eyes, nose, mouth, and chin.
- **Texture analysis**: The details in the skin, wrinkles, and contours that contribute to the uniqueness of an individual's face.
- **Biometric measurements**: The overall structure of the face, including its width, height, and shape.

Through training, AI algorithms learn to identify these patterns and can then match facial images to those in a given database or across the internet.

In simple terms, the process works as follows:

- **Capture Image**: A face is detected in an image or video.
- **Feature Extraction**: The system identifies unique facial features, creating a mathematical model of the face.
- **Comparison**: The model is compared to known faces in a database (such as social media platforms, public records, or image repositories) to identify potential matches.
- **Confidence Score**: The system assigns a confidence score to indicate how likely a match is, based on the similarity between the two faces.

Popular AI and facial recognition tools include:

- **Clearview AI:** A controversial tool used by law enforcement agencies that scrapes public images from social media platforms to build its facial recognition database.
- **Face++:** A tool offering facial recognition and analysis services, allowing users to identify individuals from images and compare faces.
- **Microsoft Azure Face API**: A cloud-based AI tool that provides facial detection and identification capabilities, used for various applications, including in security and identity management.
- **Amazon Rekognition**: A service that uses deep learning to identify and analyze faces in images and videos, offering functionality for both security and analysis of public data.

8.2.2 Applications of AI & Facial Recognition in OSINT

Facial recognition tools powered by AI have significant applications in OSINT investigations. Here are several scenarios where these tools can be extremely helpful:

1. Identifying Unknown Individuals in Images

One of the most direct applications of facial recognition technology is identifying individuals in images or videos. When investigating a person's background, OSINT investigators may encounter photographs or videos of individuals whose identity is unknown. AI-powered facial recognition tools allow them to upload these images and search for matches across publicly available databases, such as social media profiles, news websites, and other publicly accessible repositories.

Example: A news report may feature an image of a protestor, but the individual's name is not included. Using AI and facial recognition, an investigator can run the image through a facial recognition tool to identify the person, cross-referencing the match with social media profiles or other public records to confirm their identity.

2. Verifying Alleged Identities

In cases of fraud or deception, AI-based facial recognition can help verify the true identity of individuals who claim to be someone else online. Whether it's identifying a scammer using a fake photo on a dating app or uncovering the true identity of an individual posing as a public figure, facial recognition can help confirm if the person in question is who they say they are.

Example: An individual who claims to be a famous celebrity may have used publicly available images of the celebrity for their fake profile. Facial recognition tools can scan the web for similar images to match the profile photo with actual public images of the celebrity, thus exposing the deception.

3. Cross-Referencing Facial Data with Social Media

Many social media platforms are increasingly integrating facial recognition technology to automatically tag people in photos. This provides an excellent opportunity for OSINT investigators to cross-reference facial data and extract valuable intelligence from social media networks. By using facial recognition software, investigators can identify an individual's social media profiles, posts, friends, and interactions, potentially uncovering significant personal and professional information.

Example: If an OSINT investigator encounters an image of a suspect or person of interest in a publicly available social media photo, facial recognition software can be used to search for similar images. This may lead to discovering other social media accounts the individual has, revealing additional information such as their friends, affiliations, or even recent activities.

4. Monitoring & Tracking Individuals

Facial recognition tools can also be used for ongoing surveillance and monitoring. By analyzing video footage from public spaces (such as airports, train stations, or city streets), investigators can track a person's movements and interactions in real time or over a period. This application is widely used by law enforcement agencies, but it can also play a role in OSINT when investigating people of interest.

Example: A suspect captured on CCTV in a public place could be identified and tracked across multiple locations over time, allowing investigators to gather information on their activities and whereabouts. This is especially useful in cases where the individual's location or movements are important for understanding their behavior or potential involvement in criminal activities.

5. Investigating Historical Data & Events

Facial recognition is not only useful for current investigations but can also help analyze historical data. For example, a public figure's facial data could be matched against old photographs or media coverage of events, helping to track their involvement in specific incidents or uncover previously unknown connections.

Example: In a historical investigation, AI-powered facial recognition can match an individual's face in an old news archive photo with a modern image, helping investigators determine if they were involved in certain key events or circumstances, or if their identity has changed over time.

8.2.3 Ethical & Legal Considerations in Facial Recognition OSINT

While the capabilities of AI-powered facial recognition are impressive, they also raise a host of ethical, legal, and privacy concerns, especially when used in OSINT investigations. The following points highlight the key issues to consider when using these technologies:

1. Privacy Invasion

Facial recognition tools have the potential to infringe on individuals' privacy rights, as they can be used to track people without their consent or knowledge. In many jurisdictions, laws around the collection and use of biometric data are still evolving, and the use of facial recognition in public spaces can raise serious privacy concerns.

2. Consent & Data Protection

Facial recognition often relies on scraping images from social media platforms or publicly available databases, which may not always be done with the consent of the individuals involved. This can lead to potential violations of data protection laws such as the General Data Protection Regulation (GDPR) in the European Union.

3. Accuracy & Bias

AI facial recognition systems are not perfect and can sometimes produce false positives or misidentify individuals, especially when it comes to people of certain ethnic backgrounds. Bias in AI algorithms has been a significant concern, as studies have shown that facial recognition systems may have higher error rates for people of color, women, and younger individuals.

4. Misuse of Technology

The ease with which facial recognition tools can identify people raises the risk of misuse. Governments, private companies, or malicious actors may use these tools for surveillance or other unethical purposes, such as stalking, harassment, or profiling individuals based on appearance.

8.2.4 Conclusion

AI-powered facial recognition tools are transforming the way OSINT investigators identify and track individuals online. From identifying unknown people in images and videos to verifying the authenticity of online personas, these tools provide unprecedented capabilities for modern intelligence gathering. However, their use also raises significant ethical and legal concerns, particularly around privacy, consent, and the potential for misuse.

As AI and facial recognition technologies continue to advance, it will be important for OSINT practitioners to balance their powerful investigative potential with ethical responsibility, ensuring that these tools are used in a way that respects individuals' rights and complies with relevant laws. With proper oversight and awareness, facial recognition can be an invaluable tool in the OSINT arsenal, enhancing the ability to uncover the truth and solve complex cases.

8.3 Extracting Metadata from Photos for Additional Clues

In the digital age, photos have become an integral part of online communication, often shared across social media platforms, blogs, and websites. Beyond their visual appearance, these photos contain hidden data that can provide a wealth of information—referred to as metadata. For OSINT investigators, metadata is a goldmine of potential clues, offering details that can help track down an image's origin, its creator, and the context in which it was taken. Extracting and analyzing this metadata can uncover key information, making it an essential part of any investigation.

Metadata in photos typically includes technical details such as the camera model used, timestamps, geolocation coordinates, and more. This data, when examined thoroughly, can reveal patterns, expose discrepancies, or serve as crucial evidence in a case. In this section, we'll delve into the importance of photo metadata, how to extract it, and the role it plays in OSINT investigations.

8.3.1 What is Metadata in Photos?

Metadata in photos refers to the embedded information about the image itself, often stored in a format called EXIF (Exchangeable Image File Format). EXIF metadata is typically embedded by cameras, smartphones, or image editing software at the time the photo is taken or modified.

Some common types of metadata found in photos include:

- **File Information**: This includes the file name, file size, and file format (e.g., JPG, PNG, TIFF).
- **Camera Information**: The make and model of the camera or smartphone used to capture the image, including settings like the aperture, exposure time, ISO, and focal length.
- **Timestamp**: The date and time when the photo was taken, which can be essential for verifying an image's authenticity and tracking the timeline of events.
- **Geolocation**: GPS coordinates embedded in the photo, indicating the exact location where the photo was taken (if the camera or device had location services enabled).

- **Orientation**: The rotation or alignment of the image (i.e., whether the photo is oriented upright or sideways).
- **Software Information**: The software or app used to edit or process the photo, which may indicate if the image has been altered.

Some metadata can also be manually added to images, such as keywords or descriptions, which can be useful for organizing or categorizing images, but this type of data is less common in OSINT investigations.

8.3.2 How to Extract Metadata from Photos

Extracting metadata from photos is an essential part of an OSINT investigator's workflow. There are several methods and tools available to extract metadata, ranging from manual examination to automated tools that streamline the process.

1. Checking Metadata with Built-in Tools

Many operating systems and photo management applications have built-in functionality to view metadata. For example:

- **Windows**: On Windows, you can right-click an image file and select Properties, then navigate to the Details tab to see the metadata.
- **Mac OS**: On a Mac, you can right-click on an image and select Get Info, which provides basic metadata such as the date and time the image was created.

However, these methods typically provide only basic metadata, and may not show hidden geolocation or camera details.

2. Using Online Metadata Extraction Tools

For a more in-depth analysis, OSINT investigators often turn to online tools designed to extract EXIF metadata from images. These tools typically allow users to upload an image and automatically extract and display its metadata in a readable format. Some popular tools include:

- **ExifTool**: A powerful command-line application that can extract and display a comprehensive range of metadata from images. ExifTool is a preferred choice for experienced investigators due to its versatility and depth of data extraction.
- **MetaPicz**: An easy-to-use online tool that allows users to upload an image and view its metadata, including geolocation data (if available).

- **Get-Metadata.com**: A simple web-based tool for extracting and viewing metadata from images, with support for various file types.

These tools are helpful when dealing with larger batches of images, as they can quickly extract all available metadata in an organized format.

3. Mobile Apps for Metadata Extraction

Mobile apps also provide convenient ways to extract metadata directly from images on smartphones. Apps like Photo Investigator for iOS and Exif Pilot for Android are designed to quickly read and display EXIF data from images taken on mobile devices.

8.3.3 Applications of Metadata in OSINT Investigations

Once metadata has been extracted from an image, it can be analyzed for valuable clues that might help investigators uncover the identity of individuals, verify the authenticity of photos, or track the location of key events. Here are some practical ways metadata can assist in OSINT investigations:

1. Verifying Image Authenticity

Metadata can help confirm whether an image is genuine or has been manipulated. For example, if an image has been edited or altered, it may show signs of modification in the software section of the metadata. Alternatively, a timestamp or camera information that doesn't align with the event depicted in the photo could indicate that the image is fake or doctored.

Example: A photo posted online showing a political figure at a protest may be suspicious, but upon examining the metadata, the timestamp could show the image was taken weeks earlier, at an unrelated event. This discrepancy helps reveal that the photo is being misused for propaganda purposes.

2. Geolocation & Tracking Movement

If geolocation data is available, investigators can pinpoint the exact location where the photo was taken. This can be extremely helpful in cases involving crime scenes, missing persons, or tracking the whereabouts of a subject over time. The GPS coordinates from a photo can be cross-referenced with maps or other location data to identify specific locations or landmarks.

Example: A photo of a protestor holding up a banner can be traced to a specific location using embedded GPS coordinates, confirming the exact spot where the image was taken. If the protestor's face is visible, facial recognition tools could then be used to identify them, providing further leads in an investigation.

3. Identifying Time & Date of Events

The timestamp embedded in a photo can be crucial in establishing timelines, particularly in fast-moving investigations. Whether it's to confirm the timing of a newsworthy event, such as a crime or a political rally, or to verify the date a particular photo was taken, the date and time information is often one of the first pieces of metadata that investigators examine.

Example: In a missing persons case, investigators may receive an image from a witness or anonymous tipster that allegedly shows the missing person at a particular location. The timestamp in the photo's metadata may confirm whether the image was taken around the time the person disappeared, narrowing down the timeline of the investigation.

4. Investigating Online Fraud & Scams

Metadata can reveal clues about the origin of fraudulent images used in scams, such as fake product listings, phishing attempts, or fraudulent online identities. By checking the metadata of an image shared in a scam or fraudulent post, investigators can determine the source and potentially identify the individuals behind the deception.

Example: A scammer may post a fake job listing with a professional-looking photo. By analyzing the image's metadata, investigators could uncover the original source of the image, possibly linking it to a legitimate company or another individual, thereby revealing the scam.

5. Tracking Photo Edits & Alterations

In cases where photos have been edited or manipulated, metadata can reveal the software or app used for the edits, or even the date of the last modification. This information is vital for investigators who need to verify the authenticity of visual evidence.

Example: A photo showing a suspect in a crime scene may be heavily edited. Metadata analysis could reveal that the photo was edited using software like Photoshop, and the date of modification could be inconsistent with the events shown in the image. This suggests the image may have been tampered with.

8.3.4 Challenges in Metadata Extraction

While extracting metadata from photos is a powerful investigative tool, there are certain limitations and challenges:

- **Loss of Metadata**: Many social media platforms strip metadata from images when they are uploaded. This can make it difficult to extract valuable information from images shared on sites like Facebook or Instagram.
- **Editing & Manipulation**: Some individuals intentionally remove or alter metadata to obscure the origin or history of an image. While metadata can reveal much about a photo, it's important to remember that it can also be intentionally altered or deleted.
- **Privacy Concerns**: Using metadata extraction for investigative purposes can raise privacy concerns, particularly when GPS coordinates reveal sensitive location information. Investigators must be mindful of the ethical and legal implications of using metadata in their work.

8.3.5 Conclusion

Extracting metadata from photos is a crucial aspect of OSINT investigations, providing valuable information that can verify identities, authenticate images, track locations, and uncover hidden clues. Whether it's examining timestamps, camera details, or GPS coordinates, metadata analysis is an essential tool for investigators seeking to uncover the truth in a digital world.

By utilizing the right tools and techniques, investigators can leverage metadata to gain insights into the origins, authenticity, and context of photos, ensuring that every detail is thoroughly examined. However, it's important to be aware of potential challenges, such as the removal or alteration of metadata, and to handle this data with sensitivity to privacy concerns. In the end, metadata can be the key to unlocking vital information in OSINT investigations, providing a deeper understanding of the people, events, and locations at the heart of any inquiry.

8.4 Identifying Fake & AI-Generated Profile Pictures

In the world of digital investigations, the proliferation of fake identities and AI-generated images presents a growing challenge. Many individuals and organizations engage in the creation and use of fake profiles, often by employing sophisticated tools to generate synthetic photos that look authentic. These fake profile pictures are commonly used on social media platforms, dating sites, and fraudulent business pages. For OSINT investigators, identifying and analyzing these types of images has become a crucial skill in uncovering deceit and tracking down the true identity of individuals behind such profiles.

Artificial intelligence (AI) has advanced to a point where it can generate hyper-realistic images of people who do not exist, making it increasingly difficult to distinguish between a real person and a fabricated one. In this section, we will explore how investigators can identify fake and AI-generated profile pictures using a variety of techniques and tools. We will discuss the methods for detecting synthetic images, the implications for OSINT investigations, and provide insights into how these images can be traced back to their origins.

8.4.1 What Are Fake & AI-Generated Profile Pictures?

Fake profile pictures are images that have been deliberately created or modified to deceive others. These photos can either be taken from real people (i.e., images stolen from social media or other online sources) or they can be entirely fabricated using artificial intelligence.

AI-generated profile pictures, often referred to as deepfakes or synthetic images, are created through algorithms trained on vast datasets of real human faces. These technologies, like Generative Adversarial Networks (GANs), are capable of creating hyper-realistic images that look like real people, even though they don't exist. Some AI programs allow users to generate entirely new faces based on specific parameters, like age, gender, or ethnicity, while others can alter or manipulate existing images.

For OSINT investigators, identifying whether a profile picture is fake or AI-generated is essential, particularly when dealing with cases involving online fraud, scams, or impersonation.

8.4.2 Identifying Fake Profile Pictures: Key Indicators

Detecting fake profile pictures requires a careful eye for detail. Here are some of the most common indicators that may suggest a photo is not genuine:

1. Inconsistencies in Image Quality

Fake profile pictures, especially those generated by AI, often have subtle flaws in the image quality. These flaws might not be immediately obvious to the casual observer but can often be detected by closer inspection. Look for:

- **Unusual lighting or shadows**: AI-generated faces often have lighting that doesn't match the environment. Shadows might appear inconsistent or unnatural.
- **Unrealistic skin textures**: Synthetic faces may exhibit overly smooth or overly textured skin, often with a lack of visible pores or freckles, which is unnatural for real human faces.
- **Distorted facial features**: While AI-generated faces can be strikingly realistic, they may have odd quirks like mismatched eyes, irregularly shaped noses, or disproportionate mouths and ears.

2. Unusual or Synthetic Features

Many fake profile pictures exhibit telltale signs of being generated by AI or altered through digital means. Some of these features include:

- **Unnatural eyes**: In many AI-generated images, the eyes may appear too large, too symmetrical, or have odd reflections.
- **Blurred or inconsistent hairline**: The hair may not align properly with the scalp, or it may have a synthetic sheen that doesn't match the texture of real human hair.
- **Blurry backgrounds**: AI-generated photos often struggle with rendering coherent backgrounds, leading to distortion or blurry elements behind the person's face.

3. Untraceable Image Sources

One key sign of a fake profile picture is its lack of online presence. If you reverse-search the image using tools like Google Reverse Image Search, Tineye, or Yandex, and find that the image doesn't appear anywhere else on the web or doesn't show up in credible image repositories, it may be a synthetic or stolen image.

4. Symmetry & Perfection

AI-generated faces are often unnaturally symmetrical, and while this might seem like an ideal feature for an image, real human faces usually have small asymmetries. A perfectly symmetrical face might be a sign that an image was created or altered by artificial intelligence.

8.4.3 Tools and Techniques for Detecting Fake & AI-Generated Images

There are several advanced tools available for OSINT investigators to detect fake and AI-generated profile pictures. These tools rely on algorithms and machine learning to spot inconsistencies and anomalies in digital images.

1. Reverse Image Search

Reverse image search tools like Google Images, TinEye, and Yandex are essential for investigating whether a photo has been used elsewhere on the internet. If the image is associated with multiple fake profiles or websites known for scam activities, it could indicate that the profile picture is either stolen or part of a broader fraudulent campaign.

2. Deepfake Detection Tools

Deepfake detection technologies have been developed to specifically target AI-generated images. Some of the most effective tools include:

- **Deepware Scanner**: This tool scans images and videos for signs of AI-generated content and can help investigators determine if a face is synthetic.
- **Sensity AI**: Sensity AI provides tools for detecting deepfakes and manipulated images. It uses machine learning to analyze images and detect inconsistencies in facial features, lighting, and textures.
- **Microsoft Video Authenticator**: Though primarily used for video deepfakes, this tool also analyzes photos to check for signs of manipulation and synthetic creation.

These tools are designed to catch the subtle signs of AI manipulation that might be missed by the human eye, especially as AI-generated images become more realistic.

3. EXIF Data Analysis

While not always conclusive, analyzing the EXIF metadata of an image can offer valuable insights. For example, synthetic images might not have EXIF data that is consistent with a real photo—such as camera model, exposure settings, or geolocation information. Lack of EXIF data altogether or inconsistent metadata could be a red flag that the image was manipulated or generated artificially.

4. Image Forensics

Advanced image forensic tools, such as FotoForensics, analyze photos for signs of tampering, including inconsistencies in the image's pixel structure, which can often reveal the use of Photoshop or other editing software. These tools are designed to help investigators find traces of manipulation in an image that might not be visible to the naked eye.

8.4.4 Best Practices for Investigating Fake & AI-Generated Profiles

When encountering a suspicious profile picture during an OSINT investigation, there are several best practices to follow to determine its authenticity:

1. Cross-Reference Profiles

Check if the same profile picture is being used on multiple social media platforms or websites. Cross-check the image against multiple sources to see if the account shows any suspicious signs of being fabricated, such as having a new account with limited posts or a lack of meaningful connections.

2. Investigate Profile Activity

Examine the activity and behavior of the individual behind the profile. If the account is constantly interacting with other fake accounts or participating in scammy behavior (like spamming links), this can be an indication that the profile picture is fake. Use social media analysis tools to check if the account has been flagged for suspicious behavior.

3. Use AI Image Recognition

Utilize specialized AI image recognition software to help identify whether an image is likely to be AI-generated. These tools analyze thousands of data points in the image and compare them against known datasets of synthetic and real images, offering a likelihood score of authenticity.

4. Investigate the Profile's History

Look at the history of the account. Does the user have a full profile with past interactions, a network of friends or followers, or does it appear to be freshly created with minimal interaction? Fake profiles often have incomplete or highly irregular histories, making them easier to spot.

8.4.5 Conclusion

The rise of AI-generated images and fake profile pictures has added a new layer of complexity to OSINT investigations. Identifying fake or synthetic images requires a combination of digital forensics, reverse searching, and specialized tools that can detect subtle anomalies. As AI technology continues to improve, investigators must stay vigilant, utilizing the latest tools and methods to ensure that they can accurately identify fake profiles and uncover the truth behind digital facades.

Whether you are tracing a fraudulent online identity, exposing a scam, or verifying the authenticity of an image, the ability to spot fake or AI-generated profile pictures is an essential skill for OSINT practitioners. By combining image analysis techniques with cross-referencing and advanced detection tools, investigators can uncover hidden truths and bring deceptive individuals or organizations into the light.

8.5 Legal & Ethical Issues in Facial Recognition Investigations

Facial recognition technology has seen remarkable advancements in recent years, becoming an invaluable tool in OSINT (Open Source Intelligence) investigations. It allows investigators to identify individuals based on their unique facial features, either from photographs, videos, or other digital media. While facial recognition tools can significantly enhance the effectiveness of OSINT investigations—whether it's finding missing persons, identifying criminal suspects, or verifying identities—the use of this technology also raises significant legal and ethical concerns.

As facial recognition systems become more accessible and widely used, it is crucial for investigators to understand the legal and ethical frameworks that govern its application. The balance between leveraging cutting-edge technology for investigation and respecting individual privacy rights, civil liberties, and the law is a fine line. This section will explore the key legal and ethical challenges related to facial recognition in OSINT investigations, along with considerations for investigators who wish to navigate this space responsibly.

8.5.1 Legal Issues in Facial Recognition

1. Privacy Rights and Consent

One of the most significant legal concerns surrounding facial recognition technology is the right to privacy. Many countries have laws protecting individuals' personal privacy, and these protections can vary widely across jurisdictions. In many places, the use of facial recognition technology to track or identify individuals without their consent may be a violation of privacy laws.

For example:

- **GDPR** (General Data Protection Regulation) in the European Union places strict limitations on the collection and processing of personal data, including biometric data such as facial images. Collecting and storing facial data without explicit consent can lead to severe penalties for individuals or organizations.
- **CCTV footage and facial recognition**: In certain regions, public surveillance systems equipped with facial recognition can raise red flags. In some cases, the use of facial recognition technology to track individuals in public places could be considered an infringement on personal freedoms and privacy rights.

Facial recognition is a type of biometric data, which is considered sensitive personal information in many jurisdictions. Before utilizing facial recognition tools in an OSINT investigation, it is critical to assess whether obtaining and processing facial data is permissible under applicable privacy laws.

2. Data Protection and Storage

The legal implications extend beyond just the collection of facial images; investigators must also be aware of data protection laws concerning the storage, use, and sharing of such data. Storing facial images or other biometric information requires heightened security protocols to avoid data breaches and unauthorized access.

- **Data Minimization**: In many jurisdictions, data protection laws require that only the minimum necessary amount of data should be collected. If an investigator collects facial data during an OSINT investigation, it should be done with the specific intent of furthering the investigation, rather than indiscriminately amassing personal data.
- **Retention Period**: The law may also govern how long investigators are allowed to store biometric data. In some cases, data may need to be deleted or anonymized after a specific period or once the investigation is concluded.

Failure to comply with these data protection standards can result in legal repercussions, including fines, lawsuits, or other sanctions.

3. Use of Public vs. Private Data

The use of facial recognition technology in public spaces versus private platforms also presents legal challenges. While images taken in public spaces may have less privacy protection, investigators must still consider the context in which facial recognition is being used:

- **Public Surveillance**: In many places, public spaces such as streets, parks, and airports are considered to have a lower expectation of privacy. However, even when facial recognition is used in these spaces, it can still raise concerns about potential surveillance without consent.
- **Private Platforms**: On social media or private websites, facial recognition tools used without consent can violate both platform policies and legal regulations. Many social media platforms have strict guidelines regarding how facial data can be used. In some cases, platforms like Facebook and Instagram have been involved in legal disputes due to the unauthorized use of facial recognition systems.

Investigators should be cautious and ensure that facial recognition use complies with the terms and conditions of the platform or service hosting the data. Unauthorized use of facial recognition on private platforms could lead to legal action from the platform or individual users.

4. Potential for Misuse and Discrimination

Facial recognition systems are not perfect and can be prone to errors, such as false positives or false negatives. The legal implications of such errors can be significant, especially if facial recognition is used in the context of criminal investigations or security operations.

There is also the risk that the technology could be used for unlawful surveillance or targeting vulnerable individuals. For instance, facial recognition might be misused by governments or organizations to track activists, journalists, or marginalized groups, violating their civil liberties. Additionally, if a facial recognition system disproportionately misidentifies people of a certain race, gender, or age group, it could lead to discriminatory practices or unjust consequences.

In light of these concerns, some jurisdictions have implemented legal restrictions on the use of facial recognition by law enforcement or other public entities, citing potential abuse and harm. Investigators need to be mindful of these concerns and ensure they are using the technology responsibly and in a way that minimizes harm.

8.5.2 Ethical Issues in Facial Recognition Investigations

1. Respect for Human Dignity and Autonomy

Facial recognition can be intrusive, as it involves analyzing and identifying individuals based on their biometric data. In ethical terms, this may conflict with an individual's right to autonomy and dignity. Using facial recognition technology to investigate people without their consent—especially when they are unaware they are being surveilled—can be seen as an infringement on personal freedoms and autonomy.

Ethical guidelines for OSINT investigators emphasize the importance of respecting individuals' dignity by using facial recognition technology in a way that prioritizes their rights and personal boundaries. Investigators should consider whether their actions are truly justified or if they are encroaching on personal privacy unnecessarily.

2. Transparency and Accountability

One of the ethical dilemmas with facial recognition technology is its lack of transparency in terms of how and why it is being used. When investigators use facial recognition tools, it is essential to be transparent about the reasons for its application and the methods being employed. Failure to provide clear reasoning or accountability could lead to misunderstandings or misuse of the technology.

Moreover, investigators should be mindful of who has access to the results of facial recognition searches and how this data is shared. Sharing such data irresponsibly or without appropriate oversight can lead to exploitation or manipulation.

3. Consent and Informed Decision-Making

A critical ethical issue in facial recognition investigations is informed consent. Whenever possible, investigators should ensure that individuals are aware that their faces might be analyzed or used for identification purposes. Informed consent is a key principle in ethics, and respecting it helps ensure that the rights of individuals are upheld.

In some cases, obtaining explicit consent for facial recognition may not be practical, especially in the context of OSINT investigations. However, it is still important for investigators to balance the need for information with the ethical imperative to protect privacy and ensure fairness.

4. Potential for Harm

Facial recognition investigations, if conducted recklessly, can lead to harm. Investigators must be cautious not to perpetuate harmful stereotypes, stigmatize individuals, or damage reputations. Investigating someone's identity based on a facial image without proper context or verification can lead to misinformation, wrongful accusations, or even defamation.

Ethically, investigators must use facial recognition technology responsibly and avoid rushing to conclusions based on a match that may not be conclusive. Confirming the identity of an individual with additional verification steps is crucial to ensuring that no harm is done.

8.5.3 Conclusion

The use of facial recognition technology in OSINT investigations can provide valuable insights, but it is accompanied by significant legal and ethical challenges. Investigators must be aware of privacy laws, data protection regulations, and the ethical implications of using such powerful technology. Legal concerns such as the need for consent, the protection of personal data, and the potential for discrimination are central to responsible facial recognition use.

Ethically, investigators must respect individuals' autonomy, ensure transparency in their methods, and avoid causing harm through reckless or invasive use of facial recognition tools. As facial recognition technology continues to evolve, it is essential that investigators navigate these legal and ethical challenges thoughtfully, ensuring that their use of the technology aligns with both legal standards and moral principles. By doing so, they can ensure that their OSINT investigations are both effective and responsible.

8.6 Case Study: Finding a Missing Person Using Facial Recognition

Facial recognition technology has become an essential tool in the field of OSINT investigations, particularly in cases where individuals go missing, and every lead is critical. This case study will explore a hypothetical scenario in which facial recognition technology played a pivotal role in locating a missing person. The case demonstrates not only the potential of facial recognition but also the challenges, ethical concerns, and importance of responsible usage in such investigations.

The Case: Disappearance of Emma Thompson

Background

Emma Thompson, a 28-year-old woman, was reported missing after she failed to return home from work one evening. The police were initially called in to investigate, and they conducted a search of her known whereabouts, including her home, workplace, and social spaces. However, after several days of no leads and limited progress, the authorities turned to OSINT experts for assistance.

The missing person case was particularly troubling because Emma had no history of mental health issues, had never gone missing before, and there were no signs of foul play at her home. Her disappearance was sudden and left her family and friends in distress. With the case quickly turning cold, the family, desperate for answers, allowed law enforcement to leverage facial recognition technology to help locate her.

Step 1: Gathering Data for Facial Recognition

The first step was to gather images of Emma from publicly available sources that could be used for facial recognition analysis. OSINT investigators combed through her social media profiles (Facebook, Instagram, and LinkedIn), where they found numerous photos of Emma in various settings, from personal outings to professional events.

Some of the most relevant images came from her Instagram account, where she frequently posted pictures of herself at social gatherings, along with occasional selfies and photos with friends and family. Investigators also obtained images from her Facebook account and scanned her publicly available photos from friends' posts and tagged photos.

The investigators also requested access to Emma's images from her workplace, where a company security system had occasionally captured her in the office building. These images were of a lower quality but were still usable for facial recognition purposes. Investigators made sure to gather a broad selection of photos to account for different angles and lighting conditions, which would improve the accuracy of facial recognition analysis.

Step 2: Running Facial Recognition Across Various Platforms

Using a specialized OSINT tool that leveraged a facial recognition algorithm, the investigators uploaded the photos to search through publicly available video surveillance footage, social media platforms, and online databases. They also cross-referenced various databases, such as known public facial recognition services and other investigative platforms.

The first lead came from a CCTV camera at a local coffee shop, just a few miles from her home. The footage showed Emma entering the shop, where she purchased coffee just before she disappeared. The investigators extracted the timestamp from the footage and used facial recognition to compare the image of Emma's face with those in publicly available databases.

This first match provided a strong clue—Emma had been seen at the coffee shop, but where did she go after that? Investigators turned to social media and public video feeds to try and track her further. They uploaded the same facial recognition search to platforms like Facebook, Instagram, and Snapchat to search for images posted after that day.

Step 3: Analyzing Social Media Leads

The next breakthrough came from Instagram. A user, unaware of Emma's disappearance, had posted a photo at a nearby bar later that evening. The photo included Emma in the background, clearly identifiable in the shot, although she was not the focal point of the image. Using facial recognition, investigators were able to confirm that Emma was at the bar at the time, based on the timestamp and the matching facial features.

At this point, investigators began to narrow down the possible locations where Emma might have gone after leaving the bar. They identified other photos from social media posts showing Emma with two other individuals. These people were identified through further facial recognition matching, as well as cross-referencing their social media profiles, and they were soon flagged as persons of interest.

Step 4: Geolocating and Verifying the Trail

With several confirmed locations, the investigators turned to geolocation tracking and analyzed data from both the facial recognition software and Emma's social media. Many of her social media posts were tagged with geolocation information, revealing places she had visited prior to her disappearance. The combination of location data and facial recognition results allowed investigators to follow her movements from the coffee shop to the bar and then to a restaurant nearby, where she had been seen with the two people.

Using public satellite imagery and tools like Google Maps and Street View, they were able to identify areas around the restaurant where Emma could have gone afterward, including nearby public transportation hubs and less populated areas. Based on this trail of evidence, investigators were able to hypothesize a potential location where Emma might be located.

Step 5: Reaching the Final Location

With the accumulated data—facial recognition matches, geolocation from social media, and the identification of individuals seen with Emma—the investigators were able to work with local law enforcement to narrow down potential safehouses or addresses associated with the suspects. Using further OSINT techniques, such as public property records and business registration searches, they tracked down the addresses linked to the suspects.

At one of the properties linked to the individuals seen with Emma, law enforcement found her, safe but disoriented. It turned out that she had been coerced by one of the suspects, who had posed as a friendly acquaintance, and was kept at the location against her will. Thankfully, facial recognition and OSINT tools allowed authorities to trace her whereabouts, leading to her rescue.

Challenges and Ethical Considerations in the Case

While the outcome of this investigation was ultimately successful, several challenges and ethical considerations arose during the process:

Accuracy of Facial Recognition: One of the first concerns was the accuracy of the facial recognition software used. The investigators had to ensure that the technology did not falsely identify individuals or link innocent people to the investigation. The system's accuracy was paramount, particularly when dealing with sensitive personal information.

Privacy Concerns: Although the investigators worked with law enforcement, the use of facial recognition without explicit consent still raised privacy concerns. Social media accounts were analyzed to obtain images, and several of these were from friends and acquaintances who may not have been aware their photos could be used for such purposes. Ethical practices in facial recognition investigations require ensuring that the data is collected responsibly and does not infringe on others' rights.

Data Protection: The investigators had to be cautious when storing and processing the facial recognition data, ensuring it was done in compliance with data protection regulations such as GDPR in Europe or similar laws elsewhere. Any mishandling or leakage of personal information could have jeopardized the investigation and led to legal consequences.

Consent from Family: Emma's family consented to the use of facial recognition in the investigation, but in many cases, obtaining consent from family members can be a sensitive issue. Investigators must ensure that they have clear consent for any methods that may involve sensitive personal information or data collection.

Conclusion

This case study highlights the tremendous potential of facial recognition technology in solving missing person cases. By leveraging OSINT tools and combining facial recognition with other investigative techniques such as social media analysis, geolocation tracking, and public databases, investigators can significantly improve the chances of locating individuals who may otherwise remain untraceable. However, the ethical and legal challenges presented by such technologies must not be ignored, as they require careful management to ensure that individuals' privacy and rights are respected.

Ultimately, while facial recognition played a crucial role in finding Emma Thompson, investigators must always balance the power of this technology with the need for responsible usage and respect for privacy. As this field continues to evolve, ethical guidelines and legal frameworks must evolve alongside it to ensure that OSINT remains a force for good.

9. Dark Web & Identity Theft Investigations

The dark web is a hidden corner of the internet where stolen identities, leaked data, and illicit activities thrive. This chapter delves into OSINT techniques for uncovering compromised personal information, monitoring darknet marketplaces, and investigating identity theft cases. You'll learn how to safely navigate the dark web using Tor, track down breached credentials, and analyze identity fraud patterns. Additionally, we'll discuss legal considerations, ethical boundaries, and proactive measures to protect against identity theft in an increasingly vulnerable digital landscape.

9.1 Understanding the Dark Web & Its Role in Identity Theft

The dark web is a part of the internet that is not indexed by traditional search engines, making it harder to access and often used for anonymous activity. While the deep web encompasses all parts of the internet not indexed by conventional search engines (such as private databases and password-protected sites), the dark web represents a more secretive and, at times, illicit segment that requires specialized tools, like Tor (The Onion Router), to access. It is home to a variety of activities, both legal and illegal, with a particularly concerning role in identity theft.

In the context of identity theft, the dark web is a marketplace where stolen personal data, including Social Security numbers, credit card details, and other sensitive information, is traded. It provides an avenue for criminals to buy, sell, and exchange information that can be used for fraudulent purposes, such as financial theft, identity impersonation, or creating fake documents.

This chapter will explore the dark web's structure, its role in identity theft, and how investigators can navigate it to uncover illicit activities related to stolen identities. It will also discuss the tools and techniques employed in tracking down stolen personal information and combating the growing threat of identity theft facilitated by dark web interactions.

The Structure of the Dark Web

The dark web is often misunderstood as a place solely for illegal activity, but it encompasses a broad range of uses. While criminal activities such as drug trafficking, illegal arms sales, and human trafficking are prevalent on the dark web, many individuals use it for legitimate purposes, such as whistleblowing, evading censorship, and privacy protection. However, its anonymity and lack of regulation make it a haven for cybercriminals who engage in illicit activities, including identity theft.

The dark web is part of the deep web, which itself is not indexed by traditional search engines like Google. Accessing the dark web requires special software, such as Tor or I2P, that allows users to browse websites with anonymity. Websites on the dark web have .onion or .i2p domains, which are not accessible using regular browsers. These platforms provide an environment where individuals can hide their identities and avoid government surveillance or detection.

While the dark web is technically a subset of the deep web, it is distinct due to the higher level of encryption and anonymity it offers to its users. This makes it both a valuable resource for legitimate users looking for privacy and an attractive marketplace for criminals involved in various illegal activities.

Role of the Dark Web in Identity Theft

One of the most significant threats associated with the dark web is the sale and purchase of stolen personal data. Cybercriminals have discovered that there is a significant demand for stolen identities, and the dark web serves as a perfect venue for these transactions.

1. Stolen Personal Information for Sale

The dark web is home to a variety of illegal marketplaces where criminals can buy and sell stolen personal data. These stolen identities often include:

- Social Security Numbers (SSNs)
- Credit card details (including both physical and virtual card numbers)
- Bank account numbers and login credentials
- Driver's license numbers
- Passports and other government-issued IDs
- Medical records and other sensitive health-related information

These stolen records can be sold to other criminals or used to carry out fraudulent activities, such as applying for loans or credit cards in someone else's name, draining bank accounts, or even creating fake identities for illegal purposes. The sale of such information is common on dark web marketplaces, where price tags for these data sets can vary based on the type and completeness of the information.

For example:

- **Credit card information**: A full set of credit card details (including the card number, expiration date, and CVV) can be sold for as little as $10-$20, depending on the card's type and location.
- **Full identity sets (including name, address, SSN, birthdate, and more):** These can be sold for hundreds of dollars, especially if they are accompanied by additional information such as banking credentials or access to government accounts.

In some cases, cybercriminals can also sell entire databases of stolen identities to buyers who wish to conduct large-scale fraudulent schemes.

2. Identity Theft Methods on the Dark Web

Identity theft on the dark web can take many forms, and criminals often combine different methods to exploit stolen data. Some of the most common ways stolen identities are used on the dark web include:

- **Credit card fraud**: Criminals may use stolen credit card details to make unauthorized purchases online or withdraw cash at ATMs. They often use cloning technology to create counterfeit credit cards or engage in online transactions that bypass detection.
- **Account takeover**: Criminals can use stolen personal information, such as email addresses, social media profiles, or login credentials, to take over victims' accounts and gain unauthorized access to their online bank accounts, e-commerce profiles, and social media accounts.
- **Phishing and spear-phishing**: Cybercriminals may use stolen data to craft convincing phishing emails, targeting victims or their associates to steal even more information, such as login credentials, and trick them into transferring money or revealing sensitive information.
- **Synthetic identities**: In some cases, stolen personal data is combined with fake information to create new, synthetic identities that are used to apply for loans, credit cards, or government benefits. These synthetic identities are difficult to trace because they do not correspond to any one person in official records.

The ability to sell or use stolen personal data anonymously on the dark web makes it an attractive option for criminals looking to commit identity theft on a large scale. This ease of access to personal information has made the dark web a central hub for cybercrime.

Investigating Identity Theft on the Dark Web

For investigators and cybersecurity professionals, tracking down stolen identities and preventing identity theft on the dark web presents a number of challenges. However, it's not impossible, and several investigative techniques can help uncover illicit activity involving stolen identities.

1. Monitoring Dark Web Marketplaces

Investigators can monitor dark web marketplaces where personal data is sold and exchanged. Several specialized tools and platforms are available to assist in searching the dark web, such as dark web scanners or OSINT tools designed to track stolen data. These tools can help locate stolen personal information, including credit card numbers, usernames, passwords, and Social Security numbers.

By regularly scanning dark web forums and marketplaces, investigators can identify when certain types of sensitive data appear for sale and work with law enforcement to intercept and trace the origin of the information.

2. Using Threat Intelligence Tools

Many cybersecurity firms provide dark web monitoring services that collect and analyze dark web data to identify when stolen personal information is being sold or traded. These tools use automated crawlers to search for specific identifiers, such as email addresses or account numbers, across dark web sites.

These intelligence feeds can help businesses, banks, and individuals stay aware of potential identity theft threats by flagging compromised data. For example, if a company's employee credentials are discovered for sale on the dark web, the organization can immediately take steps to mitigate the impact, such as resetting passwords and notifying affected individuals.

3. Law Enforcement Cooperation

Due to the international and encrypted nature of the dark web, investigating identity theft often requires collaboration between multiple law enforcement agencies across various jurisdictions. International law enforcement organizations like Europol and Interpol work with local authorities to track down criminals who operate on the dark web, sometimes engaging in large-scale takedowns of illicit markets.

Investigators may use traceable data (such as IP addresses, transaction logs, or blockchain transactions) to identify criminals behind dark web identity theft activities. Through these collaborations, authorities have successfully dismantled dark web marketplaces, arrested perpetrators, and disrupted fraud schemes.

Conclusion

The dark web is a double-edged sword: it can offer privacy for those who seek to avoid censorship or harm, but it also serves as a haven for criminals engaged in identity theft. Understanding how the dark web operates and the role it plays in the trade of stolen personal data is critical for combating this growing threat. Investigators must stay informed of the latest trends in cybercrime and use cutting-edge tools to track stolen identities and prevent further exploitation of personal data.

As dark web marketplaces continue to evolve, so too must investigative strategies, requiring a combination of advanced OSINT techniques, cybersecurity measures, and cooperation between law enforcement to combat identity theft in the digital age. By navigating the dark web cautiously and responsibly, both investigators and consumers can help mitigate the risks posed by this shadowy corner of the internet.

9.2 Searching for Stolen Credentials & Personal Data Leaks

One of the most significant and ever-growing threats in the digital age is the leakage of personal data, particularly credentials such as usernames, passwords, Social Security numbers (SSNs), and banking details. With the rise in cybercrime and hacking activities, personal data can often be found in massive breaches, making it vulnerable to exploitation. The dark web is a key platform where stolen credentials and personal data leaks are traded, bought, and sold, contributing significantly to the rising instances of identity theft and fraudulent activity.

For investigators, security professionals, and individuals concerned with protecting their identities, the task of searching for and identifying stolen credentials or personal data leaks is essential to prevent further exploitation of sensitive information. This chapter focuses on methods for searching for such breaches, tools and techniques for tracking leaked data, and how to respond when you discover that your or someone else's credentials have been exposed.

Understanding the Impact of Data Breaches

Data breaches occur when sensitive personal or corporate data is accessed, stolen, or exposed without authorization. In recent years, breaches have affected millions of people, leaving sensitive information exposed and at risk of being misused. Personal data leaks can occur in a variety of forms, including:

- **Account credentials**: Usernames, email addresses, and passwords.
- **Financial information**: Credit card numbers, bank account details, and payment information.
- **Personal identifiers**: Social Security numbers, national ID numbers, driver's license numbers, etc.
- **Medical records**: Health-related data and insurance information.
- **Employment information**: Employment history, job titles, and compensation data.

While data breaches can happen to large corporations or government agencies, they can also occur on smaller platforms, such as local businesses or community websites. Cybercriminals target these leaks for a wide variety of purposes, including identity theft, financial fraud, and social engineering attacks.

The dark web plays a central role in the trade and sale of this stolen information, as its anonymity makes it difficult for law enforcement to track and prevent the illicit activity. Once credentials and personal data are compromised, they are often sold on underground marketplaces where criminals can purchase and use them for a wide range of malicious purposes.

1. Understanding Where to Look for Stolen Credentials

In the context of OSINT (Open Source Intelligence) and cybersecurity investigations, searching for stolen credentials involves scouring various sources for evidence of data leaks. Below are some common areas where personal information may be leaked and traded.

a. Dark Web Marketplaces

Dark web marketplaces are among the most prominent places for trading stolen personal data. Websites operating on the Tor network (with .onion domains) host a variety of illegal marketplaces where cybercriminals trade stolen credentials, credit card data, and other sensitive information. Examples of these marketplaces include sites like AlphaBay, Silk Road, and Dream Market, although many of them have been taken down by law enforcement.

Here's how you can search for stolen credentials on the dark web:

- **Marketplace Scanning**: Investigators often scan known dark web marketplaces for data leaks using specialized tools or monitoring services. Some tools allow investigators to set up alerts for specific keywords (such as "stolen credit card" or "SSN") to track when new data is being traded.
- **Keyword Searches**: By searching for specific keywords or identifiers such as email addresses, usernames, or even company names, investigators can determine if any credentials or personal data associated with these terms have been compromised.
- **Purchase History and Listings**: Criminals often list stolen data in bulk or in "packs," and these listings can be searched for information like database dumps, which may contain millions of exposed accounts.

b. Public Data Breach Repositories

Some repositories have been set up specifically to track large-scale data breaches, making it easier to determine if personal credentials have been exposed in these incidents. For example, platforms like Have I Been Pwned provide users with an easy way to check whether their email or other accounts have been part of publicly known data breaches.

- **Have I Been Pwned (HIBP):** This is one of the most well-known databases for checking whether personal information has been exposed in data breaches. Users can input an email address or username to see if it has been part of a public breach.
- **BreachAlarm**: Similar to HIBP, BreachAlarm allows users to check whether their email addresses are in breach databases and offers additional monitoring tools.
- **Firefox Monitor**: Mozilla's Firefox browser offers a tool that allows users to check their email addresses against data breach records, alerting users if their credentials have been exposed.

These platforms allow individuals to check if their credentials (such as email addresses and passwords) have been exposed and then take the necessary steps to protect their accounts, such as changing passwords or enabling two-factor authentication.

c. Paste Sites and Forums

In addition to marketplaces, the dark web hosts numerous forums and paste sites where hackers or data brokers share stolen data. These paste sites often provide a place for large volumes of dumped data to be posted publicly or semi-publicly, including login credentials, usernames, and passwords. Some of the most popular paste sites for criminals include:

- **Pastebin**: Although Pastebin is legitimate for code-sharing, it is frequently used by cybercriminals to share large dumps of stolen personal data.
- **GitHub**: Similarly, GitHub, primarily used for version control and coding, has been exploited by hackers to share stolen credentials and data leaks in public repositories.
- **Other Paste Sites**: There are a range of less known pastebin-like sites where hackers and cybercriminals post stolen data dumps. These sites can often be monitored by investigators to track sensitive data leaks.

d. Leaked Databases and Data Sets

Hackers often distribute entire leaked databases that contain vast amounts of stolen personal information. These databases may be sold as a whole or shared publicly. Once exposed, they provide access to an entire range of sensitive information, including personal identification numbers, passwords, and email addresses.

Investigators may monitor various sources, including Hacking Team data leaks, Cloudflare leaks, or collection dumps, where massive data files are uploaded for public access.

2. Using OSINT Tools to Search for Stolen Data

Open Source Intelligence (OSINT) tools play a crucial role in investigating stolen credentials. There are several specialized tools that help track and identify data leaks, monitor for stolen credentials, and provide insights into cybercriminal activity. These tools can be extremely helpful for security professionals, businesses, and investigators seeking to mitigate the risks associated with stolen data.

Some popular OSINT tools for monitoring and searching for stolen credentials include:

- **DarkSearch.io:** A search engine designed for the dark web, allowing users to search for leaks and stolen personal data across various dark web marketplaces and forums.

- **Tor Browser**: While Tor is the tool for accessing the dark web, it can also be used in combination with other tools to trace data leaks, access criminal activity reports, and search for specific stolen credentials.
- **Censys**: A search engine that allows security researchers to discover exposed personal data and leaked credentials. It also provides detailed information about security breaches and other vulnerabilities.
- **Shodan**: A tool that searches for devices connected to the internet, including exposed databases or accounts that may be part of a data leak.

By using these tools, investigators can monitor data leaks in real time, trace the origins of stolen credentials, and assess the scale of the exposure.

3. Responding to Stolen Data and Credentials Leaks

When stolen data or credentials are identified, it is crucial to take swift and appropriate action. Here are some of the steps that should be followed when responding to a data leak:

a. Change Passwords and Use Multi-Factor Authentication (MFA)

The first and most important step is to change the affected passwords. If the credentials were part of a breach, immediately updating passwords across all platforms is essential. Additionally, enabling multi-factor authentication (MFA) on accounts adds an extra layer of security, making it harder for cybercriminals to gain unauthorized access.

b. Notify Affected Parties

If the breach involves third-party systems (such as in the case of a corporate data leak), it's important to notify the affected individuals or businesses. For example, if personal credentials such as Social Security numbers are leaked, those individuals should be alerted so they can take steps like freezing their credit.

c. Monitor Accounts and Financial Activity

After a data breach, monitoring accounts for suspicious activity is essential. This includes checking bank accounts, credit reports, and online activity for signs of identity theft or fraud.

Conclusion

The dark web and other online platforms play a critical role in the trade of stolen credentials and personal data leaks, making it a crucial area of focus for cybersecurity professionals, investigators, and individuals concerned with protecting their personal information. By leveraging OSINT tools, dark web monitoring, and breach repositories, investigators can track down exposed data and work to prevent further exploitation. Additionally, prompt response and protection strategies are essential for mitigating the damage caused by such leaks. In the ever-evolving landscape of data breaches and identity theft, staying vigilant and informed is key to minimizing risks and securing sensitive data.

9.3 Investigating Cybercriminal Forums & Marketplace Transactions

The rise of the internet has transformed the landscape of cybercrime, enabling a thriving underground economy. Central to this digital black market are cybercriminal forums and dark web marketplaces, where illicit activities—including the sale of stolen credentials, hacked data, malware, and other illegal goods and services—take place. These platforms provide anonymity and a degree of safety for cybercriminals looking to buy and sell digital assets or recruit others for malicious activities.

For investigators, law enforcement agencies, and cybersecurity professionals, identifying and monitoring these forums and marketplace transactions is critical to preventing, mitigating, and responding to cybercrime. By understanding how these forums and marketplaces operate, how transactions occur, and how they can be traced, investigators can gather valuable insights to uncover criminal activities, track cybercriminal networks, and identify key actors involved in illegal transactions.

This chapter delves into how cybercriminal forums and marketplace transactions can be investigated using open-source intelligence (OSINT) methods, the challenges faced when navigating these environments, and the tools and techniques used to track down illicit activities.

Understanding Cybercriminal Forums & Marketplaces

Cybercriminal forums and marketplaces are distinct but interconnected spaces on the dark web where cybercriminals interact, exchange information, and carry out illicit activities. These forums and marketplaces facilitate the exchange of everything from stolen personal data and credit card details to malware, hacking tools, and ransomware. Some of the most prominent cybercriminal forums and dark web marketplaces include:

1. Cybercriminal Forums

Cybercriminal forums are places where hackers, fraudsters, and other criminals gather to share knowledge, techniques, and tools. These forums often feature a range of discussions, from technical topics like exploiting vulnerabilities and bypassing security measures to the buying and selling of stolen data. Some forums offer private sections where members can freely trade illegal items, while others operate more openly but with coded language to avoid detection.

Examples of well-known cybercriminal forums (often previously active) include:

- **Hack Forums**: A popular forum where hackers share coding knowledge, tutorials on hacking techniques, and discuss illicit activities, including the sale of compromised accounts and tools.
- **XSS**: A cybercriminal forum focused on web application security vulnerabilities and the tools used to exploit them.
- **The Hub**: A forum catering to various cybercriminal activities, including fraud, identity theft, and hacking techniques.

Cybercriminals use these forums to exchange information and recruit others into their illegal activities. Investigators often monitor these forums for signs of new data breaches, the sale of personal information, and recruitment of hackers for cyberattacks.

2. Dark Web Marketplaces

Dark web marketplaces are digital marketplaces where criminals can buy and sell a variety of illicit goods and services. These marketplaces, often operating on the Tor network using .onion domains, are built around anonymity and untraceable transactions. They provide a secure environment for criminals to trade stolen data, hacking tools, and services like ransomware-as-a-service, DDoS attacks, and fake IDs.

Some of the best-known dark web marketplaces (both current and previously active) include:

- **AlphaBay**: Once one of the largest dark web marketplaces, it facilitated the sale of stolen data, drugs, weapons, and counterfeit currencies before being shut down by law enforcement.

- **Dream Market**: Another major marketplace that offered the exchange of illicit goods, including stolen credit cards, bank account details, and ransomware.
- **Empire Market**: A highly active dark web marketplace that hosted a wide variety of illicit items, including malware, stolen credentials, and other digital goods.

The dark web marketplace ecosystem operates on cryptocurrency payments, which further hides the identities of buyers and sellers. Transactions are typically protected by escrow services to ensure fair trade, but there is always the risk of fraud or scams.

How Cybercriminal Forums & Marketplaces Operate

Understanding how cybercriminal forums and marketplaces function is key to conducting a successful investigation. These platforms are characterized by their anonymity and structure, which facilitate the ease of illegal transactions and protect users from law enforcement scrutiny. Below are the key operational aspects of these environments:

1. Anonymity via Tor and Cryptocurrency

Both cybercriminal forums and dark web marketplaces depend heavily on anonymity to shield users from law enforcement. The Tor network provides encrypted browsing through its .onion domain system, allowing users to access these forums and marketplaces without revealing their IP addresses or physical locations.

Additionally, payments on these platforms are made using cryptocurrency, such as Bitcoin, Monero, or Ethereum, which provide a layer of pseudonymity. Cryptocurrencies, by nature, are decentralized, making it challenging to trace the identities behind transactions. However, blockchain analysis tools can be used to identify patterns and trace crypto transactions.

2. Reputation & Trust Mechanisms

Forums and marketplaces often use reputation systems to build trust between buyers and sellers. On cybercriminal forums, members build credibility through their participation in discussions and successful trades, while in marketplaces, sellers are often rated by their customers. This reputation system provides a level of assurance for transactions, but it can also be manipulated, as some sellers may fake positive feedback.

Investigators looking to track down cybercriminals need to monitor these reputation systems closely, identifying trusted actors and following their activities across forums and marketplaces. Escrow services used in marketplaces act as intermediaries between buyers and sellers, protecting funds until the transaction is completed, which reduces fraud but also introduces another layer of complexity for investigators.

3. Classified Ads & Data Listings

On cybercriminal forums, users may post classified ads offering services or stolen goods for sale. Common items listed include stolen credit card information, login credentials, malware tools, data dumps, and phishing kits. Some criminals also offer hacking services, such as launching DDoS attacks or engaging in social engineering.

Marketplaces provide a more formalized structure for listing stolen data and illegal services. Vendors often list their products in categories such as credit card details, databases of personal information, or software vulnerabilities. Investigators searching these marketplaces can identify bulk data dumps, which may contain millions of stolen records from breaches.

Techniques for Investigating Cybercriminal Forums & Marketplace Transactions

To effectively investigate cybercriminal forums and marketplaces, law enforcement agencies and cybersecurity professionals employ various open-source intelligence (OSINT) techniques, tools, and methods. Below are some of the primary investigative techniques used:

1. Monitoring Forums for Keywords & Patterns

OSINT tools can be used to monitor cybercriminal forums for specific keywords or patterns of activity. By searching for terms like "stolen data," "credit card dump," "database leak," or "ransomware," investigators can identify new threats and emerging trends within these communities. Setting up automated alerts for certain keywords can help track activity in real-time.

- **Alert Systems**: Services like DarkSearch and Cyberscan provide real-time alerts when specific keywords are mentioned in dark web forums or marketplaces.
- **Social Media Monitoring**: Some cybercriminals cross-post activity from forums to social media platforms like Telegram or Twitter, making them an additional avenue for tracking down illicit activity.

2. Tracing Cryptocurrency Transactions

Despite the pseudonymity provided by cryptocurrencies, some investigators can trace the flow of funds using blockchain analysis tools. By monitoring transactions through tools like Chainalysis, Elliptic, or CipherTrace, investigators can track illicit crypto transactions, identify high-value wallets, and uncover links to cybercriminal activities.

3. Investigating Seller Profiles & Reputation

On dark web marketplaces, seller profiles and transaction histories provide valuable information about the cybercriminal ecosystem. Investigators can trace the activities of high-profile vendors who specialize in selling stolen data or malware. By analyzing transaction histories, communication patterns, and rating systems, investigators can track the activity of certain sellers across multiple platforms.

4. Data Dump Analysis

Data dumps, often shared in forums or marketplaces, contain large amounts of stolen information that can be analyzed for identifying details. Investigators can examine these dumps to identify compromised personal information or trace the source of the data breach. Specialized tools can be used to automate the extraction and analysis of data dumps.

5. Network Analysis

By following the digital footprints left behind by cybercriminals, investigators can perform network analysis to uncover links between various forums, marketplaces, and specific criminal groups. This helps build a larger picture of how cybercriminals interact across different platforms and how their networks function.

Challenges in Investigating Cybercriminal Forums & Marketplaces

Investigating cybercriminal forums and dark web marketplaces is fraught with challenges, including:

- **Anonymity**: The use of Tor and cryptocurrencies creates significant barriers to identifying cybercriminals and tracing their activities.
- **Encryption & Obfuscation**: Many forums and marketplaces use encryption or coded language to avoid detection, making it harder to understand their activities.
- **Jurisdictional Issues**: The international nature of the dark web means that investigators often face jurisdictional issues, as criminal activities may span multiple countries and legal systems.

Conclusion

Investigating cybercriminal forums and marketplace transactions is crucial for identifying emerging threats, tracking down criminal actors, and preventing cybercrime. By employing a combination of OSINT techniques, blockchain analysis, and dark web monitoring tools, investigators can gain insight into the activities of cybercriminals, trace stolen data, and mitigate the impact of criminal activity. While challenges abound, the ability to effectively track and investigate these platforms is critical in the ongoing fight against cybercrime and identity theft.

9.4 Tracking Stolen IDs, Passports & Credit Card Fraud

The digital age has dramatically changed the landscape of identity theft and financial fraud, with criminals using stolen personal information to commit a wide range of illicit activities. Among the most common and valuable types of stolen information are identification documents, such as passports, driver's licenses, and Social Security numbers, as well as credit card details. These stolen assets are often sold on the dark web, used for committing fraud, or exploited for a variety of other malicious purposes, from committing financial crimes to impersonating individuals in various forms.

Tracking these stolen assets through open-source intelligence (OSINT) techniques is a critical task for investigators, financial institutions, and law enforcement agencies. Detecting and tracing stolen IDs, passports, and credit card information can help prevent financial losses, disrupt criminal activity, and ultimately lead to the identification of criminals involved in identity theft.

In this section, we'll explore the methods used to track stolen IDs, passports, and credit card fraud, including the use of dark web monitoring, OSINT tools, and investigative techniques for identifying patterns and tracing stolen data to its sources.

The Scope of Stolen IDs, Passports, and Credit Card Fraud

Identity theft is one of the fastest-growing crimes in the digital age. Criminals steal individuals' personal data to gain access to their financial resources, engage in fraudulent activities, or even commit crimes in the victim's name. Stolen passports and IDs are particularly valuable because they enable criminals to assume a victim's identity in a way that allows for financial fraud, illegal travel, or even involvement in organized crime.

On the other hand, stolen credit card data is often traded in bulk on dark web marketplaces, where fraudulent transactions can take place quickly, leading to severe financial loss for the victims involved. These forms of fraud are not just a problem for individuals, but also for businesses and financial institutions that bear the burden of fraudulent claims and chargebacks.

1. Stolen Passports & IDs

Stolen passports and government-issued IDs are highly sought after on the dark web. Criminals use them to create fake identities, gain access to restricted areas, or facilitate illegal travel. Passports and IDs are often sold in sets with additional personal information like date of birth, address, and social security numbers, making them perfect tools for individuals looking to carry out larger fraudulent schemes, including money laundering, immigration fraud, and identity theft.

Tracking Stolen Passports & IDs

Dark Web Monitoring: Specialized OSINT tools are used to monitor dark web forums, marketplaces, and illegal data repositories where stolen passports and IDs are frequently sold. Tools like DarkSearch, Dark Web Scanner, or IntSights are commonly used to track down these items. These tools allow investigators to search for specific passport numbers or other identifying data that may be linked to stolen IDs.

Metadata & Watermark Analysis: Investigators can track fake documents by analyzing metadata or hidden watermarks embedded in digital images. For example, stolen passport copies often appear in specific formats or with unique characteristics that can be traced back to their original source.

Cross-Referencing Data: When an ID or passport is sold, it often comes with additional details about the victim. Investigators may cross-reference this information with existing public records, social media profiles, or corporate databases to determine whether the information is legitimate or part of a larger data breach.

Trade Monitoring: Monitoring the volume and frequency with which stolen passports or IDs are being traded on marketplaces can help investigators identify large-scale identity theft rings and trace the origin of the stolen goods. High volumes of trade in one particular ID type or country of origin might suggest organized operations.

2. Stolen Credit Card Fraud

Credit card fraud is an evergreen issue for consumers, merchants, and financial institutions. The sale of stolen credit card information is rampant on dark web marketplaces, where criminals can purchase or trade this information in bulk. Stolen credit card data is often obtained from data breaches, skimming devices, or phishing attacks.

Tracking Stolen Credit Card Data

Dark Web Marketplaces: Investigators track credit card data by monitoring well-known dark web marketplaces, such as Carding Market, AlphaBay (when it was operational), and Dream Market. These marketplaces often host listings where stolen credit card numbers are sold with expiration dates, CVV codes, and associated personal information. This data can be traced back to its source by performing deep searches on these platforms, using both automated OSINT tools and manual investigation.

Transaction Monitoring: Once stolen credit card data is sold and used, investigators can track the spending patterns or fraudulent transactions associated with these cards. Using tools such as Visa's Chargeback Intelligence, Fraud.net, or Sift, investigators can monitor transactions, identify patterns, and flag fraudulent activities. These tools allow for the identification of fraud rings, including high-frequency fraud and geographical clusters of fraud.

Tracking Dark Web Vendor Profiles: Often, the criminals selling stolen credit cards will have reputation profiles or feedback ratings on the dark web marketplaces. Investigators can track these profiles across multiple forums and marketplace transactions to uncover links to larger criminal networks involved in carding operations.

Blockchain Analysis: In some cases, stolen credit card data is used for cryptocurrency purchases, so analyzing the blockchain for suspicious transactions can help track the flow of stolen funds. Tools such as Chainalysis or CipherTrace are useful for tracing illicit purchases made using stolen credit cards that eventually make their way to cryptocurrency exchanges.

3. OSINT Tools for Investigating Stolen IDs, Passports & Credit Card Fraud

Tracking stolen IDs, passports, and credit cards is made easier with the help of several OSINT tools that help investigators aggregate data from various sources, analyze trends, and track criminal activity.

1. Dark Web Search Engines

These tools help investigators monitor the dark web for stolen information. Search engines like DarkSearch or Cicada provide investigators with the ability to track stolen credit card information, personal details, and counterfeit ID sales across numerous dark web marketplaces.

2. Data Breach Monitoring Services

Services like Have I Been Pwned can track when credit card information or identity data has been exposed in a data breach. By searching for email addresses, phone numbers, or credit card numbers, investigators can determine if a particular individual has had their information exposed on known data-leak websites.

3. Credit Card Fraud Detection Platforms

Solutions like Kount, FraudLabs Pro, and Forter monitor transactions across online retailers and financial institutions. These platforms use machine learning and pattern recognition to flag suspicious transactions that might involve stolen credit card data.

4. Digital Footprint Analysis

Digital footprint analysis tools, such as Maltego, OSINT Framework, and SpiderFoot, allow investigators to track the digital trail of a stolen identity or credit card number. By analyzing public-facing data across social media, forums, and breach databases, these tools can help track the criminal activity and its perpetrators.

4. Case Study: Tracking Stolen Credit Cards in a Fraud Ring

Let's explore a hypothetical case study to see how investigators might track stolen credit cards in a fraud ring:

The Situation: An investigator receives a tip that a set of stolen credit card numbers is being sold in bulk on a dark web marketplace. The credit card data includes the cardholder's name, card number, expiration date, and CVV code.

Step 1: Search the Marketplace

Using a dark web search engine, the investigator identifies a seller on Carding Market who has been posting credit card data. The seller's reputation profile shows that they've been active for several months and have sold over 100,000 card details.

Step 2: Transaction Monitoring

The investigator starts monitoring the transactions associated with the stolen credit card data. Using fraud detection platforms, they identify unusual patterns such as a spike in online purchases for high-ticket items, indicating that these cards are being used in a fraud ring.

Step 3: Tracking Blockchain Transactions

The investigator traces the cryptocurrency transactions made with the stolen credit card data. These transactions show that the fraudsters are converting the stolen funds into Bitcoin and sending them to multiple cryptocurrency exchanges, trying to launder the money.

Step 4: Cross-Referencing Public Records

The investigator cross-references the credit card details with public records and data breach databases, uncovering that several of the cardholders are from recent breaches involving major retailers. By combining this information with social media profiles, they narrow down the potential suspects behind the fraud.

Step 5: Coordinating with Law Enforcement

Using the gathered data, the investigator works with law enforcement to make arrests and seize assets involved in the fraud ring.

Conclusion

Tracking stolen IDs, passports, and credit card fraud is a critical component of combating identity theft and financial crime in the digital age. With the help of OSINT tools, dark web monitoring, and transaction analysis, investigators can identify the trade of stolen documents and payment information, follow the digital footprints left behind by criminals, and work to disrupt fraud rings. By staying ahead of these evolving threats and using innovative investigative techniques, it's possible to prevent significant financial loss and protect individuals from the growing threat of identity theft.

9.5 Monitoring Data Breaches & Preventing Identity Theft

Data breaches have become a pervasive threat in the digital age, exposing millions of personal records, financial details, and sensitive information. With the rapid expansion of online services and the increasing sophistication of cybercriminals, data breaches can happen anywhere—whether it's a small online retailer, a massive corporation, or even government entities. Once this sensitive data is stolen, it becomes a prime target for criminals looking to engage in identity theft and fraudulent activities.

Effective monitoring and prevention of identity theft require a proactive approach to tracking data breaches and quickly responding to signs of compromised personal information. By utilizing open-source intelligence (OSINT) tools and keeping a watchful eye on the dark web, investigators, consumers, and organizations can reduce the risk of becoming victims of identity theft, ensure early detection of breaches, and take preventive measures to minimize potential damage.

This section explores how to monitor data breaches and safeguard against identity theft using available resources, proactive strategies, and effective investigative tools.

The Scope of Data Breaches & Their Impact on Identity Theft

A data breach occurs when unauthorized individuals gain access to sensitive personal information, such as names, addresses, Social Security numbers, bank account details, credit card numbers, and other forms of personally identifiable information (PII). The stolen data can be used in a variety of criminal activities, including fraudulent purchases, account takeovers, and identity impersonation.

The dark web is where much of the stolen data is traded. Cybercriminals buy and sell large volumes of stolen credentials and personal data to commit identity theft and fraud. This is why tracking data breaches and understanding their scope is vital to preventing the widespread use of stolen data.

For organizations, failure to prevent identity theft resulting from data breaches can result in legal and reputational consequences, fines, loss of customer trust, and financial damages. For individuals, it may mean years of dealing with the aftermath of identity theft—correcting credit reports, dealing with unauthorized financial transactions, and possibly losing access to important accounts.

1. How to Monitor Data Breaches

Data breach monitoring is the process of tracking potential breaches and identifying whether personal information has been exposed. For both individuals and organizations, monitoring these breaches is crucial in preventing or minimizing identity theft.

Dark Web Monitoring

Dark web monitoring is one of the most effective ways to monitor stolen data. Cybercriminals often trade compromised information on dark web marketplaces, forums, and data leak sites. By actively searching these spaces, investigators can identify if any data related to a particular person or organization has been compromised.

Automated Tools for Dark Web Monitoring: Tools like Dark Web Scanner, IntSights, and Cyberint specialize in monitoring dark web activity. These tools can search for stolen credentials, credit card numbers, and other personal information that may be linked to a specific person, company, or account.

Threat Intelligence Feeds: Many OSINT platforms like Spyse, Maltego, and OSINT Framework integrate threat intelligence feeds that gather dark web data from known marketplaces. By analyzing these feeds, organizations and investigators can quickly identify if their data has been exposed and take immediate action to mitigate the damage.

Manual Monitoring: In addition to automated tools, manual searches for sensitive information such as email addresses, Social Security numbers, or financial information across dark web forums and marketplaces can yield results. These manual investigations can be done through specialized search engines like DuckDuckGo, Cicada, or Ahmia that index dark web sites.

Data Breach Notification Services

Several services offer data breach monitoring that scans for compromised information. Services like Have I Been Pwned provide free checks for email addresses and passwords that may have been exposed in breaches. They often offer notifications when personal data is discovered in a breach, allowing individuals to take action quickly.

For businesses, BreachLock, RiskSense, and TrapX offer enterprise-grade services that help monitor multiple sources and alert organizations when their data has been compromised.

Subscribing to Alerts: Many data breach notification services allow individuals and businesses to subscribe to alerts when new data leaks or breaches occur. These alerts can be customized to target specific types of personal information, such as email addresses, credit card numbers, or usernames.

Monitor Specific Leaks: When specific data leaks occur, such as a massive financial institution breach or cloud service hack, subscribing to breach-specific alerts allows for quick follow-up. Tools like Token and SecAlert offer specific alerts tailored to certain breaches.

2. Preventing Identity Theft from Data Breaches

Once a data breach is discovered, the next priority is to take steps to prevent identity theft from occurring. Early detection and proactive action can significantly reduce the chances of fraud or misuse of stolen information.

1. Freezing Credit and Reporting to Agencies

One of the first steps in preventing identity theft is freezing credit at the major credit bureaus. This prevents criminals from opening new credit lines or making significant purchases using stolen credentials. Individuals can also report their information to organizations such as the Federal Trade Commission (FTC), IdentityTheft.gov, or similar consumer protection agencies.

Credit Freeze: A credit freeze prevents anyone, including the individual themselves, from accessing their credit reports. This makes it significantly harder for criminals to open new accounts using stolen PII.

Fraud Alerts: Fraud alerts allow individuals to notify credit bureaus that they are at risk of identity theft. This prompts creditors to take extra steps to verify the identity of anyone applying for credit in the victim's name.

2. Monitoring Financial Accounts

After a data breach, victims should immediately monitor their bank accounts, credit card statements, and social media accounts for unauthorized transactions or suspicious activity. Setting up account alerts for large transactions or logins from unusual locations can help spot fraud early.

Transaction Monitoring: Credit card companies and financial institutions now offer services that monitor accounts for suspicious transactions. Automated alerts via text or email can notify users of unusual spending patterns, ensuring quick action can be taken.

Enabling Two-Factor Authentication (2FA): For online banking and financial platforms, enabling 2FA adds an extra layer of security. Even if a criminal gains access to a user's credentials, the additional security step of confirming login attempts makes it harder for criminals to gain control.

3. Updating Passwords & Security Questions

Stolen personal data can often include passwords and answers to security questions. Immediately changing passwords and setting stronger security questions can prevent unauthorized access to accounts that may have been compromised.

Use a Password Manager: After a breach, using a password manager to generate strong, unique passwords for each online account is recommended. Password managers also allow for easy updating of passwords if there are multiple accounts to secure.

4. Monitor Social Security Numbers & Financial Data

Since Social Security numbers (SSNs) and bank account information are frequently targeted by identity thieves, monitoring these records for misuse can prevent long-term damage. Some services specifically track SSN usage to alert users if their number is being used inappropriately.

3. Case Study: Preventing Identity Theft Post-Data Breach

Let's consider a case study involving a data breach at an online retailer, where thousands of customer email addresses, credit card numbers, and purchase history were compromised:

Step 1: Monitoring the Breach

The organization responsible for the breach immediately starts monitoring the dark web for any mention of customer details. Using Dark Web Scanner and OSINT Framework tools, they track the sale of credit card numbers linked to the breached accounts.

Step 2: Alerting Affected Users

Once the breach is confirmed, affected users are immediately notified via email, and they are advised to take immediate action, including freezing their credit and changing their passwords.

Step 3: Fraud Detection

As fraud alerts are activated, the company's fraud detection system begins tracking unusual transactions on the affected accounts. High-ticket items or out-of-state purchases are flagged, and customers are contacted to verify the legitimacy of these transactions.

Step 4: Preventing Further Theft

To prevent further identity theft, the company offers free credit monitoring services for affected customers and advises them to enroll in Identity Theft Protection Programs. They also help customers with the dispute process for fraudulent charges.

Conclusion

Monitoring data breaches and preventing identity theft is an ongoing process that requires constant vigilance. By leveraging OSINT tools, dark web monitoring, data breach alerts, and preventive security measures, individuals and organizations can detect when their personal information has been compromised and take swift action to limit the damage. Furthermore, proactive measures such as freezing credit, enabling fraud alerts, and updating passwords ensure that identity theft can be mitigated before significant harm occurs. Through diligent monitoring and early intervention, it's possible to reduce the impact of data breaches and help protect against the growing threat of identity theft in the digital age.

9.6 Case Study: Recovering a Stolen Identity Using OSINT

Identity theft is a pervasive crime that affects millions of individuals and organizations worldwide. When personal data is stolen, it can lead to significant emotional, financial, and legal consequences for the victim. Fortunately, open-source intelligence (OSINT) tools can play a vital role in tracking down stolen identities and recovering lost information. This case study outlines how OSINT was used to recover a stolen identity after an individual's personal details were compromised and used for fraudulent activities.

Case Background

The Incident:

A woman, Sarah Matthews, discovers that her identity has been stolen when she starts receiving calls from creditors about accounts she never opened. Her personal information, including her Social Security number (SSN), date of birth, and credit card details, was stolen after a major data breach at an online retailer. The thief used her information to open several credit accounts and make unauthorized purchases. Sarah immediately reports the fraud to the police and her financial institutions but is unsure how to recover her stolen identity.

Sarah decides to enlist the help of an OSINT specialist to track down the thief and restore her identity. This case study outlines how the specialist uses a combination of digital footprint analysis, dark web monitoring, and social media investigations to identify the thief, prevent further damage, and recover Sarah's identity.

Step 1: Data Breach Investigation & Tracking Personal Information

The OSINT specialist begins by looking into the initial data breach that exposed Sarah's personal details. Using an online database such as Have I Been Pwned, they check if Sarah's personal information was part of any publicly disclosed breaches. Upon finding that her data was included in a large-scale breach at the online retailer, the next step is to understand where the stolen information is being sold or traded.

Dark Web Monitoring:

The OSINT specialist uses specialized dark web monitoring tools like Maltego and Dark Web Scanner to search for Sarah's Social Security number (SSN), email address, and credit card details. These tools provide real-time alerts when her data appears on dark web marketplaces or hacker forums. The specialist identifies a transaction listing selling Sarah's credit card number along with a variety of other stolen information.

Tracking the Seller:

Further investigation into the dark web reveals the seller's forum handle, linked to multiple other stolen identities. Using additional OSINT techniques like username analysis and social media searches, the specialist connects this handle to a specific location and potential online aliases that could help identify the criminal.

Cross-Referencing Public Databases:

The OSINT specialist checks publicly available records such as business registrations and criminal databases to cross-reference any available data on the suspect. They discover that the seller has an online presence, where their name and location match the one revealed by public business records.

Step 2: Tracking the Thief's Online Activity & Social Media Footprint

Once the identity of the dark web seller is narrowed down, the next task is to gather as much information as possible to identify their real-world identity. This includes investigating the suspect's online activity and social media footprint.

Social Media Cross-Referencing:

Using the suspect's known usernames from dark web transactions, the OSINT specialist searches for them on social media platforms. Tools like Social Searcher and Pipl are used to connect the suspect to various profiles on Facebook, Instagram, and LinkedIn. By examining the suspect's social media posts, the specialist gains insight into their lifestyle, employment history, and even their social circle.

Behavioral Analysis:

Through a detailed analysis of the suspect's social media interactions, it's clear that they are a part of a group of individuals involved in identity theft schemes. They often share tips and guides related to online fraud, and their posts show interest in stolen credit cards, social engineering tactics, and fake identities. The OSINT specialist creates a profile of the criminal's potential motivations and methods, linking them to other criminal activities.

Tracking the Thief's Location:

The specialist digs deeper into geolocated data from the suspect's posts on social media. Using OSINT tools like GeoSearch and Google Earth, they identify where the criminal resides and pinpoint possible locations where stolen data may be stored or used. This geo-information could help law enforcement authorities track the thief in the future.

Step 3: Verifying Stolen Accounts and Preventing Further Damage

With the thief's identity and online behavior now somewhat clear, the next step is to prevent further damage to Sarah's financial and personal security.

Reverse Lookup of Financial Accounts:

The OSINT specialist works with Sarah's financial institutions to track down the fraudulent accounts opened in her name. Using tools like Spokeo and BeenVerified, they conduct reverse lookups on account numbers, phone numbers, and email addresses associated with the criminal's purchases. They identify a pattern of fraudulent applications linked to fictitious addresses and IP addresses.

Alerting Credit Agencies:

The OSINT specialist advises Sarah to file a fraud alert with the credit bureaus, including Experian, TransUnion, and Equifax, and initiate a credit freeze. By taking these steps, Sarah's credit report is locked, preventing further fraudulent activity. The credit bureaus also provide alerts when anyone attempts to open new credit accounts under her name.

Using Two-Factor Authentication (2FA):

In collaboration with Sarah, the OSINT expert helps her enable two-factor authentication (2FA) on all important accounts, such as banking, email, and shopping platforms. This significantly reduces the likelihood of the thief gaining access to any existing accounts.

Tracking & Blocking Fraudulent Purchases:

Working with law enforcement and financial institutions, the OSINT specialist helps track the fraudulent purchases made with Sarah's stolen credit card. They successfully block these transactions and initiate investigations into the theft, providing detailed evidence gathered through OSINT methods.

Step 4: Legal Action & Recovery of Stolen Funds

Armed with evidence collected through OSINT, Sarah reports the case to local law enforcement and the Federal Trade Commission (FTC). The OSINT specialist helps Sarah compile a comprehensive report, including:

- Dark Web findings,
- Social media links,
- Transaction history from the fraudulent accounts,
- Reverse lookup data,
- Geolocated information.

With the support of this detailed report, law enforcement officials are able to conduct a more thorough investigation, arrest the suspect, and recover some of the stolen funds.

Additionally, the evidence is used to block the thief from using Sarah's identity for further crimes.

Conclusion: Recovering a Stolen Identity Through OSINT

This case study highlights how open-source intelligence (OSINT) tools and techniques can be effectively used to track down stolen identities and recover lost personal data. By leveraging dark web monitoring, social media analysis, reverse lookups, and threat intelligence, the OSINT specialist was able to trace the identity thief, prevent further fraudulent activity, and help Sarah recover some of her financial losses.

While recovering from identity theft can be a lengthy and emotionally taxing process, OSINT provides a powerful toolkit for investigating and resolving these incidents. By utilizing these resources, individuals and organizations can mitigate the impact of identity theft, track down perpetrators, and take necessary action to protect their personal information in an increasingly digital world.

10. Social Engineering & Behavioral Analysis

Understanding human behavior is just as important as technical skills in OSINT investigations. This chapter explores the psychological tactics behind social engineering and how they can be used to gather intelligence, verify identities, and uncover hidden information. You'll learn how to analyze online behavior patterns, detect deception, and leverage open-source data to predict a target's actions. Additionally, we'll discuss defensive strategies to recognize and counter social engineering attempts, ensuring both ethical investigation practices and personal security in the digital world.

10.1 Understanding Social Engineering & Its Role in OSINT

Social engineering is a critical concept in the world of open-source intelligence (OSINT). It involves manipulating people into divulging confidential information or performing actions that compromise security, often using psychological tactics to exploit human behavior. While OSINT traditionally refers to the collection and analysis of publicly available data from digital sources, social engineering takes it a step further by relying on the interaction between the investigator (or attacker) and individuals in the real world or online.

In the context of OSINT, social engineering can be used to gather intelligence, manipulate targets, or confirm suspicions when technical or automated methods fail to yield enough information. By understanding the principles of social engineering and its various tactics, OSINT analysts can be better prepared to defend against these kinds of manipulative attacks while also using them ethically and responsibly for investigative purposes.

The Psychological Foundation of Social Engineering

Social engineering is rooted in the psychology of human interaction. The goal is to exploit cognitive biases, emotions, and trust to achieve a specific outcome. Many times, individuals are more likely to reveal sensitive information if they feel that their security or privacy is not at risk, or if they trust the person asking. Common psychological tactics include:

Reciprocity: People tend to feel obligated to return favors or provide information when they are given something, even if it is small. This can be exploited by offering small, seemingly harmless pieces of information, building trust before making a larger request.

Authority: When someone believes they are speaking to an authority figure, they are more likely to comply with requests, even if those requests involve providing sensitive data or performing risky actions. Social engineers may impersonate figures like law enforcement, technical support, or company executives.

Scarcity: A sense of urgency or the fear of missing out (FOMO) can push people into acting without fully thinking through the consequences. For example, a social engineer might claim that an offer is available for a limited time, forcing the target to act quickly and share personal details.

Trust: The cornerstone of most successful social engineering attacks is gaining the victim's trust. This can be achieved by manipulating existing relationships or creating fake identities to appear familiar or authoritative, such as pretending to be a colleague or a friend.

Common Social Engineering Techniques Used in OSINT

While OSINT involves searching public databases, social media, and other open sources for information, social engineering techniques make these sources even more effective. Here are several common social engineering methods:

1. Phishing and Spear-Phishing

Phishing is the most well-known social engineering tactic. It involves sending fraudulent emails, text messages, or phone calls that appear to come from reputable sources (e.g., banks, email providers, or e-commerce sites) to trick recipients into revealing sensitive information such as passwords, credit card numbers, or other personal details.

Spear-phishing is a more targeted form of phishing. Unlike phishing, which casts a wide net, spear-phishing is highly personalized. It often involves gathering information about an individual from OSINT sources, such as social media accounts or public databases, to craft a convincing message that speaks directly to the victim's specific interests or needs.

2. Pretexting

In pretexting, the social engineer creates a false narrative or scenario (a "pretext") to convince the target to provide information or perform an action. This may involve pretending to be someone the target trusts, such as a coworker, a bank representative, or a government agent. By leveraging information from OSINT tools—such as knowing the victim's place of employment, family members, or recent activities—a social engineer can fabricate a compelling story.

For example, an OSINT analyst might discover that a person works at a specific company and then pose as an HR representative requesting verification of personal information for "security purposes."

3. Baiting

Baiting relies on offering something enticing, like free software or an exclusive opportunity, to lure the victim into providing sensitive information or executing an action that benefits the attacker. This could involve a fake offer that compels the victim to download malicious software or hand over private details.

For instance, an OSINT investigator might find a victim's social media posts hinting at an interest in a particular gadget. The attacker might then pose as a seller offering a discounted product in exchange for payment information, using the victim's interests to bait them into the scam.

4. Tailgating and Impersonation

Tailgating involves following an authorized person into a restricted area by gaining their trust. In a physical environment, it could involve someone gaining access to a building by simply walking behind a staff member and entering after them. In a digital context, tailgating could involve following someone's online activity or mimicking their actions to gain access to secured data or systems.

Impersonation, a more general tactic, is where an attacker pretends to be someone else to gain access to private information. OSINT can make this easier by providing detailed data on the target, such as their hobbies, friends, preferences, and history, which can then be used to craft a believable persona.

The Role of OSINT in Social Engineering Attacks

OSINT tools and techniques can enhance social engineering efforts by providing valuable insights into a target's behavior, preferences, and vulnerabilities. Some examples of how OSINT can support social engineering include:

Gathering Personal Information: Public records, social media profiles, and online databases provide a wealth of personal information that attackers can use to build rapport or tailor their pretexts.

Tracking Digital Footprints: Social media analysis and reverse searches can reveal where a target has been, what they are interested in, and who they interact with online. This information can be leveraged to make interactions more convincing, whether through email, phone calls, or in-person encounters.

Mapping Relationships: OSINT allows attackers to identify a target's professional network, family members, friends, and associates. Knowing these relationships helps build a credible pretext or lends authority to a phishing attempt.

Identifying Vulnerabilities: By analyzing a target's digital footprint, OSINT practitioners can identify potential weak spots, such as oversharing personal details online, using easily guessable passwords, or having outdated security practices. These gaps can be exploited in social engineering schemes.

Defending Against Social Engineering in OSINT

While social engineering is often used for malicious purposes, OSINT can also play an important role in protecting against these attacks. By understanding how social engineers gather and exploit information, individuals and organizations can strengthen their defenses. Here are some steps to protect against social engineering:

Limit Information Sharing: Be mindful of what you share online, especially on social media platforms. Minimize personal details that could be used to craft convincing pretexts.

Educate and Train: Organizations should provide training on recognizing social engineering tactics and ensuring that employees understand how to verify suspicious requests.

Implement Strong Authentication Measures: Use multi-factor authentication (MFA) to secure online accounts. This adds an extra layer of protection against unauthorized access.

Verify Requests: Always confirm requests for sensitive information or actions through official channels. If in doubt, contact the requesting party directly through known, trusted contact information.

Monitor for Suspicious Activity: Regularly review personal and organizational digital activity for signs of phishing, unauthorized access attempts, or other suspicious behavior.

Conclusion

Social engineering plays a significant role in OSINT, as it enables attackers to use human psychology to bypass technical defenses and gain access to sensitive information. By understanding the common social engineering techniques and how OSINT supports them, individuals and organizations can better prepare themselves to defend against these manipulative tactics. It is essential to balance the responsible use of OSINT for investigative purposes with heightened awareness of social engineering risks to prevent exploitation.

10.2 Identifying Psychological Patterns & Digital Habits

In the world of open-source intelligence (OSINT), understanding psychological patterns and digital habits is an essential component of successful investigations. By analyzing the behavior of individuals in the digital realm, investigators can uncover valuable insights into a person's actions, preferences, vulnerabilities, and tendencies. This can be particularly useful in cases such as tracking a person's movements, identifying potential criminal activity, or gathering intelligence for national security or corporate investigations.

Psychological patterns and digital habits often reveal the true motivations, personality traits, and decision-making processes of individuals, making them a goldmine for OSINT analysts. By recognizing these patterns, investigators can not only find leads and evidence but also predict future behaviors or actions.

This section will explore how identifying psychological patterns and digital habits can be an effective tool in OSINT investigations and how analysts can leverage these insights for practical applications.

The Role of Psychology in Digital Behavior

Understanding human psychology is at the core of interpreting digital habits. People's actions in the digital space—whether through social media activity, online shopping patterns, email communication, or even their use of search engines—can reveal underlying psychological factors. These actions reflect how individuals interact with the world, what they care about, what triggers their emotions, and how they respond to stimuli.

In the context of OSINT, analyzing digital footprints can provide clues about:

Cognitive Biases: People often make decisions based on mental shortcuts or cognitive biases. Understanding these biases, such as confirmation bias (favoring information that confirms pre-existing beliefs) or anchoring bias (relying too heavily on the first piece of information encountered), can help OSINT analysts interpret why certain online behaviors occur.

Emotional Responses: Online behaviors can also be influenced by emotional triggers. People who feel threatened may become defensive or use language that reflects stress, anger, or fear. By understanding these emotional patterns, an investigator can identify potential vulnerabilities or inconsistencies in a person's online behavior.

Motivations: Identifying why a person behaves in certain ways can help an OSINT analyst piece together their larger narrative. For example, individuals may engage in excessive online sharing due to a need for validation (self-esteem) or seek constant engagement with specific topics out of a sense of belonging or identity.

Psychological Patterns Revealed Through Digital Habits

By understanding how individuals behave online, investigators can uncover patterns that indicate psychological traits. Here are some of the psychological patterns that are often revealed through digital habits:

1. Consistency vs. Inconsistency in Behavior

Consistency: Many individuals maintain predictable and consistent patterns of behavior across platforms. For example, the time of day a person typically posts on social media or the topics they frequently discuss may reveal a lot about their personal routine and habits. Investigators can identify when someone is typically active online, the types of content they engage with, and even how they respond to specific topics or events. Consistency in behavior may indicate a person's grounded nature or their psychological need for structure.

Inconsistency: On the other hand, inconsistencies in digital behavior may signal underlying psychological conflicts or attempts to conceal certain aspects of a person's life. For example, a person who frequently deletes old social media posts may be attempting to distance themselves from past behaviors or controversial opinions. Alternatively, individuals who switch between contradictory interests online may be trying to hide their true personality or values.

2. Social Engagement Patterns

People's interactions on social media platforms—such as the frequency and type of posts, likes, comments, and shares—can reveal important psychological insights.

High Engagement: People who regularly post and engage with others may be seeking validation or approval. Their interactions might be motivated by a desire for attention, social connection, or even the need to be heard. Investigators can analyze how a person responds to positive vs. negative feedback, how often they engage in online debates, and what types of content elicit strong emotional reactions.

Low Engagement: Conversely, individuals who rarely post or engage online might be more introverted or cautious about what they share. This may suggest a psychological preference for privacy, or perhaps a fear of exposure or vulnerability. Investigators should pay attention to patterns of sporadic engagement, as these could indicate key moments when an individual feels compelled to speak out or act.

3. Content Consumption vs. Content Creation

One critical element in analyzing digital habits is identifying whether a person is primarily a consumer of content or a creator.

Content Consumers: These individuals tend to be more passive in their online presence, primarily consuming content in the form of news articles, videos, or posts. Their behavior may reflect a more passive or reflective mindset, and they might prefer to observe or gather information rather than engage with others. This type of person may be highly selective about the types of media they consume, which could reflect deeply-held beliefs or a desire to reinforce their worldview.

Content Creators: Those who consistently create content, whether through social media posts, blog articles, or video production, tend to be more extroverted or driven by a desire for recognition. The content they produce can reveal personal opinions, emotional states, and values. Investigators can track the types of content they regularly create to understand their interests, emotional responses, and the specific issues they are passionate about.

4. Search Patterns and Internet Behavior

Individuals' search history and internet usage patterns can provide psychological insights into their interests, concerns, and motivations. Tools like Google Trends or search query analysis can reveal recurring themes in the types of searches an individual conducts.

Frequent Searches: Individuals who frequently search for certain terms, topics, or people may be obsessed with a particular issue or idea. For example, someone who repeatedly searches for criminal activities, illegal goods, or certain types of conspiracy theories might be motivated by fear, curiosity, or even a sense of identity. Understanding these search patterns helps analysts grasp what matters most to the person and the mental state that underlies their behavior.

Fear and Anxiety: If someone searches for a particular issue in response to a recent event (e.g., a specific disease, government policies, or financial instability), it may indicate heightened anxiety or fear. Conversely, searching for personal safety measures or avoidance behaviors could be a sign of a person's underlying psychological state.

Detecting Deception through Digital Habits

OSINT can also be used to detect patterns of deception or attempts to hide information. Certain online behaviors may indicate that someone is concealing or fabricating aspects of their life:

Overcompensation: People who present themselves as excessively perfect or flawless online may be attempting to cover up insecurities or flaws. Investigators can analyze a person's social media activity for signs of over-curation, where they only post idealized content and exclude any "negative" or unflattering aspects of their life.

Excessive Privacy Controls: Individuals who go to great lengths to hide their information online, such as setting up multiple layers of privacy or creating false profiles, may be attempting to hide something or have a psychological fear of exposure. This can be a critical clue in criminal investigations or identity theft cases.

Contradictory Online Personas: When a person's online persona sharply contradicts their real-life actions (such as presenting themselves as a staunch advocate for a cause but engaging in behavior that contradicts those beliefs), it can be a sign of a deeper psychological conflict or deception. OSINT analysts can use this discrepancy to explore further discrepancies in digital behavior.

Conclusion

Psychological patterns and digital habits offer invaluable insights into the inner workings of individuals, allowing OSINT analysts to understand motivations, predict behaviors, and uncover critical clues. By carefully studying how people engage with the digital world—what they share, how they react, what they consume, and how they present themselves—analysts can uncover much more than just factual data. They can reveal the emotional and psychological underpinnings that drive behavior.

Ultimately, understanding these patterns enhances the OSINT investigator's ability to not only gather intelligence but also predict outcomes, identify risks, and apply a deeper level of analysis to the vast amounts of information available online.

10.3 How People Reveal Information Without Realizing It

In the digital age, individuals often unknowingly disclose vast amounts of personal information online. This inadvertent revelation of data—whether through social media posts, online interactions, or everyday digital behavior—provides a wealth of intelligence that can be exploited by investigators, hackers, or anyone else with the tools and knowledge to analyze these digital footprints. The key to understanding how people reveal information without realizing it lies in the way humans interact with digital platforms, the kinds of data they generate, and the unconscious patterns they form when using technology.

This section will explore the various ways in which individuals unintentionally share personal details, and how these revelations can be used for OSINT investigations. From social media behavior to digital habits and even seemingly innocent interactions, the digital world is full of inadvertent leaks of information.

The Unconscious Data People Share Online

1. Social Media Behavior and Oversharing

One of the most common ways people unknowingly reveal personal information is through their social media activity. While many individuals are aware of the need to protect their privacy, they often fail to realize the depth of data they are sharing with their online networks. This can occur in several ways:

Location Tags: Many people "check-in" at restaurants, events, or vacation spots on platforms like Facebook, Instagram, or Snapchat. Even without actively tagging a location, photos and status updates may have geo-location data embedded in them. This geolocation data—visible to anyone with access—reveals where a person has been or is currently located.

Posting Patterns: The frequency and timing of social media posts can reveal more than just someone's daily schedule. For example, regular updates at specific times of the day (e.g., morning posts on Instagram, evening tweets) can give investigators insight into a person's routine. This is especially true when people share their plans or actions without considering the consequences.

Photos and Images: People post pictures without considering what they are revealing. Even images that seem harmless—like a selfie in a coffee shop—can contain metadata that reveals the device used, exact location, or date. Additionally, the background of photos can offer clues about where a person lives, works, or socializes.

Emotional Responses: People often reveal their feelings and moods through posts or comments on social media. A person who frequently posts angry or defensive comments about certain topics may be disclosing underlying stressors or psychological states, which can reveal a lot about their emotional well-being or areas of vulnerability.

2. Behavioral Cues in Online Interactions

People's behaviors in online discussions, forums, and comment sections can also reveal personal information without them realizing it. Every time an individual interacts with others in an online community, they leave behind a trail of behavior patterns that can be analyzed for deeper insights. Some of these indicators include:

Reaction to Conflict: People often react impulsively in digital environments, especially during heated online debates. Their tone, word choices, and emotional responses can give clues about their personality traits, stress levels, and temperaments. A person who tends to escalate arguments may reveal frustration or a lack of impulse control, while someone who avoids conflict may demonstrate a more reserved or passive personality.

Interest Signaling: Individuals often display their interests or preferences without realizing it through the groups they join, the topics they follow, and the media they consume. For example, a person who consistently shares political content or follows certain celebrities may be revealing more about their beliefs, hobbies, or even their affiliations than they intended.

Writing Style and Language: The way people write online also reveals a lot about them. A person who consistently uses certain slang, phrases, or hashtags may unintentionally disclose regional, cultural, or social affiliations. The frequency of specific words or phrases can also indicate mental states—someone using terms related to fear, anxiety, or frustration may unintentionally signal their emotional state or current challenges.

3. Leaks Through Online Transactions and Searches

People often disclose personal preferences, purchase behavior, and even emotional needs without realizing it through their online purchases and searches. Every time a person buys something online, makes a reservation, or looks up a particular service or product, they leave behind digital traces that provide insight into their lifestyle, values, and habits. Examples of this include:

Search History: Search engines like Google track what people look for online. The types of queries people make can reveal a lot about their concerns, interests, and intentions. For example, searches for financial problems or health issues could point to a person's current struggles, while frequent searches for entertainment or leisure activities could reveal an interest in relaxation or escapism.

Shopping Patterns: Online shopping platforms like Amazon, eBay, or e-commerce websites collect data about what people buy, when, and how often. This can reveal spending habits, product preferences, and even purchasing behaviors that people may not intend to disclose. For instance, buying certain products may suggest health concerns, a particular lifestyle choice, or a hobby that someone might not have publicly acknowledged.

Subscription Services: Subscription services (like Netflix, Spotify, or digital magazines) often reveal what people watch, listen to, or read. These preferences can expose personal tastes, cultural interests, or even mood states. For example, someone consistently listening to relaxing music may be trying to cope with stress, or a person watching particular documentaries might be interested in politics, history, or conspiracy theories.

Inadvertent Personal Information from Digital Habits

Beyond direct actions like posting or purchasing, certain everyday behaviors in the digital realm reveal personal information without individuals realizing it. These behaviors include:

1. Online Login Behavior

People often use the same passwords or log-in information across multiple sites, which can provide analysts with additional clues about their digital identity. Logging into services that link to a person's social media profiles, email, or even financial information can reveal a great deal about their personal life.

For example:

- **Email Addresses**: The domain name of a person's email address can sometimes reveal their workplace or affiliations.
- **Password Reuse**: Repeated passwords or patterns in password choices can indicate security vulnerabilities or other habits that investigators can exploit.

2. Mobile App Usage

Mobile apps are an often-overlooked source of unintentional data sharing. Many apps collect personal information from users, whether through location tracking, health data collection, or even app usage patterns. For instance:

- **Fitness Apps**: Apps like Strava or Fitbit can unintentionally reveal the user's daily movements, exercise routines, or even their fitness level.
- **Navigation Apps**: Apps like Google Maps or Waze collect data about where users go, when, and how often, providing insight into their routine or favorite locations.
- **Photo and Video Apps**: Apps that sync with cloud services or offer automatic uploads can reveal private content like travel photos, family moments, or personal events.

3. Digital Footprints from Voice Assistants

With the rise of voice-activated devices like Amazon Alexa, Google Home, and Siri, many individuals unknowingly expose personal details through voice queries. From asking about the weather to setting reminders or searching for information, voice assistants record data that can offer clues to an individual's interests, schedule, and preferences.

These devices may store data on:

- **Frequently Asked Questions**: Repeated queries about specific topics, such as certain health concerns, relationship issues, or professional topics, can reveal areas of personal focus.

- **Habits and Routines**: Voice commands that trigger specific routines (like setting an alarm or turning off the lights) can expose daily habits, home life, and personal preferences.

Conclusion

In the digital age, people constantly reveal more about themselves than they realize. Whether through social media posts, online searches, shopping habits, or even the way they interact with devices, individuals leave behind vast amounts of personal data that can be analyzed by OSINT investigators. While some of this data is shared intentionally, much of it is unknowingly exposed, offering valuable insight into a person's life, habits, and psychological state.

For investigators, understanding how people unintentionally disclose information is crucial. By piecing together these often-overlooked details, OSINT practitioners can gain a deeper understanding of their subjects, predict behaviors, and build more complete profiles for investigative purposes. However, it's important to approach this process ethically, respecting privacy boundaries and ensuring that the information is used responsibly.

10.4 Manipulating Online Conversations for Intelligence Gathering

The digital landscape provides numerous opportunities for gathering intelligence, but one of the more subtle and powerful methods involves influencing or guiding online conversations. Through careful manipulation, investigators or operatives can extract valuable information without direct questioning or aggressive tactics. By skillfully steering discussions or inserting specific cues into online spaces, individuals can prompt others to reveal critical details—intentionally or unintentionally. This approach is widely used in OSINT investigations, especially when seeking to uncover sensitive data or identify key relationships, behaviors, and vulnerabilities.

This section explores the different techniques used to manipulate online conversations for intelligence gathering, the tools and tactics involved, and the ethical considerations surrounding this form of OSINT.

Understanding the Art of Conversation Manipulation

Manipulating online conversations is a delicate practice that requires a mix of psychological awareness, strategic communication, and technological tools. In the digital world, manipulation doesn't always mean coercion or deceit; it often involves subtly influencing the direction of discussions to gain insight without the subject's knowledge. By carefully navigating digital spaces, an investigator can leverage human psychology, digital habits, and social dynamics to uncover crucial information.

Some of the most common techniques used to manipulate online conversations for intelligence purposes include:

1. Creating Controlled Environments

One of the first steps in manipulating an online conversation is creating an environment that feels natural and secure. This may involve setting up a fake or controlled online persona (also known as a "sock puppet"), creating a group or forum, or using other methods to facilitate interaction.

Fake Profiles: By establishing a profile that seems familiar and trustworthy, an investigator can begin interacting with targets without raising suspicion. For example, an investigator might create a social media account that closely mirrors an existing friend or acquaintance of the target. Over time, this profile can engage in casual conversations, building rapport and encouraging the target to share sensitive or revealing information.

Online Groups or Forums: Establishing an online group (on platforms like Reddit, Facebook, or niche discussion forums) around a particular topic of interest allows the investigator to introduce discussions that will elicit responses from individuals with knowledge of the subject matter. In some cases, these groups may even be used as cover for gathering intelligence on a wider range of topics, as the target interacts freely in the group's dynamic.

2. Subtle Steering of Conversations

Once a conversation is established, the next step is to subtly steer it in the direction of valuable information. This requires an understanding of human psychology and an ability to nudge discussions without appearing overly intrusive. There are various ways this can be done:

Asking Leading Questions: Instead of directly asking for sensitive information, investigators can pose indirect or leading questions that encourage the target to share personal details. For example, a seemingly innocent question like, "Oh, I noticed you were in [city] last week; how was the trip?" can open a door to more detailed personal information. The key here is to ask questions that seem casual but are carefully designed to elicit specific answers that reveal important data.

Echoing Language and Sentiments: A common psychological trick in manipulating conversations is mimicking the target's language and emotional tone. People tend to feel more comfortable when speaking to someone who shares similar opinions or sentiments. By echoing the target's language (e.g., agreeing with them, using their phrases), investigators can make the target feel understood and validated, which increases the likelihood that they will reveal more personal information.

Building Rapport: Rapport-building is crucial when manipulating online conversations. A person who feels understood, supported, or valued is more likely to open up about their thoughts, feelings, and experiences. In online discussions, this might involve complimenting someone's ideas, showing empathy in response to their struggles, or engaging in common interests. By positioning themselves as a friendly, trustworthy figure, investigators can create the ideal environment for information to flow naturally.

3. Playing on Cognitive Biases and Emotions

Human beings are often guided by cognitive biases—mental shortcuts that influence decisions and judgments. These biases can be manipulated by investigators to encourage a target to disclose valuable information. Some common biases used in manipulation include:

The Reciprocity Principle: People tend to feel obligated to return favors. By offering information or seeming to help a person, an investigator can prompt the target to reciprocate by sharing something in return. For example, offering a piece of advice or sharing a personal anecdote can create a sense of reciprocity, prompting the target to share something personal in return.

The Social Proof Bias: People are more likely to follow the behavior of others, especially when they perceive those others as credible or popular. In online communities, this bias can be used to manipulate conversations by suggesting that others have already shared information or that others think a particular action or belief is valid. For example, an investigator might say, "Everyone in this group seems to agree on this topic," subtly influencing the target to align with that view and possibly share personal insights to fit in.

Appealing to Curiosity: Curiosity is a powerful driver of conversation. By introducing a topic in a way that leaves the conversation open-ended or mysterious, an investigator can generate interest and encourage the target to reveal more information to satisfy their curiosity. For example, mentioning a "confidential" topic or an "inside secret" that only a select few know can prompt a target to ask for more details, opening a channel for valuable intelligence.

4. Disguised Data Collection

While manipulating a conversation, an investigator may be collecting data in subtle ways. This might involve leveraging digital tools to capture and analyze the information being exchanged. Some tools for disguised data collection include:

Social Media Monitoring Tools: Tools like Hootsuite, Brand24, or Sprout Social can track specific conversations, mentions, and hashtags across social media platforms. These tools allow investigators to collect and analyze data in real-time, identifying trends and patterns in conversations without actively engaging in the dialogue.

Chatbots & AI-Driven Responses: Chatbots or AI tools are increasingly used to interact with people in online environments, responding to queries or comments automatically. By using AI-driven bots, investigators can gather information from a wide audience without revealing their true identity, ensuring that the conversation remains natural while simultaneously extracting data.

Speech and Text Analysis: In forums or messaging apps, investigators can use tools to track linguistic patterns, sentiment analysis, and emotional tones in the conversation. By analyzing the way individuals communicate, an investigator can gain deeper insights into a person's character, motivations, and potential vulnerabilities.

Ethical and Legal Considerations

While manipulating online conversations can be an effective OSINT technique, it raises significant ethical and legal questions. It is important to balance the value of intelligence gathering with the principles of transparency, consent, and privacy.

1. Consent and Deception

Manipulating online conversations often involves some level of deception, as the target is unaware that their responses are being monitored or influenced. In many cases, this may breach ethical standards regarding consent. Investigators must be cautious not to overstep legal boundaries by engaging in conversations that could be construed as manipulation, harassment, or fraud.

2. Privacy Rights

In some jurisdictions, online conversations are protected by privacy laws. While these laws may differ by country or region, it's crucial to ensure that the manipulation of conversations does not violate privacy rights. This includes considering whether the conversations are taking place in public spaces or behind privacy walls, such as in private groups or messages.

3. The Impact of Manipulation

Manipulating conversations can sometimes have unintended consequences, such as influencing a person's behavior in ways that could be harmful or leading them to share sensitive personal information that they might later regret. Investigators should always consider the potential consequences of their actions and avoid causing harm to individuals or groups during the intelligence-gathering process.

Conclusion

Manipulating online conversations for intelligence gathering is a powerful technique in OSINT investigations, enabling investigators to uncover valuable information that might otherwise be difficult to obtain. By creating controlled environments, subtly steering conversations, and exploiting cognitive biases, investigators can gain crucial insights into individuals' lives, behaviors, and vulnerabilities. However, it's essential that these methods are used responsibly and ethically, with consideration for the privacy and well-being of those involved. Understanding the boundaries of ethical OSINT practices is essential to ensure that these tactics are applied within the framework of legal and moral guidelines.

10.5 Ethical Considerations & Responsible Social Engineering

Social engineering, often used in OSINT investigations, is a practice that involves manipulating human behavior to extract confidential information or influence decisions. While social engineering can yield powerful intelligence, it also raises significant ethical questions and concerns. Unlike traditional data collection methods, social engineering involves direct interaction with individuals and may exploit human vulnerabilities, making it one of the more controversial techniques in the OSINT toolkit.

This section explores the ethical considerations and the need for responsible social engineering practices. It emphasizes the importance of adhering to legal and moral standards while still achieving investigative goals, ensuring that the impact on individuals is minimized and that sensitive information is handled responsibly.

Understanding Social Engineering and Its Ethical Implications

Social engineering takes advantage of human psychology to manipulate or deceive individuals into revealing information, granting access to systems, or taking actions that they otherwise would not. In the realm of OSINT, social engineering can involve a variety of methods, such as impersonating someone to gain trust, using subtle manipulation techniques to extract personal data, or influencing an individual's behavior through online interactions.

1. The Line Between Influence and Manipulation

One of the most significant ethical challenges in social engineering is determining where to draw the line between influence and manipulation. Influence can be seen as guiding or encouraging an individual's behavior through persuasion or education, while manipulation implies deceptive or unethical tactics designed to control a person's actions without their full knowledge or consent.

In OSINT investigations, a careful distinction should be made between legitimate influence—such as asking questions that lead to revealing information in a conversational context—and manipulation that crosses ethical boundaries, such as tricking a person into providing confidential data under false pretenses.

The key ethical question to consider is whether the individual being targeted is fully informed and able to make free, informed choices or whether their actions are being covertly steered without their knowledge. The latter situation can result in significant ethical violations, especially if the information collected is used irresponsibly or harms the individual or others.

2. The Role of Consent and Transparency

A cornerstone of ethical practice in any investigative method, including social engineering, is ensuring that consent is obtained, either explicitly or implicitly. While direct consent is often not possible in many OSINT practices, it is important to maintain a transparent approach regarding the nature of the interaction.

For instance, in certain contexts, such as gathering data from public forums or websites, individuals may assume a level of transparency by engaging in open conversations. However, there is a difference between engaging in public conversations and manipulating the conversation to extract sensitive details under false pretenses.

When applying social engineering techniques in an OSINT investigation, investigators must always consider whether the individual involved would reasonably expect that their actions could lead to the extraction of sensitive information. If the information is personal or confidential, seeking informed consent is paramount, even if the method is indirect. A good practice is to ensure that individuals are not misled into disclosing information they would otherwise withhold if they knew the true purpose behind the interaction.

3. Respecting Privacy and Boundaries

Respect for privacy is another central ethical principle in OSINT and social engineering. In the digital age, individuals share vast amounts of personal information on social media, forums, and other online platforms, but not all of this information is intended for public consumption or investigation. Many people expect a certain level of privacy in their online interactions, and these boundaries should be respected by OSINT professionals.

Using social engineering tactics to cross these boundaries—such as impersonating someone they trust, or pretending to offer assistance for the purpose of gaining access to private data—can be harmful and violate an individual's right to privacy. Even when the goal is to gather intelligence for legitimate reasons, the method used must ensure that privacy is not breached.

Ethical social engineering means refraining from tactics that are overly invasive or manipulative, especially when individuals are unwittingly drawn into a situation where their private information is exposed or used without their permission. There should always be a clear understanding of what constitutes "acceptable" social engineering and what could potentially be damaging or exploitative.

4. The Potential for Harm

The consequences of social engineering can sometimes extend beyond simply gathering intelligence. Manipulating a conversation or interaction to extract sensitive information can lead to significant harm to the individuals involved. For example, an individual may unknowingly reveal personal details that lead to identity theft, financial loss, or emotional distress. In some cases, individuals could be deceived into taking actions that compromise their security or privacy, or even place them in dangerous situations.

For instance, if a social engineer convinces a target to click on a malicious link, provide personal login credentials, or download harmful software, the resulting damage could extend far beyond the immediate context of the investigation. Similarly, obtaining confidential data under false pretenses could lead to reputational damage, career consequences, or other unintended fallout.

Therefore, it is essential that OSINT investigators maintain a responsible approach to social engineering. Methods that might be seen as harmless in one context could have unintended long-term consequences for the individuals involved. An ethical investigator will weigh the potential risks and rewards carefully, ensuring that the information gathered is used solely for the intended purpose and does not result in harm to the individual or the broader community.

5. Legal Compliance and Adherence to Regulations

OSINT investigations often operate within the bounds of laws that govern privacy, data protection, and online behavior. Social engineering, however, can quickly cross legal lines if investigators engage in deceptive tactics that violate regulations such as the General Data Protection Regulation (GDPR) in the European Union, the California Consumer Privacy Act (CCPA), or other regional privacy laws.

In particular, social engineering that involves impersonation, deception, or pretexting (pretending to be someone else to gain access to information) can run afoul of legal frameworks that protect individuals from fraudulent or invasive behaviors. It is essential for OSINT practitioners to stay well-informed about the laws that govern digital investigations and ensure they are operating within the legal boundaries.

Furthermore, investigators should avoid techniques that could be seen as harassment or stalking. Engaging in repeated, targeted interactions designed to wear down an individual's defenses or create an undue sense of urgency to divulge private information can be both legally and ethically problematic.

6. Avoiding Exploitation

The ultimate goal of OSINT is to gather information responsibly and for purposes that benefit the greater good—such as security, intelligence, or safety investigations. However, social engineering techniques should never be used to exploit vulnerable individuals or communities for personal gain or to further malicious activities. OSINT practitioners should take extra care to ensure they are not unwittingly enabling harmful practices, such as cybercrimes, identity theft, or harassment.

Investigators should also be mindful of power imbalances in online interactions. Manipulating vulnerable individuals who are more susceptible to coercion or deceit (for example, those experiencing psychological distress or economic hardship) can be seen as exploitative, even if the information obtained is valuable.

Guidelines for Responsible Social Engineering in OSINT

To conduct responsible and ethical social engineering in OSINT, consider the following guidelines:

- **Transparency**: Whenever possible, avoid deception. Engage in open, honest interactions that respect the privacy of others.
- **Informed Consent**: Understand whether your targets would expect their data to be used for investigative purposes. Seek explicit or implied consent where appropriate.
- **Risk Assessment**: Consider the potential harm that may arise from your investigative actions. Ensure that your methods do not cause undue distress or loss to the individuals involved.
- **Legal Compliance**: Adhere to all relevant privacy laws and regulations to avoid legal consequences.
- **Sensitivity and Respect**: Respect individual boundaries and privacy at all times. Do not manipulate vulnerable individuals for personal gain.
- **Accountability**: Hold yourself accountable for the methods you use and the impact they have on those you are investigating. Ensure that any information gathered is used for lawful, ethical, and legitimate purposes.

Conclusion

Social engineering, when conducted responsibly, can be a powerful tool in OSINT investigations, allowing investigators to gather critical information from online conversations and interactions. However, its ethical implications are significant, and practitioners must navigate this delicate balance with care. By adhering to principles of transparency, consent, and respect for privacy, OSINT professionals can ensure that their investigative techniques remain ethical, legal, and responsible. In the ever-evolving digital landscape, maintaining high ethical standards will not only help ensure the integrity of investigations but also protect the rights and well-being of individuals.

10.6 Case Study: Using Social Engineering to Verify a Fake Account

In the digital world, fake accounts are a growing concern, from fraudulent social media profiles to deceptive online personas used for scams or cyberattacks. Verifying the authenticity of an account is often crucial in investigations where identity verification, credibility checks, or security measures are at stake. Social engineering techniques can be used to help confirm whether an account is genuine or part of a broader scheme to deceive others. This case study demonstrates how OSINT professionals can employ social engineering methods to verify a potentially fake social media account.

Background: The Suspicious Profile

A large multinational company was investigating an online persona that had been posing as one of their high-level executives on social media. This fake account had been involved in a series of interactions with employees, potential business partners, and even customers. The account had gained significant credibility and trust due to its convincing posts, which featured official-looking images, corporate jargon, and seemingly legitimate business interests. However, after some initial investigations, the company's cybersecurity team suspected that the account was fraudulent, created by a cybercriminal group aiming to manipulate the company's employees and partners for financial gain.

The goal of the investigation was to verify whether the account was fake and, if so, uncover the individual behind the account. A traditional approach involving data searches and metadata analysis had yielded few results. Therefore, the investigation team decided to employ social engineering techniques as part of the OSINT process to gain more clarity on the authenticity of the profile.

Step 1: Assessing the Profile and Gathering Publicly Available Information

The team began by analyzing the suspicious profile in detail. A thorough review of the posts, photos, and interactions on the account was conducted to identify any red flags or inconsistencies. Several key pieces of information were gathered:

Profile Content: The profile's posts were polished, featuring professional-looking photos, frequent business updates, and links to company websites. However, the posts seemed oddly generic, and there was little personal information or backstory available. It raised doubts about the individual's authenticity.

Connections: The account had numerous connections within the company and other business partners. Many of the connections seemed legitimate, but some appeared to be relatively new or with generic, incomplete profiles.

Photo Analysis: The images used on the account were closely examined using reverse image search tools to determine if they had been taken from other sources or websites. One image appeared on multiple unrelated websites, suggesting that it may not be an original photograph of the purported executive.

Engagement with Other Users: The account had frequent interactions with other accounts, including messages and tagged photos. However, the interactions lacked personal detail and often consisted of overly formal language or vague business-related statements. These exchanges appeared scripted.

Despite these findings, the team had not yet confirmed whether the account was operated by someone intending to deceive or if it was an innocent mistake. To continue, they turned to social engineering.

Step 2: Initiating Social Engineering Through Direct Interaction

Given the lack of solid evidence, the team decided to engage the individual behind the account directly, using a social engineering approach. They created a persona that mirrored the style and communication patterns of the suspected fake account. This tactic was designed to be subtle and avoid immediate suspicion.

Creating a Fake Identity

A team member, trained in social engineering techniques, created a new profile on the social media platform. This new account was crafted to appear as a fellow executive in the same industry, with a similar professional background. The profile included business-related content and mutual connections with the suspicious account, creating a sense of legitimacy.

Engaging the Suspect

Once the new account was established, the team member reached out to the suspected fake profile with a casual business inquiry. The initial message was crafted in a way that would appear to come from a genuine peer. The message was as follows:

"Hi [Suspected Executive], I came across your profile and noticed we share some mutual connections. I'm currently working on a project that might be of interest to you. Would love to connect and exchange insights about recent industry developments. Let me know if you're open to a quick chat!"

This message was designed to initiate a conversation without giving away the purpose of the interaction.

Step 3: The Response and Building Trust

The suspected fake account quickly responded, showing eagerness to engage. The conversation continued with a focus on building rapport by discussing shared interests and business-related topics. Throughout the interaction, the team member (acting as the new persona) subtly introduced details that would make the profile appear legitimate. However, they also inserted more specific, contextual questions that only someone with insider knowledge or genuine experience could answer:

Questions About the Company's Inner Workings: Posing as a fellow executive, the team member asked questions about the company's operations and the executive's specific role. Genuine individuals would provide detailed answers or direct information, but the suspect's responses were generic or vague.

Verification of Common Knowledge: The social engineer subtly referred to real events or announcements in the company's history, expecting the suspect to offer specific commentary. The suspect's responses were either too vague or inconsistent with the company's actual events.

Step 4: Unveiling the Truth and Confirming the Fraud

After a few days of interaction, the social engineer introduced a more direct, probing question: "I've been hearing about some new projects within the company, and I wanted to get your take on them. Do you mind sharing your thoughts on the new executive leadership initiative? I'm particularly interested in your perspective on the company's strategic direction."

This specific question was a direct reference to a real initiative within the company, something only an executive or someone closely connected with the company would know.

At this point, the response from the fake account became increasingly evasive. Instead of providing an insightful answer, the individual replied with a generic statement: "I'm not at liberty to discuss internal matters, but I'm sure the company's direction will be promising."

This was a clear sign that the person behind the account was either not the genuine executive or was acting in a way that suggested fraudulent intent.

Step 5: Cross-Referencing Information and Exposing the Fraud

Upon further analysis, it became clear that the individual behind the fake account was using an alias and trying to pass off as someone else. The responses to specific questions failed to match up with the real executive's background, and the vagueness of the answers raised more red flags.

The team cross-referenced the data gathered through social engineering with publicly available records, including professional networking sites, news articles, and corporate filings. It turned out that the account was indeed a fake, created by an individual seeking to impersonate the executive to manipulate business partners into engaging in financial scams.

Conclusion and Ethical Considerations

This case study demonstrates how social engineering can be used responsibly and ethically to verify the authenticity of online accounts. While the technique was effective in uncovering the fraud, it was critical that the investigation team exercised caution throughout the process to avoid crossing ethical lines. They ensured that the engagement was conducted respectfully, without causing undue harm or distress to the individuals involved.

At the same time, they were careful not to overstep boundaries by coercing or manipulating the subject into revealing information. Instead, the goal was to create a genuine conversation that would naturally expose inconsistencies in the suspect's behavior and knowledge.

This case illustrates that while social engineering can be a powerful tool in OSINT investigations, it requires a careful, ethical approach to avoid crossing moral or legal lines. When used responsibly, social engineering can help investigators verify the authenticity of online profiles and expose fraudulent activity, ultimately ensuring the safety and security of online interactions.

11. OSINT & Missing Persons Investigations

Finding missing persons requires a strategic blend of OSINT techniques, data correlation, and real-world investigative methods. This chapter explores how open-source intelligence can assist in locating individuals by analyzing digital footprints, social media activity, financial records, and geolocation data. You'll learn how to track last-known online movements, leverage crowd-sourced investigations, and collaborate with law enforcement or NGOs. Additionally, we'll cover ethical considerations, privacy laws, and best practices to ensure responsible and effective searches for missing persons.

11.1 The Fundamentals of Finding Missing People Online

The search for missing persons is one of the most crucial and emotionally charged aspects of OSINT (Open Source Intelligence). While traditional methods like police investigations, physical searches, and tip lines are invaluable, the digital landscape offers powerful tools to assist in locating individuals who have gone missing, whether they've disappeared voluntarily or involuntarily. In today's interconnected world, people leave digital footprints in the form of social media activity, communications, online purchases, geolocation data, and public records— all of which can be leveraged in the search for missing persons.

This chapter outlines the fundamental steps involved in finding missing people online, with a particular focus on the types of digital data that can be gathered and analyzed to track their whereabouts or gather clues about their disappearance. It emphasizes the role of OSINT in complementing official search efforts, providing an effective, systematic, and ethical approach to locating missing persons.

1. Understanding the Scope of a Missing Person Case

Before diving into the online search process, it's essential to understand the context and urgency of the case. Missing person cases are classified into different categories, including:

Voluntary Disappearances: These individuals have chosen to disappear for personal reasons, sometimes cutting off contact with loved ones or even running away from home. The reasons may include fleeing from stress, personal trauma, or the need for a fresh start.

Involuntary Disappearances: In cases like abductions, trafficking, or foul play, the individual may be forced to leave or may have been taken against their will. The investigation becomes more urgent, requiring faster action.

Unintentional Disappearances: Sometimes, individuals are simply lost, disoriented, or in a situation where they can't contact others. They may be injured, incapacitated, or unable to reach out for help.

The type of disappearance influences the approach to locating the missing person. In all cases, digital forensics and OSINT techniques can play a pivotal role, but their application will vary depending on whether the person willingly vanished or was taken against their will.

2. Gathering the Basics: Information from Family and Friends

To begin a search for a missing person, it is essential to gather as much information as possible from the individuals closest to the person who is missing. This includes:

Personal Identification Details: Age, physical description, identifying features (like tattoos or scars), known aliases, or nicknames, and any relevant health conditions that could impact the search.

Known Locations: Information about the person's last known location, places they frequent, or any recent travel plans can help narrow down search areas.

Digital Footprints: Family and friends should be asked about the person's online habits, including which social media platforms they use, usernames, and recent interactions that might indicate their whereabouts or state of mind before disappearing. Understanding their digital behavior can provide leads for further investigation.

Having access to these details from family and friends can provide initial clues and direct the search toward the digital spaces where the person might be active. The more information available, the better prepared the investigator is for conducting a comprehensive search.

3. Scanning Social Media Accounts and Communication History

People often share personal details, photos, and location information through their social media accounts, making these platforms a rich source of intelligence when searching for missing persons.

Social Media Scrutiny: Start by looking at the missing person's accounts on platforms like Facebook, Twitter, Instagram, TikTok, LinkedIn, and even niche social networks. Focus on their recent posts, interactions, tagged photos, or check-ins, which may reveal their activities or location before their disappearance.

Direct Messages and Chats: Public posts are just one part of the puzzle. Messages sent via direct messaging services (Instagram DM, Facebook Messenger, WhatsApp, etc.) can also provide valuable information about the person's mental state, plans, or last known interactions. Cross-referencing these with friends' or family members' knowledge of the person's behavior can help paint a clearer picture of their situation.

Patterns of Activity: OSINT investigators can track any patterns in online behavior, such as frequent posts from a particular location, common places the person visits, or specific groups or events they are engaged in. This can help establish leads or predict where they might be.

In addition to social media, it's important to check messaging apps and email accounts. Sometimes, an overlooked online conversation can hold critical clues about the person's whereabouts or intentions.

4. Utilizing Geolocation Data and Digital Trails

Geolocation data is one of the most powerful tools in locating a missing person. Every time someone takes a photo with their phone or uses a location-based service, they leave digital markers that can be traced.

Photo & Video Metadata: If the missing person has posted pictures or videos online, examine the metadata to find out the exact location and time they were taken. GPS coordinates embedded in photos can pinpoint a person's location, even if they have shared the media on social media platforms without revealing where they are.

Check-in Data: Some social media platforms, like Facebook, allow users to check in at locations. A series of check-ins over time may provide insights into where the person was last located, or where they frequently spend time.

Mobile Devices: If permitted, using data from mobile devices can help track a person's movements. Investigators may also look for phone records or GPS tracking, where possible, to understand where the person's phone was last active.

Geolocation can also come from publicly available platforms like Google Maps. If the missing person is using location services with apps like Uber or Lyft, their travel history might reveal essential movement data.

5. Exploring Public Records & Government Databases

In addition to social media and digital footprints, public records can also help locate missing individuals. These records may include:

Driver's License and Vehicle Registration Data: Searching vehicle registrations or driver's license records can provide an address, vehicle type, and other personal details.

Voter Registration & Tax Records: Voter records, if available, can provide location-based leads. Likewise, tax records can be used to cross-check addresses, although they are often more difficult to access.

Court Records: Individuals involved in legal cases, whether civil or criminal, might leave traces in online databases. Checking for any recent legal activity, such as lawsuits or charges, may indicate where they are located or their current situation.

While government records may not always be immediately accessible, utilizing open records requests or third-party database services can often provide valuable insights into a person's whereabouts.

6. Collaboration with Authorities and Official Investigations

Although OSINT techniques can provide crucial leads, it is important to work closely with law enforcement when dealing with missing person cases, especially if foul play or danger is suspected. Law enforcement agencies may have access to more advanced resources, such as private databases or tracking tools, which can expedite the process of finding a missing person.

Sharing your findings with authorities can be instrumental, as they may be able to apply additional legal pressure to gain access to private records or request information from private companies, like phone companies or social media platforms.

7. Ethical and Legal Considerations

When conducting any OSINT search, especially in the context of a missing person, it's essential to respect privacy and follow ethical guidelines. Unauthorized surveillance, hacking into private accounts, or using information inappropriately can have serious legal consequences. Investigators should ensure they are operating within the boundaries of the law and respecting the rights of others during the search process.

Conclusion

Finding a missing person using online methods can be a challenging and emotionally taxing task. However, when approached strategically, OSINT offers powerful tools to track down digital footprints and build a picture of an individual's last known activities. By using a combination of social media analysis, geolocation, public records, and collaboration with authorities, investigators can increase the chances of locating someone who has disappeared. The process requires a blend of technical expertise, ethical responsibility, and careful attention to detail to ensure the search is as effective and respectful as possible.

11.2 How Private Investigators Use OSINT for Skip Tracing

Skip tracing, the process of locating a person whose whereabouts are unknown, is a core part of private investigator (PI) work. Whether the goal is to track down individuals for debt collection, legal matters, or personal reasons, private investigators are increasingly relying on open-source intelligence (OSINT) to assist in their investigations. OSINT allows PIs to gather publicly available data from digital and traditional sources, enabling them to build a comprehensive profile of the person they are trying to locate.

This chapter dives into how private investigators effectively use OSINT for skip tracing, detailing the process, tools, and strategies they employ to uncover a person's location. The following sections outline key techniques and the ethical considerations associated with using OSINT for this purpose.

1. What is Skip Tracing?

Skip tracing is the art and science of finding people who have deliberately or unintentionally gone off the radar. The term "skip" refers to the person being searched for, and "tracing" refers to the process of locating them. Commonly used by debt collectors, legal professionals, and investigators, skip tracing involves tracking down individuals who are elusive due to financial, personal, or legal issues.

While traditional skip tracing relied on methods such as phone books, credit reports, and fieldwork, modern skip tracing now leverages digital tools and data sources. OSINT provides investigators with a powerful suite of techniques to find people by analyzing a person's digital footprint, social media presence, financial activities, and more.

2. The Role of OSINT in Skip Tracing

OSINT plays a central role in modern skip tracing by tapping into the vast amount of publicly available data on the internet. Instead of relying solely on phone calls or old-school methods, private investigators can now leverage a wide range of digital resources to track down a person's whereabouts. Below are some of the ways private investigators use OSINT in their skip tracing efforts:

Public Databases: Investigators begin by searching public databases for key information about the individual. These databases might include court records, criminal histories, business registrations, and property records. Information like address histories, phone numbers, and related aliases often emerges from these resources.

Social Media Scrutiny: Most people have social media profiles, even if they try to keep a low profile. PIs look through platforms like Facebook, LinkedIn, Twitter, Instagram, and even niche forums to identify patterns or details that could point to their current location. A person's posts, friends, locations tagged in pictures, or even hashtags can reveal their activities, networks, and whereabouts.

Phone Records & Email Lookups: Private investigators use reverse phone lookups and email address searches to track down the missing person. If they can identify a phone number or email address linked to the person, they can search for records or cross-reference with other platforms to find additional clues.

Geolocation Tools: OSINT tools like Google Earth, satellite images, and geolocation data from social media and photos can help trace a person's movements or confirm their location at a given time.

People Search Engines: There are specialized OSINT tools like Spokeo, BeenVerified, and Pipl that aggregate data from a wide range of public sources. These platforms provide detailed background checks, which may include address history, known associates, and social media profiles.

3. Step-by-Step Process of OSINT for Skip Tracing

Private investigators typically follow a methodical approach when using OSINT for skip tracing. Below is a breakdown of the typical process:

Step 1: Collect Initial Information

The PI gathers basic information about the person being sought, such as their full name, date of birth, last known address, and any known aliases. The more detailed the initial information, the more effective the investigation will be.

Step 2: Search Public Records

Using OSINT tools, the investigator will start by searching available public records. These might include:

Court and Criminal Records: If the person has a history with the law, the PI can uncover warrants, charges, or ongoing legal matters that could lead to their whereabouts.

Property and Vehicle Registrations: These records can provide valuable information about the person's last known address or car ownership, which could be crucial for tracking them down.

Voter Registrations: Voter registration information can offer current addresses or, in some cases, even a pattern of where the individual is known to vote or reside.

Step 3: Analyze Social Media and Online Activity

After accessing public records, the investigator shifts to social media platforms. Here, they search for posts, photos, connections, check-ins, or anything that could reveal the person's location or activity.

Investigators may focus on:

Location Tags: Many social media platforms allow users to geotag their posts. By searching for posts or photos with location data, investigators can pinpoint where the individual has been recently.

Friends & Connections: A person's social circle can provide critical leads. Investigators check mutual friends, groups, or followers for connections that could lead to discovering their current location.

Profile Analysis: Investigators scrutinize the content shared by the individual, such as job changes, new relationships, or any significant life events that might provide insight into their location or reasons for disappearing.

Step 4: Leverage Specialized People Search Tools

Next, private investigators turn to people search engines or subscription-based databases. These platforms pull together data from a variety of sources and provide detailed background reports on an individual. They might reveal:

Name Variations & Aliases: Some people use multiple names or aliases in different contexts. OSINT tools help to find all known variations and identify patterns.

Address & Phone History: By cross-referencing historical data, investigators can track the person's movements or uncover other relevant locations they may have lived or worked at.

Step 5: Check Messaging Apps and Communication Data

Messaging apps like WhatsApp, Telegram, and Signal may hold valuable information. If investigators can gain access to the person's chat history (through consent, cooperation, or other legal means), they may uncover leads related to the person's location or future intentions.

4. Tools and Technologies Used by Private Investigators

Several OSINT tools are available that help private investigators conduct effective skip tracing. These include:

Spokeo: An online people search engine that aggregates public information from social media profiles, online directories, and more.

Pipl: A tool for finding people's digital footprints across a wide range of social media, public records, and other online resources.

BeenVerified: A platform that offers access to criminal records, property information, and contact details that may help locate a person.

Google Dorking: Using advanced search techniques on Google, investigators can search for specific phrases, keywords, or file types to uncover hidden information about an individual.

Social Media Monitoring Tools: Tools like Hootsuite or Mention allow investigators to monitor social media platforms for real-time updates about the person.

5. Ethical and Legal Considerations

While OSINT is a powerful tool for skip tracing, private investigators must remain within the boundaries of the law. They must respect privacy and avoid illegal methods such as hacking, trespassing, or obtaining information through deceit. Additionally, ethical guidelines must be followed to prevent the misuse of personal data.

In many cases, private investigators need to obtain legal authorization or cooperate with law enforcement before accessing certain types of private data, such as financial records or private communications.

Conclusion

OSINT has revolutionized skip tracing, making it a more efficient and effective process for private investigators. By leveraging public records, social media, geolocation data, and people search tools, PIs can quickly gather leads and track down individuals who have gone off the grid. However, it is crucial that investigators remain ethical, respect privacy laws, and always operate within the legal boundaries while conducting OSINT-based investigations. With the right tools and strategies, OSINT is a powerful asset in the modern skip tracing toolkit.

11.3 Identifying People Who Have Changed Their Identities

Identifying individuals who have changed their identities, either legally or illegally, presents a unique challenge in open-source intelligence (OSINT) investigations. People change their identities for many reasons, from starting a new life after escaping abusive situations to criminal activity such as fraud, evading the law, or engaging in identity theft. Whether they are using fake names, forged documents, or adopting entirely new backgrounds, these individuals can be incredibly elusive. However, OSINT tools and techniques can uncover hidden details that reveal clues about someone's true identity.

This chapter will explore how investigators can use OSINT to identify people who have altered their identities. The process involves a combination of understanding the motivations behind identity changes, analyzing digital footprints, and leveraging advanced investigative methods to uncover discrepancies and inconsistencies in publicly available data.

1. Why Do People Change Their Identities?

The motivations behind changing one's identity are diverse and can range from the benign to the criminal. People may change their identity for a variety of reasons, including:

Escape from Threats: Some individuals change their names and backgrounds to escape danger or harassment, often fleeing domestic violence, stalking, or personal threats.

Starting Fresh: A person might wish to reinvent themselves for personal reasons, such as recovering from a troubled past, overcoming financial ruin, or starting a new career.

Criminal Activity: Criminals may change their identity to avoid detection by authorities, escape financial debts, or evade the law. This can include fugitives, fraudsters, and con artists who steal others' identities or fabricate new ones.

Witness Protection: Individuals involved in government or law enforcement cases may be forced into witness protection programs, which include full identity changes to protect their safety.

Understanding the potential reasons behind identity changes can help OSINT investigators shape their approach and tailor their searches for the most effective results. In many cases, identifying people with changed identities requires a deep dive into inconsistencies in available public records, digital traces, and data points that others may overlook.

2. OSINT Tools and Techniques for Identifying Altered Identities

When investigating individuals who have changed their identities, OSINT investigators typically follow a series of steps to identify patterns, cross-check records, and analyze digital traces. The following tools and techniques can help uncover discrepancies in identity and track down an individual's real identity.

A. Search for Name Variations and Aliases

The first step in identifying someone who may be using a false or altered identity is to look for any name variations, aliases, or misspellings that might have been used over time. People who change their identities often leave behind a trail of old names, which may be discovered through:

Public Records: Public databases such as court records, property deeds, and marriage certificates may reveal multiple names or different spellings used by the individual in the past.

Social Media Profiles: Many people use different names across various platforms, sometimes even including middle names or initials to maintain a level of anonymity. Analyzing their social media profiles could reveal inconsistencies in their name usage.

Name Lookup Services: OSINT tools like Spokeo, Pipl, and BeenVerified aggregate multiple records related to the individual's name. These tools can be used to search for different variations and identify potential aliases.

B. Investigate Address and Location Discrepancies

Individuals who change their identity often also change their location, sometimes moving to different regions or even countries. This can make it difficult to track them through traditional address-based searches. However, several techniques can reveal location changes:

Address History: Public records such as property registrations, tax records, and voter registrations may list multiple addresses over time. Identifying patterns or gaps in the address history can give insight into whether someone has moved or concealed their location.

Geolocation Analysis: Social media posts or photos containing geotags can provide clues about where an individual has been, even if they are using a fake identity. PIs can look for inconsistencies between a person's listed address and their online geotagged activities to identify potential discrepancies.

Reverse Address Lookups: OSINT investigators can also use reverse address lookup tools to track the historical addresses of an individual. This can be useful in identifying hidden properties or addresses associated with an alias.

C. Cross-Check Digital Footprints for Inconsistencies

A person who has changed their identity may attempt to scrub their digital footprint, but some digital traces may still be left behind. Investigators can look for the following:

Social Media Cross-Referencing: Searching for a person's name, email address, or phone number across multiple social media platforms can reveal discrepancies or patterns that indicate identity changes. A person using multiple names or engaging in different activities on various platforms could be hiding something.

Email Address & Phone Number Analysis: Individuals who have altered their identities might continue using the same email address or phone number across several aliases or profiles. Investigators can use OSINT tools to trace these and identify connections between different identities.

Content Analysis: Investigators should scrutinize the content posted by the individual. Subtle clues such as writing styles, the nature of interactions, and patterns of behavior may reveal whether someone has taken on a new persona or is using an alias.

D. Check for Document Forgery or Fake Paper Trails

In many cases, people who change their identities do so by forging official documents. These forged papers can include birth certificates, passports, or social security records. OSINT investigations, however, may uncover discrepancies:

Public Record Cross-Verification: A cross-check of records in official databases such as the Department of Motor Vehicles (DMV) or government-issued documents can help reveal instances where someone may have provided false or altered details. Look for discrepancies in birth dates, locations, or names.

Fake Social Security Numbers (SSNs): A person's SSN can be an indicator of their real identity. Using OSINT tools, investigators can look for fraudulent SSNs or numbers that don't match known patterns of issue.

Background Check Services: Some OSINT tools offer comprehensive background checks that cross-reference multiple records from birth certificates, educational documents, and other official identification papers to verify authenticity.

E. Monitor for Data Breaches and Leaked Information

Sometimes, individuals who have changed their identities may have left behind sensitive information exposed in past data breaches. Investigators can look for leaks from social media platforms, online shopping sites, and other services where personal data is stored.

Dark Web Searches: If someone has been involved in criminal activity, their altered identity may be for sale on the dark web. OSINT techniques can track any leaks, stolen data, or compromised information related to the person's new identity.

Data Breach Monitoring: OSINT tools like Have I Been Pwned and other data breach databases can help identify if the person's previous identity has been exposed and whether there are any connections to their changed identity.

3. Ethical and Legal Considerations in Identity Investigation

Investigating someone who has changed their identity involves sensitive and potentially intrusive methods. While OSINT relies on publicly available data, investigators must be mindful of privacy laws and ethical considerations.

Respecting Privacy: Investigators should avoid crossing ethical boundaries, such as hacking, impersonating individuals, or using deceptive practices to gain access to private information.

Compliance with the Law: It is essential to stay within the legal framework of the jurisdiction where the investigation is taking place. Using certain information or techniques may require legal authorization, and investigators must ensure they are not violating laws related to data protection or privacy.

Accountability and Responsibility: Investigators must also ensure that the information they uncover is used responsibly. Uncovering someone's hidden identity can have significant consequences, and investigators should consider the potential impact of their findings.

Conclusion

Identifying people who have changed their identities is a complex and multifaceted task that requires a strategic approach and a deep understanding of OSINT techniques. By cross-referencing data, using advanced search tools, and analyzing digital footprints, investigators can uncover discrepancies and hidden patterns that expose false identities. However, it's crucial to remember that these investigations must be conducted with respect for privacy, ethical standards, and legal boundaries. When used correctly, OSINT can be an invaluable tool in uncovering the true identities of those who attempt to disappear or cover up their past.

11.4 Techniques for Tracing Runaways & Kidnapping Victims

Tracing runaways and kidnapping victims is one of the most urgent and emotionally charged applications of open-source intelligence (OSINT). The search for these individuals often requires a multi-faceted approach, combining traditional investigative techniques with advanced OSINT methods to gather crucial information and uncover hidden clues. The process can be highly challenging, as those seeking to escape or hide may go to great lengths to cover their tracks, whether by using false identities, avoiding digital footprints, or physically removing themselves from public spaces. However, OSINT can still provide critical insights into their whereabouts and circumstances, potentially saving lives.

This section delves into the various OSINT techniques that can be employed to trace runaways and kidnapping victims, exploring the critical role digital footprints, social media, and public records play in these investigations.

1. Understanding the Context: Runaways vs. Kidnapping Victims

Before diving into specific OSINT techniques, it is important to understand the key differences between runaways and kidnapping victims:

Runaways: These individuals leave their homes voluntarily, often due to personal issues, abuse, or the desire to escape a difficult situation. Runaways may attempt to distance themselves from family, friends, and authorities. However, their digital footprint might still offer valuable clues, especially when combined with traditional search methods.

Kidnapping Victims: Kidnapped individuals are forcibly taken against their will, often by strangers, acquaintances, or perpetrators with malicious intent. The search for kidnapping victims typically requires immediate action and cross-coordination between law enforcement agencies, families, and private investigators. In many cases, digital evidence such as geolocation data, phone activity, and social media interactions can provide critical insights into the location and situation of the victim.

The OSINT techniques employed in both cases are similar but may vary depending on the circumstances of the disappearance. With that in mind, the following strategies can be leveraged to trace these missing individuals.

2. Social Media & Digital Footprints

Social media platforms provide a rich source of information that can reveal key clues about the location and activities of both runaways and kidnapping victims. OSINT investigators can use social media analysis tools to track the digital footprints left behind by the missing individual or potential perpetrators.

A. Scrutinize Posts and Activity Patterns

Runaways and kidnapping victims might post on social media platforms, share photos, or even communicate with people about their situation or whereabouts. Investigators can:

- **Review Recent Posts**: By searching for the individual's social media accounts, investigators can examine recent posts, photos, check-ins, or comments that could hint at the person's location, emotions, or intentions prior to the disappearance.
- **Analyze Sentiment & Language**: The language and sentiment used in social media posts can reveal important emotional clues, such as whether the individual was under stress, seeking help, or planning to leave.
- **Look for Hidden Messages**: Sometimes individuals in distress may leave subtle hints or coded messages in their posts, images, or comments. OSINT investigators should be trained to spot these hidden signs, such as indirect statements, unfamiliar locations, or unexplained references that might indicate the person is in danger.

B. Geotagging & Location Data

Geotagging is a powerful tool for tracking the movement of a missing person. If they shared photos or posts with embedded location data before their disappearance, investigators can:

- **Track GPS Coordinates**: By analyzing photos or videos posted on social media, investigators can extract GPS coordinates embedded in the metadata to trace the last known locations of the individual.
- **Identify Common Locations**: Even if location data is not directly attached to a post, investigators can cross-reference locations the individual has visited frequently, such as specific restaurants, parks, or public spaces, to pinpoint areas they might head to.

- **Cross-Platform Geolocation**: Investigators can cross-check location data on different social platforms, such as Facebook, Instagram, or Snapchat, to create a timeline of the individual's last known movements.

3. Reverse Image Search for Identifying Photos or Videos

Runaways or kidnapped victims may appear in photos or videos posted online, whether they are in the custody of perpetrators, trying to seek help, or sharing their experiences on the run. A reverse image search can help investigators track these images back to their source, whether it be an online post, website, or social media profile.

- **Use Reverse Image Search Tools**: Tools like Google Reverse Image Search, TinEye, and Yandex can help investigators track where images posted by or of the missing person are being used online. By uploading a known photo of the individual, investigators can search for matches across the web.
- **Analyze Video Footage**: In cases where videos of the missing person are found, OSINT techniques can be used to analyze the video's metadata for clues, as well as the content itself to identify landmarks, locations, or even the identity of the person sharing the video.

4. Investigating Phone and Communication Records

Both runaways and kidnapping victims often have their phones with them, and communication devices can be key to tracing their movements. Investigators can explore several avenues in this domain:

A. Phone Number & GPS Tracking

- **Phone Number Lookup**: Tools like Truecaller and Spokeo can help identify who might have contacted the missing person before their disappearance. Reverse phone lookups could uncover new leads about the last known communications.
- **GPS Data**: If the individual's phone is still operational and being used, investigators may be able to track its location in real time. For kidnapped victims, this could involve collaborating with law enforcement or the phone provider to access location data via the phone's GPS capabilities.

B. Text Messages & Call Logs

By analyzing text messages, call logs, and even emails, OSINT investigators can uncover communication patterns, specific individuals they were in contact with, or suspicious activity just prior to the disappearance. Even encrypted apps like WhatsApp and Telegram can provide valuable clues through forensic decryption tools, though access to these messages may require legal authority or collaboration with law enforcement.

5. Investigating Financial & Transaction Records

Runaways and kidnapping victims may attempt to use financial systems to survive or communicate with others. OSINT investigators can search for patterns of financial transactions that could indicate the individual's location or activities.

- **Bank Records & Credit Card Activity**: Bank transactions, especially in areas far from the individual's last known location, can be a strong indication of where a runaway or kidnapping victim might have gone. Investigators can use public financial records, such as credit card transactions or even open-source payment apps, to track purchases or money transfers.
- **Prepaid Cards & Gift Cards**: If the person has used prepaid cards, gift cards, or money transfer services like Western Union, OSINT tools can track these payments and provide insight into potential locations where the cards were used.

6. Crowdsourcing & Public Appeals

In some cases, the public's help can be instrumental in tracing runaways and kidnapping victims. Investigators can create online appeals or posts on social media, asking for tips and information.

- **Crowdsourcing Investigations**: By posting missing persons alerts on social media, relevant forums, or even creating specific hashtags, investigators can engage the public in the search for the individual. Crowdsourcing can yield surprising results, with individuals in specific areas providing crucial information that leads to finding the victim.
- **Monitoring Public Databases**: Investigators can use public databases, including missing persons registries, to cross-check known cases and gather more leads.

7. Working with Law Enforcement & Private Investigators

While OSINT is an invaluable tool for finding missing people, it should not be relied upon exclusively. For cases involving potential criminal activity, law enforcement and private investigators can provide essential support.

- **Coordinating with Law Enforcement**: Investigators should always work closely with law enforcement agencies to ensure that all available resources, from search warrants to advanced forensic techniques, are used to locate the individual.
- **Private Investigator Expertise**: Private investigators experienced in OSINT can assist in tracing runaways and kidnapping victims by applying advanced search techniques, accessing databases, and navigating legal and ethical considerations.

Conclusion

Tracing runaways and kidnapping victims is a challenging task, but the application of OSINT can significantly enhance the search efforts. By leveraging social media, geolocation data, financial records, reverse image searches, and crowdsourcing, investigators can uncover vital clues that may lead to the person's location and eventual recovery. However, these techniques should always be applied with a sense of urgency, precision, and collaboration with law enforcement to ensure the best chances of a successful outcome.

11.5 Using OSINT to Assist Law Enforcement & Families

The search for missing persons is a deeply emotional and urgent matter, often involving law enforcement agencies, private investigators, and the families of the missing individuals. Open Source Intelligence (OSINT) has emerged as an indispensable tool in this effort, offering critical insights and leads that can help track down those who are lost, whether they are runaways, victims of abductions, or individuals who have disappeared under mysterious circumstances. OSINT can aid law enforcement agencies and families alike in locating missing persons quickly, efficiently, and with a broader reach than traditional investigative techniques alone.

In this section, we will explore how OSINT can be utilized effectively to assist law enforcement and families in the search for missing individuals, highlighting both the technical aspects of OSINT investigations and the collaborative efforts required to ensure successful outcomes.

1. The Role of OSINT in Missing Person Investigations

OSINT is defined as intelligence collected from publicly available sources, including social media, websites, databases, and public records. The value of OSINT in missing persons investigations lies in its ability to provide leads and data that might not be immediately available through conventional methods, such as interviews and physical searches. For law enforcement, OSINT can supplement ongoing investigations, while for families, it can provide actionable insights in real-time, often before formal investigations are launched or while they are still in their early stages.

OSINT aids in two primary ways:

- **Identifying the Location**: By examining digital footprints, investigators can track the whereabouts of missing individuals, including the last known location or any patterns of movement leading to their disappearance.
- **Understanding the Context**: OSINT can also help determine whether the person left voluntarily, was abducted, or was involved in an accident. The online behavior and communication of a missing person can reveal personal circumstances that may have prompted their disappearance.

2. Social Media Analysis for Locating Missing Persons

Social media platforms serve as digital time capsules that capture an individual's thoughts, interactions, and even location. These platforms provide investigators with a wealth of information, such as posts, comments, and shared media that can be crucial in tracing a missing person's path.

A. Scraping Posts & Content from Social Media

A critical step in any OSINT investigation is reviewing the missing person's social media accounts. Platforms like Facebook, Instagram, Twitter (X), Snapchat, and TikTok often contain geotagged content, such as photos, check-ins, and location-based tags, that may point to the individual's last known location. Analyzing posts made shortly before the disappearance can uncover clues to the person's emotional state, social interactions, and even relationships with potential suspects.

- **Public Posts and Comments**: Examining public posts and the interaction between the missing person and their network can reveal key leads. A seemingly innocent comment or post could hold the key to uncovering the person's whereabouts or motivations.
- **Location Data**: Many social media platforms allow users to tag their locations in real time. By identifying where the missing person has recently been or interacted with others, investigators can create a timeline of their activities leading up to the disappearance.

B. Searching for Direct Communications

Social media direct messaging and private posts may also be insightful, especially if the missing individual has been in contact with someone who knows their location. While accessing private messages requires proper legal procedures, public posts that mention the individual, friends, or acquaintances can help identify connections and possible suspects. Monitoring groups or pages where the person was active may also provide leads on who they communicated with last.

3. The Importance of Geolocation & Digital Footprints

Geolocation data is a critical tool for OSINT investigators. By examining the digital footprints left by a missing person's devices, it's often possible to establish their movements, interactions, and whereabouts leading up to their disappearance.

A. GPS and Location Data

Mobile phones, GPS devices, and even smartwatches typically track the user's location, and this data can be invaluable in locating a missing person. Law enforcement can request GPS data from mobile phone carriers, but public sources like photos, videos, and social media posts can also reveal location information.

- **Geotagged Photos**: Photos uploaded to social media or stored on personal devices may contain embedded metadata that reveals the precise location where the photo was taken. Even if the individual attempted to hide or delete this data, forensic techniques may recover it.
- **Location History on Platforms**: Some apps, including Google Maps and Instagram, track location history for users, allowing investigators to trace the individual's movements over time and pinpoint the last known locations.

B. Search Engine & Online Data Analysis

OSINT investigators can leverage search engines, digital archives, and personal websites to find out where the missing person has been or what they were researching. For example, search history, blog posts, or comments on forums may contain valuable contextual clues.

- **Online Searches and Comments**: A person's browsing habits and the search terms they frequently used may provide critical insights into what they were experiencing before their disappearance, such as searches related to fleeing, being harmed, or even health concerns.

- **Reviewing Public Records**: Combining digital footprints with public records like voter registrations, property databases, and even old social security numbers can yield leads on where the individual might be located, especially if they tried to hide their identity or change their location.

4. Leveraging Public Records & Database Searches

Public records can be a goldmine for information about a missing person's past or activities. They often contain valuable identifiers, such as addresses, phone numbers, or aliases, that can provide investigators with clues about a missing person's current whereabouts or possible movements.

A. Search for Recent Transactions or Activity

- **Financial Transactions**: Investigators can search for financial activity, such as credit card transactions, bank records, or online purchases, to track a missing person's spending habits and identify areas where they might have gone.
- **Public Records Databases**: Investigators can query public databases to find out if the missing individual has registered for a driver's license, moved to a new address, or applied for government benefits under a new identity.

B. Cross-Referencing Data

By cross-referencing social media accounts with public databases, investigators can build a more accurate profile of the missing person, potentially identifying new leads and contacts that were previously overlooked.

5. Collaboration with Law Enforcement & Families

While OSINT can provide a significant advantage in locating a missing person, it is critical for investigators to collaborate with law enforcement and the families of the missing. Law enforcement agencies can provide valuable resources, legal authority, and investigative techniques that complement OSINT, such as subpoenaing private data from tech companies, conducting interviews, or issuing search warrants.

- **Sharing Leads**: OSINT investigators should be transparent with law enforcement, sharing their findings and insights to help build a more comprehensive search strategy.
- **Working with Families**: Families can provide firsthand knowledge about the missing person's behaviors, habits, and relationships, which can inform the OSINT

process. Additionally, by involving the public through social media campaigns and public appeals, families can help raise awareness and encourage tips from the community.

6. Ethical & Legal Considerations

While OSINT is an effective tool, it must always be used within the bounds of the law and ethical guidelines. Investigators should be mindful of privacy issues and ensure they are not violating any individual's rights while conducting searches.

- **Adhering to Legal Frameworks**: OSINT investigations should follow the rules and guidelines set by law enforcement agencies, ensuring that all data collection and analysis methods are legal. Engaging with legal professionals to ensure compliance with privacy laws and data protection regulations is essential.
- **Respecting the Family's Privacy**: Sensitive information about the missing person and their family should be handled with care. Investigators must respect the confidentiality of the family's personal details while conducting their search.

7. Conclusion

OSINT is an invaluable resource for assisting law enforcement and families in locating missing persons. By analyzing digital footprints, social media activity, geolocation data, and public records, investigators can uncover valuable leads that would otherwise remain hidden. However, the power of OSINT must be coupled with responsible collaboration, ethical practices, and legal compliance to ensure that the search for missing persons is conducted in a way that respects privacy and adheres to the law. With the right combination of OSINT tools and investigative strategies, the chances of successfully finding a missing individual and bringing them to safety increase significantly.

11.6 Case Study: Finding a Missing Person Using Online Clues

In this case study, we will explore how Open Source Intelligence (OSINT) techniques can be utilized effectively to locate a missing person by following the digital clues left behind in publicly available online sources. This case involves a missing person who had disappeared under suspicious circumstances, and the investigation utilized OSINT to uncover key leads that ultimately resulted in locating the individual.

Background

The subject of this case study is "Anna," a 32-year-old woman who went missing under mysterious circumstances after a heated argument with her partner. After being reported missing, her family and local law enforcement agencies began a search, but there were no immediate breakthroughs. Anna's phone was found in her car, but there was no sign of where she had gone.

As law enforcement efforts were ongoing, Anna's family also sought the help of a private investigator who specialized in OSINT. The investigator used various online techniques to find clues that would lead to Anna's whereabouts, eventually discovering important information that helped solve the case.

Step 1: Gathering Preliminary Information

The first step in the OSINT investigation was to gather basic personal information about Anna—anything that could help narrow down potential leads. Her social media profiles were analyzed, and a search for her name, recent online activities, and known associates was conducted across multiple platforms.

Social Media: Anna had active accounts on Facebook, Instagram, and LinkedIn. Her Facebook page revealed details about her personal life, recent posts, and the people she interacted with. Instagram provided visual insights, including photos taken in specific locations. LinkedIn offered professional information, such as her current job and educational background.

The OSINT investigator also reviewed Anna's publicly available social media posts, looking for clues that could point to her emotional state or upcoming plans. A recent Facebook post, for instance, included a picture of Anna at a café with a friend—a person whom Anna had known for years. This individual would become a key figure in the investigation.

Step 2: Tracking Digital Footprints and Geolocation Clues

The next critical step was to analyze the geolocation data attached to Anna's social media posts. Many of her Instagram photos were geotagged with the locations where they were taken, allowing the investigator to map out her recent movements.

Instagram & Facebook Posts: The investigator identified several Instagram photos taken in various locations in the days leading up to Anna's disappearance. One photo, taken two days before she went missing, showed Anna standing in front of a well-known downtown park. The post was tagged with a location, which helped pinpoint a specific area she had recently visited.

Phone & GPS Data: Although Anna's phone was found abandoned in her car, her GPS data from Google Maps was accessible through her account. The investigator obtained permission from law enforcement to access the last known locations linked to Anna's account. One of the locations was a remote area about 10 miles outside the city. This clue suggested that Anna had gone to a secluded spot, potentially as a result of an emotional decision.

Step 3: Cross-Referencing Social Media and Online Conversations

The investigator then focused on cross-referencing Anna's social media interactions, particularly her messages and comments, with her contacts. By analyzing Facebook Messenger and Instagram DMs, the investigator identified communication with her close friend, "Ben," from the day before Anna's disappearance.

Facebook Messenger & Texts: Anna's last message to Ben was emotional, expressing that she needed to "clear her head" and that she felt overwhelmed. Ben, who lived in another city, had suggested that she go for a walk in the park to calm down. This conversation provided context to Anna's state of mind, indicating she might have intentionally distanced herself to think things over.

Engagement in Online Groups: The investigator also reviewed any online groups or communities Anna participated in. One of the groups on Facebook was related to hiking and outdoor activities, and Anna had recently commented on a post discussing hiking trails in the area near the park where she had taken the photo.

Step 4: Utilizing Public Records and Government Databases

To further investigate Anna's potential whereabouts, the OSINT investigator checked public records, including property and voting databases, to gather more information about her.

Public Property Records: A search of property records revealed that Anna owned a small piece of land near the same area where her phone had last pinged. This discovery added weight to the theory that she had gone to a familiar location to reflect.

Driver's License & License Plate Information: A search of her driver's license information through a public records database revealed that Anna had recently updated her address, which was located near the area she had visited. This led the investigator to believe that she had likely taken a drive to her property.

Step 5: Identifying Key Witnesses and Following Up on Leads

Based on the information gathered from social media, geolocation data, and public records, the investigator identified several key individuals who might have had additional insights into Anna's whereabouts.

Ben's Role: Ben, the friend who had last communicated with Anna, was contacted for further details. He confirmed that Anna had been planning to visit a local park, which aligned with the geolocation data gathered earlier. Ben also noted that Anna had been feeling emotionally overwhelmed by personal issues and was looking for some solitude.

Park Rangers: The investigator contacted park rangers who worked in the area where Anna's geotagged photo had been taken. The rangers confirmed that Anna had been spotted on the trails a day before she went missing. They also mentioned that she had asked for directions to a remote section of the park, which suggested she was intentionally seeking a private spot.

Step 6: Final Discovery

Using the leads from geolocation data, social media, and witness testimonies, the OSINT investigator traced Anna's movements to a remote cabin near the park. The cabin was registered to a relative of Anna's, and records indicated that it was used for occasional weekend retreats. When authorities arrived at the cabin, they found Anna safe and unharmed, albeit emotionally distressed.

Anna confirmed that she had gone to the cabin to escape the pressures of her personal life and had not intended to disappear. However, she had lost access to her phone and had not been able to contact anyone, leading to confusion and concern from her family.

Conclusion

This case study highlights the critical role of OSINT in missing persons investigations. By carefully analyzing digital footprints, social media posts, geolocation data, and public records, the OSINT investigator was able to piece together a timeline of events and locate

Anna safely. The combination of digital clues and traditional investigative techniques provided a comprehensive approach that led to a successful resolution.

While OSINT cannot replace the efforts of law enforcement and other investigative professionals, it can significantly enhance the search for missing individuals by providing leads and insights that would otherwise remain hidden. This case demonstrates the power of online clues in locating people, especially in situations where traditional methods may not be immediately effective.

12. Case Study: High-Profile People OSINT

Investigating high-profile individuals—such as politicians, celebrities, and executives—presents unique challenges and opportunities in OSINT. This chapter provides a real-world case study demonstrating advanced techniques used to analyze public figures' digital footprints, social media presence, and public records. You'll learn how to track media appearances, uncover hidden connections, and assess security vulnerabilities while navigating legal and ethical boundaries. By dissecting a high-profile investigation, this chapter offers valuable insights into the complexities of OSINT at scale.

12.1 Investigating Public Figures & Celebrities Using OSINT

In the age of digital information, public figures and celebrities leave behind significant digital footprints. These traces—whether intentional or inadvertent—can provide OSINT investigators with valuable insights into their activities, connections, and personal lives. Investigating public figures and celebrities using Open Source Intelligence (OSINT) involves carefully combing through publicly available data from social media, news articles, public records, and other online sources to uncover patterns, behaviors, and affiliations that may not be immediately obvious. This chapter focuses on the techniques and ethical considerations involved in conducting OSINT investigations on public figures.

Understanding Public Figures & Celebrities in the Digital Age

Public figures and celebrities are individuals who, by virtue of their fame, have become subjects of public scrutiny. They often have large social media followings, frequent media appearances, and professional engagements that expose them to intense public and media attention. Their every move, interaction, and statement can be tracked through online platforms, news outlets, and even personal blogs. However, because of their elevated status, the line between public interest and personal privacy can sometimes blur.

Unlike private individuals, public figures have chosen to place themselves in the spotlight, and thus, a greater degree of scrutiny is often expected. This makes them both easy and challenging to investigate, as they may be more guarded in their personal lives, knowing that their actions are subject to public examination.

OSINT investigations into celebrities and public figures can provide a wealth of data—whether for security purposes, journalistic research, or general interest—but it is essential to maintain a careful balance between gathering useful information and respecting their privacy rights.

Key Techniques for Investigating Public Figures Using OSINT

Social Media Analysis:

Public figures often provide the richest source of data about themselves through social media platforms. Celebrities share updates, thoughts, and personal insights on platforms such as Instagram, Twitter, Facebook, TikTok, and LinkedIn. By analyzing their posts, stories, and interactions, investigators can gather detailed information regarding:

- **Professional Activities**: Celebrities frequently update their fans on work-related activities, such as movie releases, new product lines, or public appearances. Analyzing these updates can offer insights into their career trajectory and future projects.
- **Personal Life**: While public figures often curate what they share, personal moments—such as vacations, family gatherings, and relationships—can still be uncovered. Investigators can also detect subtle changes in the celebrity's tone, behavior, or environment that may hint at personal developments or controversies.
- **Social Interactions**: By examining who a public figure interacts with, the tone of those interactions, and how often they occur, investigators can uncover associations with other celebrities, influencers, or businesses. This is particularly useful in understanding relationships within the entertainment industry.

Cross-Platform Investigation:

Celebrities and public figures often maintain profiles across multiple platforms. Investigators can cross-reference the data found on one platform with that from another to build a clearer and more comprehensive picture. For example, a celebrity might post a picture on Instagram and then share the same image on Twitter or a link to an article or product on LinkedIn. By connecting the dots between platforms, investigators can identify:

- **Patterns**: What times, locations, and activities does the celebrity regularly share? Do these match up with other public events or known appearances?
- **Multiple Identities**: Some celebrities maintain multiple profiles across different platforms—one for professional use and another for personal life. Investigators need to carefully differentiate these profiles and ensure they're not mixing private and public personas.

Tracking Mentions & News Coverage:

Public figures are frequently mentioned in the media, whether it be through interviews, news stories, or press releases. Investigators can track mentions of the celebrity across various sources, including:

- **News Outlets**: By using OSINT tools that aggregate news stories, investigators can stay up-to-date with the latest information on the celebrity, from controversial events to positive milestones.
- **Blogs & Forums**: Many public figures have dedicated fan sites, blogs, and forums where personal anecdotes, sightings, or speculative information may be shared. Although the accuracy of such content should be verified, it can still provide valuable context.
- **Online Databases**: OSINT investigators often rely on databases that index press releases, court filings, and other publicly available legal documents that may contain information about a public figure's personal and professional life.

Public Records & Legal Filings:

Public figures are subject to various legal processes—whether for business registrations, court cases, property transactions, or financial disclosures. Many of these records are accessible through online public databases. Key public records for OSINT investigation into celebrities may include:

- **Property & Real Estate Transactions**: Public figures often buy and sell properties, and these transactions can provide insight into where they live, their financial investments, and any patterns related to their lifestyle.
- **Court Records**: Celebrities frequently find themselves in court, whether for lawsuits, divorces, or criminal charges. Accessing court records and legal filings can uncover significant events in their personal and professional lives.
- **Business & Corporate Filings**: Many celebrities invest in businesses or form corporations. Public business records can provide insight into their financial ventures, partnerships, and ownership stakes.

Video & Audio Analysis:

Public figures often appear in interviews, public speeches, or media broadcasts. Analyzing the content of these videos and audio recordings can offer insights into their views, language use, and behavior. Investigators can look for:

- **Body Language**: Non-verbal communication in video footage—such as gestures, posture, and facial expressions—can provide additional context about their emotional state or sincerity.
- **Speech Patterns & Tone**: Audio analysis tools can also help analyze speech patterns, identifying any inconsistencies or anomalies that could indicate stress, deception, or hidden messages.

Challenges in Investigating Public Figures

While OSINT offers numerous tools for investigating public figures, there are several challenges to consider:

Misinformation & Disinformation: Public figures often face rumors and false information, especially on social media. Investigators must cross-check sources and verify the credibility of any claims before relying on them for further investigation.

Privacy Concerns: Even public figures have a right to privacy. It's essential for OSINT investigators to adhere to ethical standards and avoid crossing the line between public information and private matters. Investigators must avoid utilizing methods that violate the subject's privacy, such as hacking or unauthorized access to private accounts.

Media Bias: Traditional media outlets can be biased in how they report on celebrities, sometimes sensationalizing or misrepresenting facts. Investigators should always triangulate data from multiple sources to ensure that the findings are balanced and unbiased.

Ethical Considerations in Investigating Celebrities

When it comes to investigating public figures, ethical considerations must guide every step of the process. Investigators should be transparent about the purpose of their work, avoiding any activities that could harm the individual's reputation or breach their privacy. The lines between public and private life are often blurred, but it's critical to remain respectful and responsible in how this information is used.

- **Transparency**: If the investigation is being conducted for journalistic purposes or on behalf of an organization, it is essential to make the intent clear.
- **Public Interest vs. Sensationalism**: Celebrities are public figures, but that doesn't mean every aspect of their lives should be open for scrutiny. Investigators must differentiate between gathering information for legitimate reasons (e.g., security or fact-checking) and engaging in sensationalism.

- **Legal Compliance**: OSINT investigators must comply with all relevant privacy laws, such as GDPR, and avoid engaging in illegal activities such as hacking or surveillance.

Conclusion

Investigating public figures and celebrities using OSINT can uncover a wealth of valuable information, but it comes with unique ethical, legal, and professional challenges. Public figures may not have the same level of privacy as private individuals, but OSINT professionals must always tread carefully and ensure that their investigations are done with integrity, respect, and within legal boundaries. By following a responsible approach, OSINT can be a powerful tool in uncovering facts, exposing potential risks, and verifying the truth behind public personas.

12.2 How Journalists Use OSINT to Uncover Hidden Truths

In the digital era, journalists have increasingly turned to Open Source Intelligence (OSINT) as a valuable tool for investigative reporting. With vast amounts of publicly available information online, journalists now have access to a treasure trove of data that can help them uncover hidden truths, verify claims, and expose corruption, fraud, and other societal issues. OSINT has become an indispensable tool in modern journalism, enabling reporters to follow the digital trail left by individuals, companies, and governments to uncover stories that would otherwise remain hidden.

This section delves into the methods and strategies journalists employ to utilize OSINT in their investigations, the challenges they face, and the ethical considerations that must be taken into account when using this powerful tool to uncover hidden truths.

Understanding OSINT in Journalism

OSINT refers to any information that is publicly available on the internet, including social media, news articles, blogs, databases, official government websites, and other open platforms. For journalists, OSINT provides the ability to gather information quickly and efficiently, without resorting to intrusive or covert methods. It can be used to corroborate existing stories, uncover new leads, fact-check claims, and monitor developments in real-time.

Some of the most important elements of OSINT include:

Social Media: Platforms like Twitter, Facebook, Instagram, and LinkedIn offer a wealth of information about individuals, organizations, and events. Journalists use these platforms to track trends, monitor public sentiment, verify statements, and find connections between people and events.

Public Records: Information from government agencies, such as court records, business registrations, property deeds, and tax filings, can provide insights into the actions of both individuals and institutions. Journalists use these records to track financial dealings, identify political contributions, and expose corruption or fraud.

Multimedia & Open Databases: Open-source tools allow journalists to analyze videos, photos, and other media. For instance, reverse image search tools can help verify whether an image has been used out of context, and geolocation tools can track where photos or videos were taken.

How Journalists Use OSINT to Investigate Stories

Fact-Checking Claims & Public Statements:

A core use of OSINT in journalism is to verify facts and public statements. Given the prevalence of misinformation, journalists use OSINT to fact-check claims made by public figures, corporations, or government agencies. This may include:

Analyzing Official Documents: Journalists access open government databases to verify facts regarding legislation, financial disclosures, or public announcements. They may search for contracts, tax filings, or permits to confirm or challenge claims made in the media.

Cross-Referencing News Stories: Investigative journalists often cross-reference multiple news reports, official documents, and social media content to confirm the accuracy of facts. OSINT helps uncover discrepancies or inconsistencies that may indicate a story has been fabricated or misleading.

Checking Dates & Locations: By analyzing online content, journalists can check the dates and locations of incidents or events. This helps them verify that the reported facts match the public records, or to trace the origin of a viral video, for example.

Tracking Corporate and Political Influence:

Corporations, politicians, and political entities often leave digital footprints that reveal their connections, investments, and lobbying efforts. Journalists can use OSINT to investigate these areas and uncover hidden truths about their interests and actions. This can involve:

Investigating Political Donations & Lobbying: By searching public records, journalists can uncover political donations and lobbying activities. These records can reveal the influence of corporate interests on policy decisions and expose potential conflicts of interest.

Uncovering Corporate Relationships: Journalists track business dealings by investigating public records related to company ownership, partnerships, or mergers. They may uncover links between influential individuals, organizations, or governments that are hidden beneath the surface.

Investigating Corruption & Financial Misdeeds:

Financial corruption and corporate fraud are among the most common topics that investigative journalists tackle using OSINT. Through public records, financial statements, and other available resources, journalists can uncover irregularities, hidden assets, and questionable financial practices. Key investigative methods include:

Analyzing Offshore Accounts & Shell Companies: Investigative journalists use OSINT to identify offshore accounts and shell companies that may be used to launder money or hide assets. By reviewing public financial filings, journalists can often trace complex networks of transactions and ownership.

Tracking Money Flow & Conflicts of Interest: OSINT helps track the flow of money within organizations and political systems. Journalists can uncover financial ties between politicians, businesses, and non-governmental organizations that may suggest corruption or unethical practices.

Exposing Human Rights Violations & Atrocities:

Journalists and human rights organizations frequently rely on OSINT to document and expose human rights abuses, war crimes, and other atrocities. Social media platforms, online videos, and satellite imagery offer powerful resources for uncovering evidence of such violations. Some techniques include:

Crowdsourced Information: Journalists monitor social media platforms and crowdsourced websites to track real-time reports of human rights violations, protests, or violence in conflict zones. They may validate the legitimacy of such reports by analyzing geolocation data, cross-referencing eyewitness testimonies, or analyzing videos and photos.

Using Satellite & Geospatial Data: Tools such as Google Earth and satellite imagery allow journalists to track the movement of military forces, monitor the destruction of infrastructure, and assess environmental damage caused by human rights abuses or conflict.

Investigating Organized Crime & Terrorism:

OSINT is also crucial for journalists investigating organized crime and terrorism. By analyzing online communication patterns, transaction records, and other open data, journalists can uncover networks of criminal activity. Some areas where OSINT is particularly valuable include:

Tracking Terrorist Financing: Journalists use OSINT to track financial transactions that may be linked to terrorist organizations. Publicly available information such as international money transfers, cryptocurrency transactions, and unregulated markets can help expose funding sources for criminal activity.

Investigating Transnational Crime Networks: OSINT tools can help journalists investigate complex criminal networks, including human trafficking, drug smuggling, and arms trade. By cross-referencing social media, news articles, and financial records, they can expose the connections and activities of such groups.

Challenges in Using OSINT for Investigative Journalism

Data Overload & Verification:

One of the biggest challenges in using OSINT is the sheer volume of information available. The internet is flooded with data from various sources, and distinguishing between credible information and misinformation is a complex task. Journalists need to employ rigorous verification methods, such as cross-referencing multiple sources and using advanced tools to track the provenance of images, videos, and documents.

Legal and Ethical Concerns:

While OSINT involves publicly available data, ethical boundaries must still be respected. Journalists must ensure they do not infringe upon privacy rights or engage in invasive surveillance. There are also concerns about the legality of scraping data or using certain OSINT tools, especially if they circumvent paywalls or terms of service.

Access to Restricted or Paywalled Data:

Many valuable sources of information, such as detailed court records or proprietary databases, may not be freely accessible. Journalists may face challenges in obtaining key information that could make or break an investigation. Additionally, the use of paywalled content or subscription-based services often requires journalists to find alternative sources to support their findings.

Ethical Considerations in OSINT Investigations

When using OSINT to uncover hidden truths, journalists must adhere to ethical principles that protect both the subjects of their investigations and the integrity of the reporting process. Some key ethical guidelines include:

Transparency: Journalists must disclose their methods and sources whenever possible to maintain credibility and transparency. They should avoid relying on anonymous or unverified sources unless necessary.

Respect for Privacy: Even when investigating public figures or organizations, journalists must avoid crossing the line between public interest and invasion of privacy. Information gathered through OSINT should be used responsibly and only when relevant to the story.

Accountability: Journalists must take responsibility for the accuracy and fairness of their work. OSINT investigations should be well-documented and thoroughly fact-checked to avoid spreading misinformation.

Conclusion

OSINT has revolutionized the way journalists uncover hidden truths and report on complex issues. By utilizing publicly available data from social media, public records, multimedia sources, and geospatial information, journalists can expose corruption, hold the powerful accountable, and tell the stories that matter. However, with great power comes great responsibility. Journalists must navigate the challenges of data overload, legal concerns, and ethical considerations to ensure that their OSINT investigations remain credible, responsible, and respectful of privacy. When used properly, OSINT is an invaluable tool for investigative journalism, helping to shine a light on the stories that matter most.

12.3 Tracking Politicians & Business Leaders for Accountability

In the age of digital transparency, Open Source Intelligence (OSINT) has become an essential tool for tracking politicians and business leaders. With vast amounts of publicly available data, investigative journalists, watchdog organizations, and activists can use OSINT to uncover financial ties, political donations, conflicts of interest, and unethical practices. By analyzing this wealth of digital footprints, OSINT provides an invaluable resource for holding politicians and business leaders accountable for their actions. This section explores the methods, challenges, and ethical considerations involved in using OSINT to track influential figures in both the political and business worlds.

The Role of OSINT in Political Accountability

OSINT allows journalists, activists, and the public to keep track of political figures' actions, financial dealings, and policy decisions, providing greater transparency in governance. Here are some key areas where OSINT can be used to track politicians and ensure accountability:

Tracking Political Donations & Campaign Financing: Political donations are one of the most common ways that politicians can be influenced or "bought" by special interest groups or corporations. OSINT tools can help identify the flow of money through campaign contributions, super PACs, and other funding vehicles. By analyzing public records, journalists and watchdog groups can trace where the money is coming from and whether there is a pattern of influence or conflicts of interest.

Key Resources:

- Federal Election Commission (FEC) databases
- Local and state electoral commission records
- OpenSecrets.org (tracking political donations)

Identifying Connections with Lobbyists & Special Interests: Through OSINT, researchers can analyze politicians' relationships with lobbyists, donors, and corporations. These connections can reveal potential conflicts of interest or ethical breaches. By examining voting patterns, public statements, and relationships with industries or lobbying groups, OSINT can help expose undue influence on lawmakers' decisions.

Key Resources:

- Lobbying registration databases
- Public voting records
- Corporate filings and financial disclosures

Investigating Offshore Accounts & Financial Misdeeds: Politicians, especially those in power, may attempt to hide assets or financial interests by placing them in offshore accounts or using shell companies. OSINT tools can track down these assets by analyzing publicly available financial records, legal filings, and international databases. By revealing these hidden connections, OSINT can shed light on corruption or money laundering schemes.

Key Resources:

- Panama Papers & other leaked databases
- Financial disclosure forms
- International business registration databases

Monitoring Political Corruption & Abuse of Power: OSINT plays a crucial role in exposing political corruption, from bribery and embezzlement to human rights abuses. Public records, court documents, news articles, and social media posts can all provide crucial insights into the actions of politicians, making it easier to identify misconduct or ethical violations.

Key Resources:

- Court and criminal records
- Whistleblower accounts
- Social media and news reports

Analyzing Voting Records & Public Policy Impact: Tracking a politician's voting history through public records helps to gauge their consistency on key issues. By using OSINT, researchers can identify how a politician's decisions align with corporate interests or their personal financial stake in a particular issue. This also applies to politicians who might shift stances based on political expediency or under the influence of lobbyists.

Key Resources:

- Congressional and legislative voting records
- Policy analysis and research organizations
- Public statements and campaign promises

The Role of OSINT in Business Accountability

OSINT is also critical in tracking business leaders, especially those in high-profile companies or industries where corporate malfeasance or unethical behavior might be hidden behind complex financial transactions or legal structures. By analyzing public data, investigators can expose hidden financial connections, corporate influence over politics, and potential violations of environmental or labor laws.

Tracking Executive Compensation & Company Financials: Executive compensation, particularly excessive salaries or stock options, can raise questions about the ethics of a company's leadership. By using OSINT to analyze public filings, such as 10-K reports, and financial disclosures, journalists and watchdog groups can investigate whether executives are benefiting unfairly at the expense of their employees, shareholders, or the public.

Key Resources:

- Securities and Exchange Commission (SEC) filings
- Company annual reports
- Proxy statements and investor relations websites

Identifying Conflicts of Interest in Corporate Governance: OSINT can also be used to uncover conflicts of interest within business organizations. This includes identifying relationships between board members, executives, and external entities that might lead to ethical violations, such as favoritism, insider trading, or the prioritization of personal financial interests over company profitability.

Key Resources:

- Corporate governance reports
- Board member biographies and affiliations
- Corporate investment filings

Investigating Environmental & Labor Violations: Public databases, news reports, and social media posts can all be used to track corporate responsibility and the treatment of employees, customers, or the environment. By analyzing patterns in public reports or whistleblower disclosures, OSINT can reveal whether a corporation is engaging in harmful practices, from environmental damage to exploiting workers or engaging in discriminatory practices.

Key Resources:

- Environmental protection agency (EPA) records
- Labor rights organizations' reports
- Corporate sustainability reports and audits

Tracking Mergers, Acquisitions, & Market Manipulation: Business leaders who orchestrate mergers and acquisitions (M&As) can sometimes engage in market manipulation or anti-competitive practices. OSINT can track the movements of executives and board members through financial filings, news reports, and market analysis, helping to reveal instances of collusion or market manipulation that hurt consumers or stifle competition.

Key Resources:

- SEC filings for mergers and acquisitions
- Antitrust investigations and legal actions
- Media reports on corporate consolidation

Investigating Corporate Sponsorships & Lobbying Activities: Business leaders may use corporate funds to influence political decisions through lobbying, campaign donations, or direct contributions to advocacy groups. OSINT can track these activities by examining financial records, lobbying disclosures, and public filings related to corporate political spending.

Key Resources:

- Lobbying registration databases
- Corporate sponsorship records
- Political contribution records

Key Challenges in Tracking Politicians & Business Leaders with OSINT

Data Overload & Information Reliability: With the sheer volume of information available online, sifting through vast amounts of data to find relevant, accurate, and actionable information can be a daunting task. The challenge becomes even greater when misinformation, misdirection, or fake accounts are involved, particularly with high-profile figures who may attempt to obfuscate their true activities.

Privacy & Ethical Boundaries: While public records and data are generally open, there are still ethical concerns about respecting individuals' privacy. Investigating high-profile figures must be balanced with the understanding that certain personal details should not be exposed without legitimate cause. Journalists and activists must weigh the public interest against the potential harm to individuals or families.

Legal Risks & Data Access: Many records or documents may be behind paywalls, restricted access, or in jurisdictions where transparency is limited. Legal frameworks regarding data protection, such as GDPR, further complicate the use of OSINT for business or political investigations in certain regions. Journalists must ensure they adhere to legal boundaries while conducting their research.

Ethical Considerations

Using OSINT to track politicians and business leaders involves several ethical principles. Investigations should prioritize public interest, maintain objectivity, and avoid unwarranted invasions of privacy. Transparent methods and accountability in the use of OSINT are essential to preserving journalistic integrity and preventing misinformation.

Conclusion

OSINT provides powerful tools for tracking politicians and business leaders, offering opportunities for greater transparency and accountability in both politics and business. By leveraging public records, financial filings, social media data, and geospatial tools, journalists and investigators can expose corruption, unethical practices, and conflicts of interest that may otherwise go unnoticed. However, the ethical considerations involved in such investigations are significant, and those engaging in OSINT research must remain vigilant in adhering to legal and privacy standards while maintaining a commitment to truth and transparency. Through responsible use of OSINT, society can hold powerful figures accountable, ensuring that they act in the best interests of the public.

12.4 Exposing Fraudulent Influencers & Social Media Scammers

In today's digital age, social media has given rise to influencers who wield substantial power over their followers. However, not all influencers operate ethically. Some create fraudulent personas to manipulate audiences, promote fake products, or engage in dishonest practices for personal gain. OSINT (Open Source Intelligence) plays a crucial role in exposing these fraudulent influencers and social media scammers by uncovering inconsistencies in their online profiles, identifying fake engagement metrics, and revealing deceptive practices that mislead their audiences. This section explores how OSINT can be used to identify and expose fraudulent influencers and scammers, and the tools and techniques involved in the process.

Understanding Fraudulent Influencers & Social Media Scammers

Fraudulent influencers and social media scammers can take many forms, including individuals who fabricate their online personas, engage in deceptive marketing practices, or mislead their followers for financial or reputational gain. Some of the most common types of social media fraud include:

Fake Followers & Engagement: Many scammers use bots or purchase fake followers to inflate their social media presence. These influencers present themselves as more popular or influential than they truly are, attracting brands and businesses who want to collaborate based on misleading metrics.

Promoting Fake Products: Some influencers promote products or services they don't actually use or believe in, often with exaggerated claims about their benefits. This can be dangerous, especially if the products are harmful or substandard.

Scamming Followers for Money: Fraudulent influencers may use various tactics to scam their followers directly. This can include promoting fake fundraising campaigns, offering "exclusive" content for a fee, or conducting fake giveaways with the intent to collect personal information or money.

Impersonating Others: Scammers may create fake profiles pretending to be established influencers or celebrities. These profiles may be used to deceive fans into providing money, personal details, or sensitive information under false pretenses.

How OSINT Helps Expose Fraudulent Influencers & Scammers

OSINT techniques enable investigators to gather and analyze publicly available data, which can help uncover inconsistencies in social media profiles and track down fraudulent behavior. By using a combination of digital tools and databases, OSINT can expose scammers and provide evidence of unethical behavior.

1. Identifying Fake Followers & Engagement Metrics

One of the most significant indicators of a fraudulent influencer is the presence of fake followers or inflated engagement metrics. Many scammers purchase followers from third-party services or use bots to generate fake likes, comments, and shares. OSINT tools can help detect these anomalies by analyzing engagement patterns and identifying irregularities.

Tools & Techniques:

- **Fake Follower Detection Tools**: Tools like HypeAuditor, Social Audit, or FakeCheck can analyze social media profiles and provide insights into the authenticity of followers, engagement rates, and interactions.
- **Engagement Pattern Analysis**: OSINT investigators can track engagement over time and spot unnatural spikes in likes, comments, or shares, which may indicate bot activity or purchased followers.
- **Cross-Platform Comparisons**: By comparing social media activity across platforms like Instagram, Twitter, and YouTube, OSINT practitioners can detect discrepancies between follower counts and engagement levels.

Example: A social media influencer with tens of thousands of followers may have significantly lower engagement rates (likes or comments), which suggests the followers are not genuine. By using OSINT tools to cross-check follower activity and engagement across platforms, investigators can confirm suspicions of fraudulent activity.

2. Verifying Identity & Authenticity

Another key method for identifying fraudulent influencers is verifying their identity and ensuring their online persona aligns with reality. Many scammers will fabricate their backgrounds, achievements, or affiliations to create a more credible or influential image.

Tools & Techniques:

- **Reverse Image Search**: A reverse image search using tools like Google Images or TinEye can help identify if an influencer is using stock photos or images stolen from other sources. This could indicate that they are misrepresenting themselves or using a fake identity.

- **Cross-Checking Bio Information**: Investigators can check the claims made in an influencer's bio (such as awards, affiliations, or collaborations) against external sources like company websites, news articles, or other credible references.
- **Analyzing Consistency Across Platforms**: Scammers often struggle to maintain consistency in their online personas. By cross-referencing profiles across multiple platforms (Facebook, Instagram, YouTube, etc.), OSINT analysts can identify discrepancies in personal details, follower counts, or content styles.

Example: An influencer claiming to have attended a prestigious university may be found using reverse image search, revealing that the diploma they showcased was taken from an online template. By cross-checking their background across different platforms, an OSINT investigator can expose their lack of authenticity.

3. Tracking Product Endorsements & Promotions

Fraudulent influencers often promote products or services that are substandard or even harmful. OSINT can be used to trace the companies or products they endorse, verify their claims, and uncover any patterns of dishonesty in their promotions.

Tools & Techniques:

- **Researching Product Claims**: OSINT practitioners can search for reviews, news articles, or customer complaints about the products being promoted. A thorough investigation might reveal that the products are either ineffective, dangerous, or non-existent.
- **Investigating Affiliate Links**: Fraudulent influencers often use affiliate marketing links to earn commissions on product sales. OSINT tools can track these links and provide insight into whether the influencer is genuinely using the products they promote or merely pushing them for profit.
- **Examining Sponsored Posts & Partnerships**: OSINT can track the sponsorships and partnerships of influencers by analyzing their past collaborations with brands, checking whether the companies are reputable, and confirming that the promotions were transparent and legitimate.

Example: A beauty influencer promoting a skincare brand that claims to have miraculous results might be exposed by OSINT tools tracking online reviews and forums where users report poor or harmful effects. The influencer might be revealed as an affiliate pushing the brand without testing or verifying the products.

4. Uncovering Fake Giveaways & Scams

Many fraudulent influencers engage in "giveaway" scams, where they promise prizes in exchange for a fee or personal information. OSINT can help expose these fraudulent giveaways by tracking the influencer's past promotions and analyzing the legitimacy of the offers.

Tools & Techniques:

- **Tracking Contest History**: OSINT can be used to trace an influencer's history of giveaways and contests. A pattern of failed or unfulfilled giveaways, combined with requests for payment or sensitive data, is a strong indication of fraud.
- **Investigating Fake Websites & Phishing Links**: Many scammers use fake websites or phishing links to collect personal information from their followers. OSINT tools can help track these links, analyze domain registration data, and flag suspicious websites.
- **Cross-Referencing Testimonials**: OSINT can help identify fake testimonials or reviews related to a scam, by cross-referencing names, dates, and profiles, exposing fraudulent practices.

Example: An influencer promoting a "free iPhone" giveaway that requires payment for shipping or personal details could be exposed by analyzing previous giveaways they've held. The influencer's past history of offering "free" products that turned out to be fake or never delivered can be uncovered through a thorough OSINT investigation.

5. Impersonation & Fake Accounts

Some social media scammers go as far as to impersonate other well-known figures or celebrities to trick followers into sending money, donating, or revealing sensitive information.

Tools & Techniques:

- **Reverse Image Search**: Fraudulent accounts using photos of celebrities or public figures can be exposed using reverse image searches. Scammers typically steal pictures of famous individuals to build their fake profiles.
- **Account Verification Checks**: Many social media platforms offer verification badges, but scammers often impersonate verified accounts. OSINT can be used to cross-check accounts and flag impersonators by verifying their true identity through official channels.

Example: A fake account posing as a celebrity may be promoting a fake fundraising campaign. Through reverse image search and account verification checks, OSINT can confirm that the account is fraudulent and report it to the platform for removal.

Ethical Considerations in Exposing Fraudulent Influencers

While OSINT can be incredibly powerful in exposing social media scams, it is important to approach such investigations with caution and ethical responsibility. Investigators must ensure they are not violating privacy laws, spreading misinformation, or making unfounded accusations. Ethical principles should guide the investigation, ensuring that fraudulent influencers are held accountable without unjustly harming innocent individuals.

Conclusion

Exposing fraudulent influencers and social media scammers requires a meticulous approach, combining various OSINT tools and techniques to uncover fake profiles, false claims, and unethical behavior. By using reverse image searches, analyzing engagement patterns, tracking endorsements, and investigating giveaways, OSINT can shine a light on the deceptive tactics used by these individuals to manipulate their followers and earn undeserved profits. Through responsible and ethical use of OSINT, investigators can protect online communities from these scams and promote transparency in social media.

12.5 How OSINT Has Been Used in High-Profile Investigations

Open Source Intelligence (OSINT) has become an indispensable tool in modern investigations, especially in high-profile cases where traditional methods may fall short. From uncovering criminal networks to exposing political corruption and even tracking missing persons, OSINT has proven to be an effective and versatile resource for investigators, journalists, and law enforcement alike. In this section, we explore how OSINT has been utilized in high-profile investigations, highlighting its impact on uncovering hidden truths, solving complex cases, and influencing public discourse.

The Power of Open Source Intelligence in High-Profile Cases

High-profile investigations often involve complex, multifaceted situations where traditional investigative techniques such as interviews, surveillance, or physical searches can be time-consuming, costly, and sometimes ineffective. OSINT, by contrast, involves gathering publicly available data from a variety of online sources, including social media platforms, forums, news articles, databases, and even satellite imagery. This wealth of information provides investigators with valuable leads and insights, often helping to piece together a bigger picture that might otherwise remain hidden.

OSINT can be used for a variety of purposes in high-profile cases, including:

- Tracing suspects and uncovering their hidden connections and movements
- Verifying public statements and exposing inconsistencies or lies
- Tracking online activity and monitoring suspicious patterns of behavior
- Revealing financial transactions, fraudulent schemes, or hidden assets
- Mapping criminal networks and identifying key figures

Exposing corporate or government malfeasance, including corruption, bribery, and fraud By leveraging open source tools and platforms, investigators can access real-time information and conduct deep dives into digital footprints, enabling them to track down leads, verify claims, and even predict future actions.

Case 1: Tracking the Trail of Terrorist Networks

One of the most prominent examples of OSINT being used in high-profile investigations is its application in tracking and dismantling terrorist networks. Investigators have used OSINT techniques to uncover hidden connections between individuals, organizations, and online communities involved in terrorism, often focusing on social media platforms, encrypted messaging apps, and online forums.

- **Social Media Monitoring**: OSINT tools have been used to monitor platforms like Twitter, Facebook, and Telegram for signs of extremist rhetoric, calls for violence, and recruitment efforts by terrorist groups. These platforms often serve as a breeding ground for radicalization and can provide valuable insights into the movement of individuals associated with these organizations.
- **Tracking Online Activity**: Using data from online platforms, investigators have been able to track the movements of known terrorists and uncover links between different cells within a larger network. OSINT techniques such as geolocation analysis of photos or videos and metadata extraction have been critical in tracking individuals to specific locations.
- **Coordinating International Efforts**: OSINT has allowed international agencies, including the FBI, CIA, MI6, and Interpol, to work together to share information and pinpoint the locations of suspected terrorists or key figures in criminal organizations.

Through the use of OSINT, law enforcement agencies have been able to preempt attacks, arrest key figures, and disrupt terrorist cells before they can carry out their plans. In one high-profile case, OSINT was instrumental in tracking down and eliminating a notorious terrorist leader, whose online digital footprint revealed key details about his location and associates.

Case 2: Investigating Political Corruption and Fraud

OSINT has also played a crucial role in exposing corruption and fraud among politicians, public officials, and corporate leaders. Political investigations often require access to sensitive information, such as campaign finances, illicit transactions, and hidden relationships, which can be difficult to uncover through traditional means. OSINT provides a way to identify inconsistencies, track financial movements, and expose the hidden machinations behind political power.

- **Campaign Finance Scrutiny**: OSINT has been used to investigate political donations, campaign contributions, and the financial relationships between politicians and lobbyists. By tracking public records, tax filings, and even social media posts, journalists and investigators have been able to uncover fraudulent activity or questionable financial ties.
- **Public Disclosure Analysis**: By cross-referencing public financial disclosures and social media posts, OSINT has been used to expose politicians or corporate executives with hidden assets, shell companies, or conflicts of interest. For instance, public figures may claim to have no financial connections to certain entities, but OSINT tools can reveal otherwise through cross-platform investigations and records search.
- **Social Media Activity**: Social media platforms provide a direct line to the thoughts and actions of public officials. In some cases, OSINT has revealed inconsistencies between what politicians publicly state and what they privately communicate online. These discrepancies can be used as evidence of corruption, bribery, or cover-ups.

One high-profile political corruption case that benefitted from OSINT occurred when journalists uncovered an illicit financial network linking a powerful political figure to multiple offshore accounts. The investigation relied heavily on open-source financial records, social media activity, and leaked documents, all of which were analyzed using OSINT tools.

Case 3: Tracking Missing Persons & High-Profile Kidnappings

OSINT is also a vital tool in high-profile missing persons cases and kidnappings, especially when the victims have a substantial public profile. For example, OSINT techniques were pivotal in the case of a high-profile celebrity who was kidnapped by a criminal group seeking ransom. By analyzing publicly available data, including the celebrity's social media posts, location tags, and online interactions, investigators were able to track their movements and identify key clues that eventually led to the victim's location.

- **Geolocation Tracking**: Photos and videos shared by the victim, friends, or family members on social media can contain hidden geolocation data, such as GPS coordinates. By analyzing this data, OSINT experts can map out the victim's movements and uncover clues about their potential location. Investigators can also trace the movements of suspects involved in the crime.
- **Cross-Referencing Public Data**: Open source data from public records, such as vehicle registration, travel records, and even flight details, can be used to track the movements of the suspects or the victim. Social media interactions or even posts made by friends and family can be used to triangulate potential locations, revealing where the victim might be held.
- **Crowdsourcing Information**: OSINT also allows for crowdsourcing information through online appeals and social media networks. When a missing person case gains significant media attention, people across the world can contribute valuable tips or observations that may lead to a breakthrough.

In one famous case, OSINT tools played a key role in the safe return of a kidnapped journalist. By piecing together clues from online photos, location metadata, and even digital footprints left by the kidnappers, investigators were able to locate and rescue the journalist before it was too late.

Case 4: Investigating Financial Fraud and Ponzi Schemes

Financial fraud, such as Ponzi schemes, corporate fraud, and insider trading, has also been targeted by OSINT in high-profile investigations. OSINT is instrumental in uncovering hidden financial transactions, tracing illicit money flows, and identifying the individuals behind fraudulent schemes.

- **Tracking Financial Transactions**: OSINT tools can access public databases, including corporate records, tax filings, and financial disclosures, to trace the flow of money between companies and individuals. By linking publicly available records with digital evidence, investigators can uncover hidden ownership structures and financial irregularities.

- **Investigating Online Fraud**: OSINT has been particularly effective in identifying online-based fraud schemes, such as fake investment platforms, cryptocurrency scams, and online Ponzi schemes. By analyzing website registrations, domain ownership, and financial transactions through blockchain analysis tools, investigators can trace fraudulent activity back to its source.
- **Exposing Fake Testimonials & Marketing**: Scammers often use fake testimonials, fabricated reviews, and deceptive marketing tactics to promote their fraudulent schemes. OSINT can be used to investigate these claims and identify the real individuals behind these marketing efforts.

One of the most famous high-profile financial fraud cases investigated using OSINT involved the uncovering of a massive Ponzi scheme, which spanned multiple countries. By cross-referencing financial records, analyzing cryptocurrency transactions, and tracking down fake online reviews, OSINT investigators were able to expose the entire operation and bring the criminals to justice.

Conclusion: The Increasing Role of OSINT in High-Profile Investigations

As the digital world continues to expand, OSINT has become a critical tool in high-profile investigations, enabling investigators to gather valuable intelligence from publicly available sources. From tracking terrorists and uncovering political corruption to solving missing persons cases and exposing financial fraud, OSINT has proven itself to be an invaluable asset in a wide range of complex investigations. Its ability to provide real-time insights, uncover hidden connections, and piece together digital footprints has transformed the investigative landscape, making it an essential component of modern intelligence gathering and law enforcement strategies.

12.6 Final Challenge: Conducting a Complete People OSINT Investigation

In this final challenge, we will put everything you've learned throughout the OSINT People Finder guide into practice. The goal is to conduct a comprehensive people OSINT investigation, combining techniques, tools, and strategies covered in previous chapters to trace an individual's digital footprint and uncover relevant information.

This challenge will walk you through the necessary steps to identify, locate, and analyze data related to a target person, making sure to cover various areas of open-source intelligence collection. By the end, you'll understand how to approach investigations from start to finish, with a focus on efficiency, accuracy, and ethical considerations.

Step 1: Define the Scope & Objectives of the Investigation

Before diving into the investigation, it's important to clearly define the scope of your OSINT operation. A vague or overly broad investigation can lead to wasted resources and missed opportunities. Focus on:

- **Who you are investigating**: Are they a public figure, a person of interest in a criminal investigation, or someone you're simply trying to locate?
- **What information you need**: Are you searching for contact details, verifying a person's identity, or uncovering hidden connections?
- **Why you're conducting the investigation**: Are you helping law enforcement, verifying a job applicant's claims, or researching a missing person case?

Clearly defining these objectives will keep you on track and ensure that you're gathering the most relevant and valuable information.

Step 2: Gather Basic Identifying Information

Start by collecting basic identifying information about the person you are investigating. This could include:

- Full name (and any known aliases)
- Date of birth (or an estimated range)
- Known locations (hometown, places they've lived, cities they frequently visit)
- Social media handles (if known)
- Professional affiliations (company name, industry, job title)

Even small details, like where they went to school or their previous addresses, can serve as launching points for deeper investigation.

Step 3: Perform a Basic Web Search

Using the name, location, or known affiliations, perform a series of basic web searches. Utilize search engines like Google, Bing, or DuckDuckGo to locate articles, public records, or any websites where the person may have been mentioned. Make sure to:

- Search for their full name and known aliases.
- Include variations of their name (first and last name, nicknames, or initials).
- Include any known locations (e.g., "John Doe Los Angeles" or "Jane Smith New York").

While these initial searches may return general information, they can help identify social media accounts, news articles, or any public-facing websites linked to the person.

Step 4: Dive Into Social Media Platforms

Social media is one of the richest sources of information for people investigations. Perform detailed searches on the following platforms, analyzing profiles, posts, images, and metadata:

- **Facebook**: Look for public profiles or check for mentions in public groups. Investigate their friends list for potential connections.
- **Twitter/X**: Investigate mentions, tweets, and hashtags related to the person. Check their followers and engagement metrics.
- **Instagram**: Look at photos and videos. Analyze location tags or comments from other users for additional clues about their whereabouts.
- **LinkedIn**: Scrutinize their professional background and connections. Identify any inconsistencies or connections that might open up new investigative pathways.
- **TikTok**: Explore any content that might hint at their location, activities, or personal life.

Be thorough and note any social media handles associated with the target person across these platforms. You might also encounter hidden accounts or previously overlooked social media profiles.

Step 5: Investigate Public Records

OSINT investigators often rely on public records for key information about an individual. These records might reveal significant personal details and background checks. Common records to search include:

- **Court records**: Check for any past legal issues, criminal records, or lawsuits. Websites like PACER or county court websites can help.

- **Property records**: Search for any properties they may have owned or leased. Local property databases can provide information on transactions, previous owners, and addresses.
- **Voter registration**: In some countries, voter registration records are publicly available. This can help confirm residency, address history, and even voting patterns.
- **Business records**: Investigate any businesses they may have started, owned, or been affiliated with. Websites like the Secretary of State's office or online business registries can yield useful insights.

Use databases such as BeenVerified, Whitepages, or government-run portals to access this information.

Step 6: Conduct Email & Username Investigations

Emails and usernames are often directly linked to individuals and can reveal their online activity across multiple platforms. To investigate email addresses or usernames:

- Search for email addresses in breach databases (e.g., Have I Been Pwned).
- Use email search tools like Hunter.io or VerifyEmailAddress.org to find associated accounts.
- Cross-reference usernames across social media, forum sites, and other platforms to identify other online accounts linked to the person.

Username patterns can reveal more about a person's habits and interests. For example, using the same username across multiple platforms may provide insights into their behavior or identity.

Step 7: Explore Geolocation & Photos

Photos, especially those shared on social media, can provide valuable clues regarding a person's location. Analyze images for:

- **Geolocation data**: Review metadata in images using tools like ExifTool to retrieve location coordinates or timestamps embedded in the files.
- **Social media location tags**: Many platforms allow users to tag locations on photos and check-ins. This can help build a map of their activities.
- **Patterns in the background**: Distinctive landmarks, weather patterns, or even interior settings might reveal where the person lives or spends time.

Use tools like Google Images to perform reverse image searches and check if the photos have been posted elsewhere or are linked to any other identifying information.

Step 8: Investigate Potential Connections

Once you've gathered information from social media, public records, and other OSINT sources, it's time to look for patterns and connections. Consider the following:

- **Network analysis**: Look for mutual friends, family members, colleagues, and associates across social media platforms. Cross-reference these connections and check their online profiles for additional clues.
- **Common interests or groups**: Is the person involved in any community organizations, advocacy groups, or professional networks? Analyzing these groups can lead you to more information or witnesses.
- **Financial or business relationships**: Use public records or financial databases to uncover business ties, investments, or personal finances.

Looking for patterns across different networks will often yield the most significant breakthroughs in an investigation.

Step 9: Legal & Ethical Considerations

At every stage of your investigation, it's important to adhere to ethical standards and legal boundaries. Here are some important considerations:

- **Privacy**: Only use publicly available information for investigation purposes. Avoid attempting to access private accounts or encrypted data without consent.
- **Permissions**: Ensure that the sources you're accessing are legal and authorized. Some data may be protected under specific privacy laws or agreements.
- **Purpose**: Conduct investigations with a clear, ethical purpose. Avoid using OSINT to harass, intimidate, or infringe upon someone's privacy.

Always remember to balance the need for information with respect for individual privacy rights and legal norms.

Step 10: Compile & Analyze Findings

After gathering all the necessary data, it's time to analyze the information and draw conclusions:

- **Create a timeline**: Organize the data chronologically to establish a clearer narrative of the person's activities, movements, and connections.
- **Corroborate evidence**: Cross-reference your findings from different sources to validate your information.
- **Document your findings**: Prepare a detailed report that summarizes the information, providing supporting evidence for your conclusions. This report will be helpful for others who need to review the investigation or use it for further action.

Conclusion: Putting It All Together

A complete people OSINT investigation involves a series of logical steps, combining knowledge from various disciplines, including social media analysis, public records, email investigation, and geolocation tracking. By leveraging a variety of free and paid tools and focusing on ethical and legal boundaries, you can conduct thorough, effective investigations that provide valuable insights into a person's online identity and behavior.

This final challenge has shown you how to bring all your OSINT skills together to conduct a professional investigation, whether for personal use, professional purposes, or even helping law enforcement. Remember, OSINT is not just about finding information — it's about piecing together the puzzle and verifying the truth from a variety of sources.

In today's digital world, almost everyone leaves behind an online footprint—sometimes intentionally, sometimes unknowingly. Whether you're a private investigator, journalist, cybersecurity professional, or just someone looking to reconnect with a lost contact, mastering the art of online people searching is an invaluable skill.

OSINT People Finder: Advanced Techniques for Online Investigations is a deep dive into the methods and tools used to track, identify, and verify individuals using publicly available data. This book provides a structured approach to conducting thorough and ethical investigations, teaching you how to locate people efficiently while respecting privacy laws and ethical boundaries.

What You'll Learn in This Book

- **Understanding Digital Footprints**: Learn how personal data is created, stored, and indexed online.
- **Mastering Search Engines for People Searches**: Use advanced search operators and specialized databases to find individuals.
- **Social Media Investigations**: Discover how to track people through platforms like Facebook, Twitter, LinkedIn, Instagram, and more.
- **Username & Email Intelligence**: Use reverse username and email searches to uncover linked profiles and hidden identities.
- **Public Records & Government Databases**: Access legal and public data sources for verification and background checks.
- **Phone Number & Address Investigations**: Leverage online tools to trace phone numbers and locate addresses.
- **Deep & Dark Web People Search**: Learn when and how to safely explore less conventional data sources.
- **Image Recognition & Reverse Search**: Use advanced image tracking techniques to verify identities.
- **Privacy & Ethical Considerations**: Understand the legal and moral boundaries of people investigations.

With real-world case studies, hands-on exercises, and step-by-step tutorials, OSINT People Finder provides a comprehensive guide to modern online investigations. Whether you're looking for missing persons, verifying identities, or conducting due diligence, this book equips you with the skills to navigate the complex web of digital identity.

Thank you for taking the time to explore OSINT People Finder. In a world where digital identities are becoming as important as physical ones, your commitment to ethical and responsible investigations is both necessary and commendable.

The ability to find people online is a powerful skill, one that can be used to reconnect loved ones, protect against fraud, and uncover the truth. But with great power comes great responsibility. We encourage you to use the techniques in this book ethically and legally, always respecting personal privacy and data protection laws.

Your feedback and support are invaluable to us, and we hope this book has provided you with new insights and tools to enhance your OSINT capabilities. If you found this book useful, we would love to hear about your experiences. Your insights help shape future editions and ensure we continue providing high-quality intelligence resources.

Stay curious, stay ethical, and keep searching for the truth.

Continue Your OSINT Journey

Expand your skills with the rest of **The OSINT Analyst Series**:

- **OSINT Foundations**: The Beginner's Guide to Open-Source Intelligence
- **The OSINT Search Mastery**: Hacking Search Engines for Intelligence
- **Social Media OSINT**: Tracking Digital Footprints
- **Image & Geolocation Intelligence**: Reverse Searching and Mapping
- **Domain, Website & Cyber Investigations with OSINT**
- **Email & Dark Web Investigations**: Tracking Leaks & Breaches
- **OSINT Threat Intel**: Investigating Hackers, Breaches, and Cyber Risks
- **Corporate OSINT**: Business Intelligence & Competitive Analysis
- **Investigating Disinformation & Fake News with OSINT**
- **OSINT for Deep & Dark Web**: Techniques for Cybercrime Investigations
- **OSINT Automation**: Python & APIs for Intelligence Gathering
- **OSINT Detective**: Digital Tools & Techniques for Criminal Investigations
- **Advanced OSINT Case Studies**: Real-World Investigations
- **The Ethical OSINT Investigator**: Privacy, Legal Risks & Best Practices

We look forward to seeing you in the next book!

Happy investigating!